M000113452

THREE
YEARS
IN HELL

BY THE SAME AUTHOR

Meanwhile Back at the Ranch

White Savage

A Traitor's Kiss

Ship of Fools

Enough is Enough

Judging Shaw

Heroic Failure

FINTAN O'TOOLE

THREE YEARS IN HELL

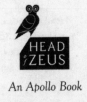

HEAD
of ZEUS

An Apollo Book

This is an Apollo book, first published in the UK in 2020
by Head of Zeus Ltd
This paperback edition first published in 2021
by Head of Zeus Ltd

Copyright © Fintan O'Toole, 2020

The moral right of Fintan O'Toole to
be identified as the author of this work has been asserted
in accordance with the Copyright, Designs and
Patents Act of 1988.

All rights reserved. No part of this publication may be reproduced,
stored in a retrieval system, or transmitted in any form or by any means,
electronic, mechanical, photocopying, recording, or otherwise,
without the prior permission of both the copyright owner
and the above publisher of this book.

9 7 5 3 1 2 4 6 8

A catalogue record for this book is available
from the British Library.

ISBN (PB): 9781838935214
ISBN (E): 9781838935221

Typeset by Adrian McLaughlin

Printed and bound in Great Britain
by CPI Group (UK) Ltd, Croydon CR0 4YY

Head of Zeus Ltd
5–8 Hardwick Street
London EC1R 4RG
WWW.HEADOFZEUS.COM

Contents

In memory of Mary O'Toole Byrne (1961–2019)

'I have been sometimes thinking, if a man had the art of second sight for seeing lies... how admirably he might entertain himself in this town, by observing the different shapes, sizes, and colours of those swarms of lies which buzz about the heads of some people like flies about a horse's ears in summer.'

JONATHAN SWIFT, 'The Art of Political Lying',
The Examiner, 9 November 1710

INTRODUCTION

Before the Golden Age

arly in the morning of 13 December 2019, Boris Johnson made his victory speech. He had used the simple thirteen-letter slogan 'Get Brexit Done' to transform the electoral map. Parts of the English Midlands and North where people used to think the official name of Johnson's party was Tory Scum had abandoned generations of loyalty to Labour and voted Conservative. Johnson had been given a parliamentary majority comfortable enough to ensure that he would, albeit in a very limited sense, get Brexit done. The United Kingdom would formally cease to be a member of the European Union on 31 January 2020. Something was certainly coming to an end. It was just not entirely clear what that something was.

Speaking at what he bathetically called 'this glorious, glorious pre-breakfast moment' (food is never far from his mind) Johnson could not contain his sense of wonder. He had managed, as he put it, to unite the nation 'from Woking to Workington; from Kensington... to Clwyd South; from Surrey Heath to Sedgefield; from Wimbledon to Wolverhampton'. Johnson can never resist an alliterative litany and this list of new and old Tory heartlands was no doubt shaped by the demands of his favourite rhetorical device. Yet in his euphoria he seems not to have noticed that seven of the eight constituencies he namechecked are in England. He could have achieved the same assonance with 'from Dumfries [in Scotland] to Don Valley' or from 'Brecon [in Wales] to Bolsover', an eternal Labour seat in the English Midlands that had miraculously passed to the Tories. But he didn't.

Johnson had, in a real sense, created a new country. Ever since Elizabeth Gaskell's classic novel of 1854, *North and South*, it has been a commonplace to speak and write of the two parts of England as if they were different countries. In the novel, the Hales, father and daughter, are to move from Helstone in the South to Milton in the North. Mr Hale explains to Margaret that in this move they would encounter 'people and scenes so different that I shall never be reminded of Helstone'. Margaret reflects: 'It would be different. Discordant as it was – with almost a detestation for all she had ever heard of the North of England, the manufacturers, the people, the wild and bleak country – there was this one recommendation – it would be different from Helstone, and could never remind them of that beloved place.'* The language would be the same if the Hales were embarking for Australia or India rather than merely moving a few hundred miles up the road.

Ever since, the notion of North and South as two different countries in everything but name has been a commonplace of English culture, reinforced by tangible differences in the economy, in wages, in educational levels, in political loyalties and even in such English institutions as fish and chips (cod in the South; haddock in the North). In the language of the 2019 general election, the term 'Red Wall' – referring to the almost geological bedrock of Labour-voting seats in the North – was repeated almost as often as 'Get Brexit Done'. It conjured an image of invasion and repulsion, as if, in addition to the old Roman fortification Hadrian's Wall, which roughly defined England's external boundary with Scotland, there were also this great political barricade running through England itself.

And Johnson completely overran it. He did, up a point, unite Wimbledon, where zero per cent of local districts are defined as 'highly deprived' and Wolverhampton North East, where 27 per

* Elizabeth Gaskell, *North and South*, Penguin Books, p. 35.

cent of them are so defined. The great political power of Brexit always lay in its ability to bring together, in one common gesture of defiance, much of the rich upper class – including the dilettante faux aristocracy to which Johnson belongs – and much of the white working class. The anti-state anarchism of the hedge fund caste was fused with the anti-Establishment rage of the post-industrial untouchables. Johnson proved in 2019 that the power unleashed when these two wires crossed was undiminished – it could burn through long-established political and social identities.

So it is not too much of an exaggeration to say that Johnson had accidentally created a new country. He deserves, perhaps, to be called the father of the nation. The only problem is that neither he nor anyone else knows what this new country is. It is certainly not, as Johnson's triumphant speech acknowledged by omission, the United Kingdom: Scotland and Northern Ireland rejected Brexit even more emphatically in the election of 2019 than they had done in the referendum of 2016 and a clear majority of voters in the UK as a whole voted in 2019 for parties that promised a second referendum and an opportunity to stay in the EU. It is not even, properly speaking, England: it includes much of Wales (Johnson did remember to namecheck Clwyd South) but excludes Greater London which voted emphatically against Johnson and Brexit.

The eerie thing is not just that this new country is nameless but that so, too, is its great unifying cause. The cause is Brexit but Brexit, in Johnson's successful framing of it, is 'done', over, gone. It has vanished. It happened already and it is not to be spoken of now. *The Huffington Post* reported shortly after the election that the word 'Brexit' was to be officially removed from public discourse, with the disbandment of the Department for Exiting the European Union and the renaming of the Brexit press team as the 'Europe and economy' unit. The anonymous country would thus have an anonymous national mission to bind it together. This seems an appropriate outcome for a project in which an unacknowledged force (English nationalism) was channelled into an undefined transformation (a Brexit that had no realistic relationship to an achievable reality). While Johnson liked to talk of 'this pivotal moment in our national story', there was neither a settled nation nor a clear story.*

This is the great paradox of the whole saga: Brexit can achieve the impossible; it's just the possible it has trouble with. It has done incredible things: shattered deeply rooted identities, united the have-nots with the have-yachts, abolished the political distinction between North and South in England, made Johnson – a figure whom almost nobody regards as honest, competent or sincere – into one of the most consequential national leaders in English history. But it struggles with the credible ones. Neither before nor after the referendum of June 2016 did its leading proponents come up with any serious plan for what Brexit would really mean in practice for Britain's economy, for its place in the world, for its very existence as a unitary state.

An aspect of this paradox is that Brexit is, on the one hand, unquestionably historic – but it is not, in the imaginations of its proponents, history. It is not an event that is unfolding in the 2020s, amid all the other realities of the time: climate change, Donald Trump, runaway technological transformations and so on. It is, rather, a flight from history. It is both literally and metaphorically escapist – the great leap out of the EU is also a giant bound out of the real, compromised, messy truths of the world in which Britain, alongside everyone else, finds itself. Into what can it escape? Only that last refuge of bankrupt utopians, the Golden Age.

A perfect little dramatisation of this clash between historic moment and ahistoric fantasy is an exchange in the House of Commons on 17 October 2019. The Plaid Cymru MP Liz Saville Roberts asked the leader of the House and arch-Brexiteer Jacob Rees-Mogg to 'do everything in his power to ensure that impact assessments are published and available for Members to see' before they voted on the withdrawal agreement that Johnson had negotiated with the EU. Rees-Mogg replied: 'There are any

---

* *Hansard*, 25 July 2019, col. 1460.

number of impact assessments that people have made, but let me give her my assessment of what will happen when we leave the European Union: it will be a golden age for the United Kingdom when we are free of the heavy yoke of the European Union, which has bowed us down for generations and made us less competitive, less efficient and higher-cost. All of that will be gone, and we will be singing hallelujahs.'*

This might be dismissed as mere facetiousness, but the Golden Age is a repeated point of reference for the Brexiteers, including Johnson. The peroration of his first major speech to the Commons after he became prime minister was: 'I believe that if we bend our sinews to the task now, there is every chance that in 2050, when I fully intend to be around, although not necessarily in this job, we will be able to look back on this period – this extraordinary period – as the beginning of a new golden age for our United Kingdom.'†
Likewise, in his speech setting out the new government's plans immediately after the election, he told parliament: 'I do not think it vainglorious or implausible to say that a new golden age for this United Kingdom is now within reach. In spite of the scoffing, in spite of the negativity, in spite of the scepticism that you will hear from the other side, we will work flat out to deliver it.'‡

That this is drivel is a given. What is striking, though, is the weird mixture of registers. Words like 'implausible' and 'work flat out to deliver it' come from a world of facts and processes. The Golden Age (as Rees-Mogg and Johnson ought to know from their Etonian education) comes from the world of cosmological myth. It is elaborated in Hesiod's *Works and Days* as a long-ago era in which people had neither facts nor processes to worry about:

Like gods they lived, with spirits free from care;
And grim old age never encroached. The feast

* *Hansard*, 17 October 2019, col. 490.
† Ibid., 25 July 2019, col. 1460.
‡ Ibid., 19 December 2019, col. 45.

Where they moved limbs to music never ceased;
Their hands and feet not ageing in the least.
They were free from every evil you could number,
And when death came, it stole on them like slumber.*

The whole point of the Golden Age is that it is outside history. It exists merely as the ideal from which humanity has been expelled forever. After it comes the age in which, as Hesiod has it:

They had no self-control, could not restrain
Themselves from wreaking outrages and pain.†

The ancient poet may not have foreseen the coming of Boris Johnson, but this does serve as fair warning. And Johnson's evocation of the Golden Age is in fact wonderfully evasive. He does not actually say that it will begin at the moment of Brexit. He says that there is a point in the future (2050) from which it will be possible to look back on 2020 as the moment at which this glorious era was inaugurated. This preserves the essence of the Golden Age – that it is always imagined in retrospect. It also lifts the idea of the fabulous transformation to be wrought by Brexit out of the realm of concrete questions (How many car plants closed? How did the chlorinated chicken go down?) and makes it a matter of future perception – perception, moreover, through the lens of myth and fantasy. Brexit is not a practical proposition to be judged by weighing costs against benefits. It is a sci-fi creation myth: this is how a future generation will understand how its existence came to be so blissful. It is not this generation's idea of its future; it is the next generation's idea of its past.

This is madness but it is also method. For the essence of Brexit is that it is impossible to disentangle fantasy from calculation, myth from manoeuvre. One of the stark facts of the great moment of

* Hesiod, *Works and Days*, Penguin Books, Kindle edition, location 735.
† Ibid., location 737.

departure in January 2020 is that it was not euphoric. There was no singing of hallelujahs – or, if there was, they were, as Leonard Cohen would have it, cold and broken. Brexit is a nationalist revolution and it strikes the pose of a small oppressed nation breaking the chains of imperial bondage. England, in Rees-Mogg's terms, is setting itself 'free of the heavy yoke of the European Union'. But precisely because this is just a pose – a performance in which the old colonial master mimics the gestures of the old colonial subjects – it cannot produce the ecstatic emotions that successful revolutions seek to generate. The real public mood in the month of liberation was revealed in a survey commissioned by the Conservative think-tank Bright Blue: 'The UK public is fairly pessimistic about the next five years. A majority of the UK public expects levels of undesirable trends – poverty (72%), crime (71%), inequality (71%) and national debt (72%) – to increase or stay the same.'*

This public pessimism is very much in keeping with the shift in the appeal of the Brexit project over the period since the referendum campaign of 2016. In the beginning, it was all gain and no pain – Britain would have all the benefits of EU membership with none of the costs or constraints. Then, as the negotiations dragged on and the political system brought itself close to a state of anarchy, it became all pain. Finally, Johnson came up with a powerful – and in electoral terms highly effective – appeal: I can make the pain go away. But the very allure of the promise to 'Get Brexit Done' was in the idea of 'done' meaning not just achieved but 'done with' – over, finished, dead. It recast the period 2016 to 2019, no longer as a glorious moment of joyful emancipation, but as a bad trip from which everyone had to come down. In the ultimate irony, Brexit had ceased to be a release from the European Union and had become a release *from itself*. In keeping with the wilfully self-generating nature of the whole episode, the relief had become purely auto-erotic.

And the truth, of course, was that even this release was illusory.

* http://brightblue.org.uk/immediate-public-expectations-of-and-priorities/

Brexit had been reshaped, as Chris Grey put it, as 'an embarrassing episode at the Christmas office party that it would be bad taste to remind anyone of in the new year'.* This is why it dare not speak its name any more. Johnson's rhetoric at the start of 2020 was at one level an appeal for amnesia: let's forget, not just all the promises we made in 2016, but all the rancour and anarchy they unleashed. Even his culinary metaphors changed. He had promised in the election that Brexit was 'oven-ready'. Now he revealed that the oven was in fact a microwave in which a prepackaged future could be reheated almost instantly and without thought or effort: 'That oven-ready deal I talked about so much during the election campaign has already had its plastic covering pierced and been placed in the microwave.'†

It might be noted in passing how bathetic the metaphors have become. The imagery of anti-Europeanism in England has always been related to food – Brexit used to be, in Johnson's notorious formulation, a fairy-tale cake that could be consumed again and again without ever diminishing. Now we have descended to Pot Noodle Brexit: Johnson will stick it in the microwave, the people will eat it and we will all forget about it as soon as we have consumed it. But even this promised junk food does not actually exist. Neither the endless and endlessly tiresome detail of trade negotiations with the EU nor the vast implications for the nature of the UK state can be 'done' at the press of a button. Instant disposable Brexit is no more real than fairy-tale cake Brexit. There is almost nothing tangible that the project can offer those who supported it. It is a point of departure, not a place of arrival. And the only place it can arrive is at an imaginary future in whose retrospective glow of approval the tedious journey will seem to have been worth making. That voyage cannot be mapped with facts. There are no impact assessments for the return of the Golden Age.

* Chris Grey, https://chrisgreybrexitblog.blogspot.com/2020/01/the-battle-between-remembering-and.html
† https://www.bbc.com/news/uk-politics-50956221

This is what makes Brexit so strange for journalists to write about. We are supposed to report on facts, on processes, on states pursuing their interests with more or less acumen, more or less success. If you live and work in Ireland, Brexit was indeed like this – there were facts, there were political processes and there was a state that had from very early on a clear sense of where its own interests lay. The story was literally grounded: the snaking, porous 500-kilometre-long border across the island is a place where you can feel political realities beneath your feet. It was also inescapably historic – if anything, too much so. No one in Ireland could think of Brexit through the metaphors the Brexiteers favoured: the clean break, the new age. There are no clean breaks on this island, just slow and delicate efforts to disentangle the present and the future from the worst aspects of the past. History may be, as James Joyce's Stephen Dedalus puts it, a nightmare from which we are trying to awake, but we know that the best you can hope to wake to is a less nightmarish history.

But facts, processes and interests are not the substance of Brexit itself. The order of priority is different. First came the gesture, then the struggle to say what it is a gesture *of*. Every commentator on it – and this very much includes the primary participants in it – feels like Mr Jones in Bob Dylan's 'Ballad of a Thin Man': 'you know something is happening but you don't know what it is / Do you, Mr Jones?' The referendum result was a statement, not of the desired destiny of the United Kingdom, but simply of what non-metropolitan England does not want. It is a big No, a void that has to be filled with content and meaning. The astonishing drama it unleashed – the resignations and elections, the picaresque rise and fall and rise again of one of English history's greatest chancers, the making and unravelling of agreements, the unprecedented constitutional conflicts between government, parliament and the courts, the surreal chaos in the House of Commons, the apocalyptic no-deal scenarios – has been a thrilling spectacle. But it is a manifestation, not a meaning.

It is said with some justice that to a man with a hammer

everything looks like a nail. The hammer in my hand is the one that every Irish person holds – a sense of how nationalism works; a fear of the ways in which, if it is poorly articulated, it can turn toxic; an awareness of the danger of imagining identity as a zero sum game; a fundamental disbelief in the possibility of extracting oneself from history. These are not examples of innate Irish wisdom – to the contrary, they are the fruits of very bitter experience. To look across the water from Ireland is to see people playing with the same fire with which we ourselves have been burned. If much of what follows here seems harsh, it is motivated merely by a hope that our neighbours would not have to learn the hard way what W. B. Yeats learned from the Irish Troubles:

> We had fed the heart on fantasies,
> The heart's grown brutal from the fare,
> More substance in our enmities
> Than in our love…

What follows here is a sort of real-time reflection on a country trying to find its substance in its enmities, seeking definition in what it does not want to be. If it has value it is not that the reflections are always right, but simply that they are an attempt to understand a historical moment as it is unfolding, without hind-sight. It is one improvised, on-the-fly attempt to fill the void with meaning. This is what Brexit felt like to one intimate outsider as it was happening. I tried, in *Heroic Failure*, to give a panoramic wide shot of the historical and cultural context. This is Brexit frame by frame. Of course, from the perspective of 2050, those looking back on the dawn of the Golden Age will find its tone appalling and its negativity incomprehensible. One can but hope that their scorn is justified by the glorious end of this strange saga.

Acknowledgements

This book brings together writings on Brexit from three main sources. The main one is my home territory at the *Irish Times*, where I have enjoyed the unfailing support of Paul O'Neill, John McManus, Conor Goodman and many other great colleagues. It is one of the most civilised newspapers in the world and I never forget my good fortune at having landed there. I am also deeply grateful to Katherine Butler, Jonathan Shainin, Paul Laity and their colleagues at the *Guardian* and to Robert Yates at the *Observer*. I am greatly indebted, too, to Jana Prikryl, Matt Seaton and the editors of the *New York Review of Books*. I am very lucky, too, to have the support, encouragement and sound advice of my editor Neil Belton and all the staff at Head of Zeus and of my agent Natasha Fairweather. The luck of having Clare Connell's patience and indulgence is the greatest windfall of them all.

Prelude: 22 May 2011

For the first time in 100 years, the British head of state is able to pay an official visit to what is now the Irish Republic. Queen Elizabeth is warmly received; protests are minimal. There is, above all, a sense of relief. A very long and often dark story seems to be over. Ireland and Britain are now good neighbours, working closely together on the peace process in Northern Ireland and as fellow members of the European Union. What could possibly go wrong?

There are, presumably, two rules the Queen has absorbed so deeply that they have become instinctive: don't take risks; don't stir emotions. She broke both rules in Ireland last week. Most of us had expected a bland occasion whose significance lay simply in the fact that it was happening at all. What we got was both challenging and moving.

The risks the Queen took were not physical. A massive security operation sealed off the events from most of the Irish public. The pathetic nature of the protests, which struggled to gather more than 200 people at a time, made the security seem disproportionate, but it was a necessary evil. And it did allow the Queen to take risks of an entirely different kind.

She stepped repeatedly on to dangerous ground. She laid a wreath at the Garden of Remembrance that is dedicated to the generations of Irish rebels who took up arms against British domination and paid with their lives. She touched the raw nerve of Bloody Sunday in 1920 when she visited Croke Park. She stirred memories of the futile sacrifice of Irish troops at Gallipoli and the Somme when she went to Dublin's long-neglected war memorial. In all of this, she was choosing to thread a path through minefields.

1

To the great surprise of those of us who have little time for monarchy, she walked that line with amazing grace. It is not simply that she didn't put a foot wrong. It is that every step seemed exactly right, from her calm humility at the Garden of Remembrance to the beautifully crafted speech that began with a few perfectly pronounced words of Gaelic. If this was a performance, it was a magnificent one. But it always seemed like something more than that.

The Queen's dignified simplicity at the Garden of Remembrance completely transformed the meaning of the visit. Most Irish people had seen it as a test of their own maturity, the ultimate way of discovering whether we could live without Anglophobia. Elizabeth, remarkably, made it something else as well: a test of British maturity.

While all the talk had been about Irish identity, British identity was being challenged too. The familiar question that was posed was whether the Irish have got over their sometimes neurotic love–hate relationship with the Brits. But it was joined by a question that was completely unexpected: have the British got over their post-imperial delusions of grandeur? Or to put it another way, is Britain's self-image now sufficiently cleansed of the stains of empire that it can treat Ireland as an equal?

It is rather extraordinary that the Queen, of all people, should be the one to deliver such a positive answer to that question. There was no handwringing and none of the apologies that most Irish people would have found embarrassing anyway. But neither was there a single moment of condescension.

This mattered a lot to Irish people, especially at a moment when Irish self-confidence has been shattered by its economic crisis. But it should also matter to the British. The subjugation of Ireland was the crucible in which Britain's 'destiny' of superiority was forged over 500 years ago. The Queen's visit closed a long chapter in Irish history, but it also signalled the end of that idea of what it means to be British. As Anglo-Irish relations are normalised, Britain, too, becomes a normal country.

TIMELINE

23 June 2016:   UK holds referendum on its membership of the EU, with the majority of voters choosing to leave the EU (51.9 per cent of the vote, versus 48.1 per cent voting to remain).

24 June 2016:   Shortly after the result is announced, Prime Minister David Cameron makes known his intention to resign.

13 July 2016:   Theresa May becomes the new UK prime minister.

2 October 2016:   In her party conference speech, Theresa May confirms Article 50 will be triggered before the end of March 2017

18 June 2016

Six days before the Brexit referendum, it seems that something profound is being created: not a mere exit from the EU but the real possibility of an English state. Yet no one seems to want to talk about it.

I t is a question the English used to ask about their subject peoples: are they ready for self-government? But it is now one that has to be asked about the English themselves. It's not facetious: England seems to be stumbling towards a national independence it has scarcely even discussed, let alone prepared for. It is on the brink of one of history's strangest nationalist revolutions.

When you strip away the rhetoric, Brexit is an English nationalist movement. If the Leave side wins the referendum, it will almost certainly be without a majority in either Scotland or Northern Ireland and perhaps without winning Wales either. The passion that animates it is English self-assertion. And the inexorable logic of Brexit is the logic of English nationalism: the birth of a new nation state bounded by the Channel and the Tweed.

Over time, the main political entity most likely to emerge from Brexit is not a Britain with its greatness restored or a sweetly reunited kingdom. It is a standalone England. Scotland will have a second referendum on independence, this time with the lure of staying in the European Union. Northern Ireland will be in a horrendous bind, cut off from the rest of the island by a European border and with the UK melting around it. Its future as an unwanted appendage of a shrunken Britain is unsustainable. Wales is more uncertain, but a resurgence of Welsh nationalism after Brexit is entirely possible, especially after a Scottish departure from the UK. After Brexit, an independent England will emerge by default.

And this is, of course, a perfectly legitimate aspiration. Nationalism, whether we like it or not, is almost universal and the English have as much right to it as anyone else. There's nothing inherently absurd about the notion of England as an independent nation state. It's just that if you're going to create a new nation state, you ought to be talking about it, arguing for it, thinking it through. And this isn't happening. England seems to be muddling its way towards a very peculiar event: accidental independence.

The first thing about the idea of England as a nation state that governs itself and only itself is that it is radically new. The Brexit campaign is fuelled by a mythology of England proudly 'standing alone', as it did against the Spanish Armada and Adolf Hitler. But when did England really stand alone? The answer, roughly speaking, is for 300 of the past 1,200 years. England has been a political entity for only two relatively short periods. The first was between the early tenth century, when the first English national kingdom was created by Athelstan, and 1016, when it was conquered by Cnut the Dane. The second was between 1453, when English kings effectively gave up their attempts to rule France, and 1603, when James VI and I united the thrones of England and Scotland.

Otherwise – and this includes all of the past 400 years – England has always been part of at least one larger entity: an AngloFrench kingdom, the United Kingdom in its various forms, a global empire, the European Union. The English are much less used to being left to their own devices than they think they are.

English nationalists can quite reasonably point out that many emerging nation states have even less experience of being a stand-alone, self-governing entity – my own country, Ireland, being an obvious example. The big difference is that other countries actually go through a process – often very long and difficult – of preparing themselves politically, culturally and emotionally for the scary business of being (to borrow a term from Irish nationalism) 'ourselves alone'. In England, there is no process. A decisive step is about to be taken without acknowledging the path ahead.

As Johnny Rotten (a typically English child of immigrants) put it: 'There is no future in England's dreaming.'

Hardly anyone is even talking about England – all the Brexit arguments are framed in terms of Britain or the UK, as if these historically constructed and contingent entities will simply carry on regardless in the new dispensation. The Brexiteers imagine an earthquake that will, curiously, leave the domestic landscape unaltered. English nationalism is thus a very strange phenomenon – a passion that is driving a nation towards historic change but one that seems unwilling even to speak its own name.

It is hard to think of any parallel for this. Successful national independence movements usually have five things going for them: a deep sense of grievance against the existing order; a reasonably clear (even if invented) idea of a distinctive national identity; a shared (albeit largely imaginary) narrative of the national past; a new elite-in-waiting; and a vision of a future society that will be better because it is self-governing.

The English nationalism that underlies Brexit has, at best, one of these five assets: the sense of grievance is undeniably powerful. It's also highly ambiguous – it is rooted in the shrinking of British social democracy but the actual outcome of Brexit will be an even closer embrace of unfettered neoliberalism. There is a weird mismatch between the grievance and the solution.

None of the other four factors applies. As a cultural identity, Englishness is wonderfully potent but not distinctive – its very success means that it is global property. From the English language to the Beatles, from Shakespeare to the Premier League, its icons are planetary. The great cultural appeal of nationalism – we need political independence or our unique culture will die – just doesn't wash. Moreover, this power of English culture derives precisely from its capacity to absorb immigrant energies. From the Smiths to Zadie Smith, from the Brontës to Dizzee Rascal, it is very hard to imagine an 'English' culture that is not also Afro-Caribbean, Asian, Irish, Jewish and so on.

Is there a shared narrative of the English past that functions even as a useful collective invention? English nationalism has a hard time integrating the past of John Ball and the Levellers, of Mary Wollstonecraft and Tom Paine with that of monarchs, generals and imperial power.

As for an elite-in-waiting, the English nationalist movement certainly has one. But the handover of elite power that will accompany this particular national revolution will surely be the most underwhelming in history – from one set of public school and Oxbridge Tories to another. And this elite's vision of a future society seems to come down to the same lump of money – the (dishonestly) alleged £350 million a week that will be saved by leaving the EU – being spent over and over on everything from the National Health Service to farm subsidies. Plus, of course, fewer immigrants, thereby creating some kind of imaginary *Lebensraum*. There is no attempt to articulate any set of social principles by which the new England might govern itself.

When it comes down to it, nationalism is about the line between Them and Us. The Brexiteers seem pretty clear about Them – Brussels bureaucrats and immigrants. It's just the Us bit that they haven't quite worked out yet. Being ready for self-government demands a much better sense of the self you want to govern.

21 June 2016

With two days to go to the vote, it seems clear to me that Leave will win. Which prompts the question: what is the attraction of self-harm?

I hurt myself today / To see if I still feel

TRENT REZNOR, 'Hurt'.

Why do people cut themselves? Obviously because they are unhappy, frustrated, angry. They feel that no one cares about them, no one listens to them. But it is still hard to understand the attractions of inflicting pain on yourself.

Two things seem to make cutting addictive. One is that it gives the pain you feel a name and a location. You can feel it and see it – it has an immediate focus that is somehow more tolerable than the larger, deeper distress. The other is that it provides the illusion of control. You choose to do it; you are taking an action and producing a result. It is a kind of power, even if the only one you can exercise that power over is yourself, and even if the only thing you can do to yourself is damage.

The thing to remember is that, even though these actions are irrational, the distress is often entirely rational. It may be well founded. Maybe it's true that nobody cares about you. Maybe your parents are so wrapped up in their own conflicts and obsessions that they don't really listen to you or pay attention to what's going on in your life. Maybe you feel powerless because you actually are powerless.

Just look at what's happening to Greece: the EU is slowly, sadistically and quite deliberately turning one of its own member

9

states into a third-world country. And it is doing this simply to make a point. No serious person now believes that the EU's Greek policies are working or will work. Greece's infamous debts were 100 per cent of GDP in 2007. The so-called bailouts have pushed them up to 180 per cent now and a projected 250 per cent by 2060. And all for what? To satisfy some crudely religious notion that sinners must be severely punished if virtue is to flourish.

A polity that inflicts such pointless suffering on some of its most vulnerable citizens is morally askew.

The EU lost its moral compass when the Berlin Wall fell. Before that, it was in a competition against communism. The generations of Western European leaders who had experienced the chaos of the 1930s and 1940s were anxious to prove that a market system could be governed in such a way as to create full employment, fair opportunities and steady progress towards economic equality.

But when the need to compete with alternative ideologies went away after the collapse of the Soviet Union, the EU gradually abandoned its social democratic and Christian Democratic roots. It also moved away from evidence-based economics – the German-led austerity drive after 2008 has been impervious to the realities of its own failure.

The social consequences have been shrugged off. Inequality has risen across the continent: the richest seven million people in Europe now have the same amount of wealth as the poorest 662 million people. There are now 123 million people in the EU at risk of poverty. That's a quarter of the EU population.

This has been allowed to happen because the fear of social and political chaos went out of the system. There is a European technocratic elite that has lost its memory. It has forgotten that poverty, inequality, insecurity and a sense of powerlessness have drastic political repercussions.

The EU was founded on a kind of constructive pessimism. Behind its drive towards inclusion and equality lay those two powerful words: or else. It was an institution that knew that if things are not held together by collective justice, things will fall apart. In the best sense, the EU itself was a Project Fear. Without that fear, the project became arrogant, complacent and obsessed with grand schemes such as the ill-conceived euro.

But Brexit is still self-harm. For the cynical leaders of the Brexit campaign, the freedom they desire is the freedom to dismantle the environmental, social and labour protections that they call 'red tape'. They want to sever the last restraints on the very market forces that have caused the pain. They offer a jagged razor of incoherent English nationalism to distressed and excluded communities and say: 'Go on, cut yourself, it feels good.'

And if Brexit happens it will feel good. It will be exhilarating and empowering. It will make English hearts beat faster and the blood flow more quickly. Until they eventually notice that it's their own blood that is flowing.

24 June 2016

It is early morning and the results are in.
Even if you expected Leave to win, it is
still hard to absorb what has happened.
This is an immediate attempt.

The English always prided themselves on not doing revolutions. Their last one, in 1688, was, for them, a curiously polite affair: the blood flowed at Aughrim and the Boyne, but not in East Anglia or Bristol.

The self-image of English conservatives is one of slow, careful, moderate change. And now, ironically, the very people who claim to revere this heritage have staged a sudden, reckless, leap-in-the-dark coup. The country that prides itself on sober moderation has made one of the most impulsive moves ever undertaken in a developed democracy. The stiff upper lips have parted and released a wild and inarticulate cry of rage and triumph.

Make no mistake: this is an English nationalist revolution.

At its heart are all of the things the English used to see as the province of other, less rational, nations: identity, difference, the deep passions of belonging and resentment. It did not, in the end, matter that no one on the Brexit side could articulate a coherent economic case for leaving the EU. It did not even matter that those who will take over from David Cameron will be right-wing market fundamentalists whose policies will deepen the very inequalities and alienation that have driven working-class voters towards Leave. It did not even matter that the very entity in whose name independence is being claimed – the United Kingdom – is surely doomed by Brexit.

What mattered was what always matters in nationalist revolutions: the appeal of Us against Them.

It helped the Leave campaign enormously that Them is both tangible and abstract, both very near and quite far away.

It is, on the one hand, the visible faces of large numbers of immigrants and, on the other, the faceless bureaucracy in Brussels. These were perfect targets for resentment, not least because they can't answer back. Immigrants and bureaucrats were not on anybody's campaigning platform. It was easy to turn them into sinister forces bent on crowding the English out of their own homeland and binding them in chains of red tape.

And it helped, too, that the European Union really is in a terrible state, that the passing of the generation of European leaders who experienced the Second World War has left a vacuum where visionary leadership ought to be. Painting the EU as a failed project is grossly simplistic, but there is enough truth in this crude portrait for people to recognise the likeness.

It helped, finally and most ironically of all, that the same Conservative Party whose internal disputes created this historic moment, is governing with the very limited legitimacy that 35 per cent of the vote confers. Britain's unreformed first-past-the-post electoral system has left huge parts of the population feeling democratically irrelevant and unrepresented. However much one might be repelled by UKIP, it is obvious that when four million people vote for a party and it gets just a single MP, Westminster itself becomes Them for many voters.

But if the Them side of the nationalist equation is strong, the Us side is dangerously weak.

This is a revolution that has scarcely spoken its own name. The English nationalism that fuelled it was not explicitly on the table – it was cloaked in talk of Britain and the UK, as if those historically constructed entities would be unshaken by the earthquake of Brexit. The English have no modern experience of national independence and the referendum campaign articulated no vision of what an independent England will actually look like.

The key word in the pro-Brexit rhetoric was 'back' – take back control; take back our country. Insofar as there is any vision behind the revolution, it is nostalgic. There is the illusion that England will now go back to the way it used to be – a vigorous world power with a secure sense of its own identity that stands defiantly alone. It's a used-to-be that arguably never was and that certainly is not going to be restored. In looking for security and stability, the English have launched themselves into one of the most unstable and uncertain periods in their modern history.

24 June 2016

As the morning wears on, an image floats up
into bleary consciousness.

D id you ever see a slightly drunk man trying that trick with the tablecloth? He thinks he can whip the cloth off the table with a fast, clean snap, but leave all the crockery perfectly intact. He gives a sharp tug and stands back with a triumphant flourish as the plates and glasses come flying to the ground and shatter all around him.

That's what Brexit is like. Those who have driven it have success-fully pulled the cloth off the table – the underlying fabric of modern Britain has been whipped away with a shocking suddenness.

They stand in triumph, sure that they have pulled off the trick of removing a whole layer of political reality without disturbing all the family tableware. They have yet to notice that so much that was on the table is now at their feet, broken, perhaps irreparably.

Brexit has achieved the breathtaking feat of causing deep cracks in four different polities at a single stroke.

One of them, most obviously, is the European Union. For the first time in its history, the EU's engine has gone decisively into reverse. At the simplest level, it has been a process of relentless ex-pansion – no large entity in modern history has grown so rapidly since the United States in the nineteenth century.

And now the steady advance has become a full-blown retreat. The whole psychology of the European project has been turned on its head – instead of ever-widening frontiers, the EU now has to think about how to prevent a retreat from becoming a rout.

The rout that must be feared is a disorderly overthrow of

15

liberal European values. When Nigel Farage speaks, as he did in his moment of triumph early today, of victory for 'the real people, the decent people', the undertone is that nearly half of the UK's voters are neither real nor decent.

England has not had the time, nor made the effort, to develop an inclusive, civic, progressive nationalism. It is left with a nationalism that is scarcely articulated in positive terms at all and that thus plugs into the darker energies of resentment and xenophobia.

But this is not just an English disease. Brexit is a huge boost to the European far right. The EU already has two member states – Poland and Hungary – that have moved towards authoritarian nationalism and away from liberal democracy. The success of the English nationalist revolution (and that is what Brexit is) will further energise those forces throughout the union.

This will please some of the Brexiteers, of course – at least until the more moderate of them realise that they are, after all, Europeans and that the fate of Europe is their fate, too. But they surely cannot be so complacent about the other three polities they have managed to crack.

One of them is the UK. A second Scottish independence referendum is inevitable – and this time the pro-independence side will have the enormous advantage of putting forward a conservative proposition that has overwhelming popular support: keep Scotland in the EU.

The utter refusal of the pro-Brexit campaigners, almost of all of whom would claim to venerate the union, to take the breakup of the UK seriously suggests that, deep down, they really don't care that much about it. English self-assertion has trumped UK preservation. The consequences will play out over the next decade: the chances are that by the tenth anniversary of what the victors are hailing as Independence Day, it will be English independence that is explicitly celebrated.

And this has deeply unsettling implications for the third cracked polity, Northern Ireland. A few pro-Remain voices, such as Trades Union Congress general secretary Frances O'Grady, tried in the referendum debates to make a gentle plea to voters to think about Ireland and the Belfast Agreement. They went unheard.

English nationalists, it turns out, wouldn't give the froth off a pint of real ale for the Irish peace process. They have recklessly imposed an EU land border between Newry and Dundalk, between Letterkenny and Derry. What grounds are there to believe that when they come to power in their own little England, they will care about (or pay for) a province they clearly regard as a closer, wetter Gibraltar, an irrelevant appendage of the motherland? It beggars belief that the Democratic Unionist Party made common cause with a movement whose logical outcome is the end of the union.

The last piece of the tableware that must now be badly fissured is the least expected: England itself. The English seem to have been utterly unprepared for how deeply divided they are, how bitter and angry the Brexit debate would be, how political assassination would return to the streets of England.

David Cameron, in one of British history's greatest miscalculations, thought of the referendum as the lancing of a boil. The bubble of nastiness that had built up in the Tory party over decades would be burst once and for all by the cold prick of economic realities. Instead, though, the referendum merely revealed how deeply the English body politic is infected with rancour and distrust.

And this raises a huge question: where is the source of authority in the brave new England? Many of the most prominent Leave campaigners are naked chancers. They made stuff up with gay abandon, but when they come to power in the autumn they will be the establishment they have told everybody not to believe.

Prime minister-in-waiting Boris Johnson is merely the winner of a Winston Churchill impersonation contest.

He has a streak of Churchill's brilliant opportunism and reckless charm, but he does not have behind him the national consensus that an existential struggle created behind Churchill and he is, in everything but girth, a lightweight.

It is not even clear that the Brexit coalition can itself hold together in any meaningful way. It is, after all, a weird conjunction. Brexit is not so much a peasants' revolt as a deeply strange peasants' – and – landlords' revolt. It is a *Downton Abbey* fantasy of toffs and servants all mucking in together. But when the toffs, as the slogan goes, 'take back control', the underlings will quickly discover that a fantasy is exactly what it is.

The disaffected working-class voter in Sunderland, rightly angry about being economically marginalised and politically disenfranchised, will wait in vain for the magical billions that are supposedly going to be repatriated from Brussels to drop from the clear blue skies of a free England.

There is, of course, a tried and trusted way to hold this kind of rickety social coalition together. It is to turn up the volume on nationalism and xenophobia, to deflect the inevitable disappointed anger on to Them.

The English nationalists have just lost their favourite scapegoat, the EU. When their dream turns sour, where will they find another?

24 June 2016

*As the result sunk in, so did the profound implications
for Northern Ireland's peace process.*

The rather patronising English joke used to be that whenever
the Irish question was about to be solved, the Irish would
change the question. And now, when the Irish question seemed
indeed to have been solved, at least for a generation, it is the English
who have changed the question.

Recklessly, casually, with barely a thought, English nationalists
have planted a bomb under the settlement that brought peace to
Northern Ireland and close cordiality to relations between Britain
and Ireland. To do this seriously and soberly would have been
bad. To do it so carelessly, with nothing more than a pat on the
head and a reassurance that everything will be all right, is frankly
insulting.

Just five years ago, when Queen Elizabeth became the first
reigning British monarch to visit southern Ireland in a century,
there was a massive sense of relief. It was not just relief that the
visit went off peacefully and well. It was much deeper than that: it
was relief from centuries of both British condescension and Irish
Anglophobia. A long story – often nasty, sometimes merely tediously wasteful – was over. There was a dignified, decent, democratic
settlement that allowed the natural warmth of a neighbourly relationship to come fully to the surface.

I never imagined then that I would ever feel bitter about England again. But I do feel bitter now, because England has done a
very bad day's work for Ireland. It is dragging Irish history along
in its triumphal wake, like tin cans tied to a wedding car.

All but a few diehards had learned to live with the partition of the island of Ireland. Why? Because the border between Northern Ireland and the Republic had become so soft as to be barely noticeable. If you crossed it, you had to change currencies, and if you were driving you had to remember that the speed limits were changing from kilometres per hour to miles. But these are just banal details. They do not impinge on the simple, ordinary experience of people sharing an island without having to be deeply conscious of division.

What will now happen is not that the old border will come back. It's much worse than that. The old border marked the line between neighbouring polities that had a common travel area and an intimate, if often fraught, relationship. It was a customs barrier. The new border will be the most westerly land frontier of a vast entity of more than 400 million people, and it will be an immigration (as well as a customs) barrier.

It will, if the Brexiteers' demands to take back control of immigration to the UK are meant seriously, have to be heavily policed to keep EU migrants who have lawfully entered the Republic from moving into the UK. And it will run between Newry and Dundalk, between Letterkenny and Derry. The Dublin–Belfast train will have to stop for passport controls. (Given that the border could not be secured with army watchtowers during the Troubles, it is not at all clear how this policing operation will work.)

Meanwhile, the cornerstone of the peace settlement, the Belfast Agreement of 1998, is being undermined. One of the key provisions of the agreement is that anyone born in Northern Ireland has the right to be a citizen of the UK or Ireland or both. What does that mean in the new dispensation? Can someone be both an EU citizen and not an EU citizen? Likewise, the agreement underpins human rights through the 'complete incorporation into Northern Ireland law of the European Convention on Human Rights'. Though not strictly required by Brexit, the Leave leadership is committed to removing the convention from UK law – in other words to ripping out a core part of the peace settlement.

But the Belfast Agreement isn't some minor memorandum. It is an international treaty, registered with the United Nations. It is also arguably the greatest modern achievement of British diplomacy, partly crafted by public servants and made possible by British politicians, especially John Major and Tony Blair. It is one of the most successful models for conflict resolution around the world. Messing around with it is an insult, not just to Ireland, but to Britain's international standing.

This fecklessness in turn is deeply unsettling for unionists in Northern Ireland. It suggests that the new English nationalism is completely indifferent to their fate. During the referendum debates, a few pro-Remain voices, such as the TUC general secretary Frances O'Grady (herself of Irish descent), tried to make a gentle plea to voters to think about Ireland and the Belfast Agreement. They went unheard. English nationalists, it turns out, wouldn't give the froth off a pint of real ale for the Irish peace process.

And if they don't care enough even to talk in any serious way about the consequences of Brexit for Northern Ireland, what grounds are there to believe that when they come to power in their own little England they will care about (or pay for) a province they clearly regard as a closer, wetter Gibraltar, an irrelevant appendage of the motherland?

Northern Ireland desperately needed a generation of relative political boredom, in which ordinary issues such as taxation and the health service – rather than the unanswerable questions of national identity – could become the stuff of partisan debate. Brexit has made that impossible.

Sinn Féin's immediate call for a referendum on a united Ireland may be reckless and opportunistic, but no more so than the Democratic Unionist Party's failure to understand that Brexit is the best gift to Irish nationalists. It is the beginning of the breakup of the union and the rise of an independent England for which Northern Ireland will be no more than a distant nuisance.

When they take power, the Brexiteers have a moral duty to think deeply and speak honestly about these effects of their victory.

But the signs are that they will pay as much attention to them as gung-ho warriors typically give to any other kind of collateral damage.

1 July 2016

A sense of Englishness is clearly at the heart
of the upheaval but what does it mean?

I f you asked any pro-Brexit campaigner in the first flush of
euphoric victory for a snatch of poetry, the repertoire would have
consisted of two items: one by William Shakespeare, the other
by William Blake. Neither is what the triumphant English patriot
thinks it is.

The first words to come to mind would have been John of
Gaunt's evocation of a sacred England in *Richard II*:

> This royal throne of kings, this scepter'd isle,
> This earth of majesty, this seat of Mars,
> This other Eden, demi-paradise,
> This fortress built by Nature for herself
> Against infection and the hand of war,
> This happy breed of men, this little world,
> This precious stone set in the silver sea...

There could be no more stirring evocation of Fortress England
as a perfect 'little world'. The imagined community of post-Brexit
England is John of Gaunt's demi-paradise, a place uniquely carved
out by nature to protect its happy breed from the infection of
foreigners.

But even as you read these lines you stumble over the word
'isle'. Gaunt in this speech is talking explicitly about 'this realm,
this England' – not about Britain. And England isn't an island. The
speech keeps claiming the idea of a land surrounded by water,

'bound in with the triumphant sea'. Gaunt's geography is strangely out of kilter.

And so is Shakespeare's history. John of Gaunt was Jean of Ghent, as in the city that is now part of Belgium. He was a French-speaking Plantagenet who spent much of his time in Aquitaine and became, for fifteen years, titular king of Castile. When the actual people of England rose up in the Peasants' Revolt of 1381, John of Gaunt was at the top of their hit list.

In any case, if you read the full speech it is not at all the hymn to English perfection suggested by its most famous lines. Shakespeare is actually making brilliant use of a rhetorical device, in this case antithesis: evoking something through what it is not.

The purpose of Gaunt's hyperbole is to point up a contrast between this imaginary England and the actual place as it is under Richard's reign: broke and mortgaged to the hilt. The imaginary island 'bound with the triumphant sea' is in reality 'bound in with shame', awash with 'rotten parchment bonds'. The speech is not a panegyric on England but a complaint about the country being in hock to bondholders.

The other poem was actually on the lips of the Leave campaigners last week. If they get the independent English state they desire Blake's 'Jerusalem' will be its national anthem:

> I will not cease from Mental Fight,
> Nor shall my sword sleep in my hand:
> Till we have built Jerusalem,
> In England's green & pleasant Land.

But the adoption of Blake's poem as a touchstone of nationalism is bizarre. It is a cry of protest at two pillars of English identity, the Industrial Revolution and the Church of England, both of which seem to be encompassed in its bitterly rhetorical question, 'And was Jerusalem builded here, / Among these dark Satanic mills?'

It embraces free love ('Bring me my arrows of desire') in the context of Blake's support for equality between the sexes. Its mystical vision of Jesus having visited ancient England is posed not as a claim to special status but as a series of disturbing questions. Like Shakespeare's 'scepter'd isle' speech 'Jerusalem' works by way of contrasts, evoking an English Utopia only as a rebuke to the present state of the country.

In its original form Blake appended to 'Jerusalem' the biblical tag 'Would to God that all the Lord's people were prophets'. The poem is a call for a freethinking, egalitarian, democratic England, in opposition to the repressive and bellicose patriotism of the era of the Napoleonic Wars, when it was written. It's a fair bet that hearing it sung by Nigel Farage, Michael Gove or Boris Johnson would have made poor William Blake puke.

These ironies are worth pointing out because they underline something that may be important in the post-Brexit dispensation. Right-wing English nationalism is on the rise, but its cultural foundations are very weak. Even its most emotive texts don't mean what nationalists think they mean.

They both raise the most problematic question of backward-looking nostalgic nationalism: when, exactly, was this golden age of Englishness you want to return to? At the end of the sixteenth century Shakespeare imagined John of Gaunt 200 years previously already complaining about how England had gone to hell in a handcart. Two centuries later Blake suggests that if you want to find the pure, holy England you have to go back to 'ancient times' – and even then with a lot of question marks over their existence.

At the end of the 'scepter'd isle' speech Gaunt says something that may in fact be more pertinent to England's current situation that his earlier hyperbole: 'That England, that was wont to conquer others, / Hath made a shameful conquest of itself.'

2 July 2016

*Boris Johnson's campaign to succeed David Cameron
collapses in farce. Donald Trump is looming as the most
likely next president of the United States.*

We are living with the politics of the fake orgasm.

The leaders of the Brexit campaign are obliged to join in with the ecstasies of their followers. They must let out a few polite yelps of satisfaction. But a week on, it is increasingly clear that theirs is a phoney consummation. The earth may have moved – but not for them.

As shown by Boris Johnson's retreat from the prospect of having to actually govern the new kingdom he did so much to create, it was all a performance. It will not be long before those they embraced – the alienated, the dispossessed – realise that they have been had in more ways than one.

Like the followers of Donald Trump in the US, white working-class Brexit voters are experiencing a new kind of political relationship. These movements may look like the reactionary populism we have seen many times before, but they are profoundly different in one crucial respect.

The old reactionary politics is utterly serious: its leaders really intend to do what they say they will do, and they really mean to reshape systems of government to allow them to do it. When they say they are going to cut out the contagion that is corrupting society – the Jews, the Catholics, the blacks, the communists – they really mean to act on their twisted obsessions, and they have every intention of creating the authoritarian systems that will allow it to happen.

What's different about the new reactionaries is that they are not at all serious. The farce of Boris Johnson's abortive leadership bid is just a token of a deeper truth: this is a game of thrones that is all game and no throne.

In the days after the Brexit vote, a number of rueful commentators were drawn to W. B. Yeats's lines from the apocalyptic poem 'The Second Coming': 'The best lack all conviction, while the worst / Are full of passionate intensity.'

But this is to miss the point of our particular political moment in the Anglophone world. It may be true that the best lack conviction, but the second part of Yeats's comparison emphatically does not apply. The worst are not full of passionate intensity; they are, to borrow from a different Yeats poem, just a pretty bellows full of faux-angry wind. They have no serious intention – no plan and no means – of doing the things they say they will do.

Here are some of the things that are not going to happen in the next few years, even if we end up with President Donald Trump and Prime Minister Michael Gove.

There will not be a wall across the Mexico/US border and Mexico will not pay for it. Muslims will not be barred from entering the United States on the grounds of their religion. Immigration into the UK will not be drastically reduced. An extra £350 million a year will not be put into the National Health Service. British fisherman will not be hauling in greatly increased catches. Vast steel plants will not reopen in Pennsylvania and Port Talbot.

The point is that neither Trump nor the Brexit leaders have ever believed for one moment that any of these promises are real.

Consider the evolution of Trump's most lurid (and, according to the polls, most resonant) proposition: the ban on Muslims entering the US. It is indeed a staggering suggestion – it would overthrow the US constitution. But we can say with some certainty that one person who has never taken it seriously is Trump.

As recently as last September, he was saying Syrian refugees should be allowed into the US: 'Something has to be done. It's an unbelievable humanitarian problem.' By December, however, he called for a 'total and complete shutdown of Muslims entering the United States until our country's representatives can figure out what the hell is going on'.

He then said customs agents would be instructed to ask incoming travellers if they are Muslim, and that those who said yes would be turned away. In May he retreated, saying the whole thing was 'just a suggestion until we find out what's going on'.

On 13 June, Trump changed his mind again, saying he would ban everyone from 'areas of the world where there is a proven history of terrorism against the United States, Europe or our allies'. (This would, of course, include Ireland, Germany and Italy.) Then he corrected this to say that it applied only to Islamist terrorism.

This is not a politician refining a serious policy proposal or even a fascist planning an outrage. It is just a spoofer trying to remember what spiel he came up with last.

Consider, too, the now infamous £350 million a week that the official pro-Brexit campaign claimed was being 'sent' to Brussels and would, after Brexit, be spent on the National Health Service. (The Leave referendum broadcasts featured a split-screen before and after hospital emergency department, one coldly indifferent and overcrowded with dark-skinned men, the other so empty the staff were only too delighted to meet the sick old lady who came in.)

This was a double lie: there was no £350 million a week, and Johnson, Gove and their allies were also promising large chunks of it to farms, education and research.

But even calling this a lie is to miss the point about the new politics. A lie has a relationship, albeit an inverse one, to the truth. The truth content of the £350 million claim is absolute zero. It floats freely above any actual intention to do something in the real world. Like Trump's Mexican wall and ban on Muslims, it is a statement of the sort invented by the linguistic philosopher Noam Chomsky: 'Colourless green ideas sleep furiously.' Chomsky pointed out that this sentence is entirely grammatical; it follows all the rules of the way we construct statements of fact. But it is still nonsense. It refers to nothing whatsoever.

When Trump says 'I will build a wall and Mexico will pay for it' or Boris Johnson and Michael Gove say 'We send the EU £350 million a week – let's fund our NHS instead', they are actually saying 'Colourless green ideas sleep furiously.' Their claims have the form and grammar of traditional political promises, but they bear no relation to anything that they actually intend to do.

The problem with pure nonsense is that it cannot be contradicted: it is no good arguing that colourless green ideas don't really sleep at all. And so it is with these claims. You can point out, for example, that even if Trump could build his wall, it would have to run through the middle of the Rio Grande. But in order to do so, you are depending on something that is entirely irrelevant to Trump's claim: the real world.

In the old politics, we know what would have happened to the £350 million claim. Once it was comprehensively proven to be a lie, the Leave side would have had to withdraw it and the Remain side would have made hay. In the new politics, however, the protestations of the Remain side that their opponents had been caught out in a huge lie were entirely ineffectual. Exposing the lie was like revealing that Snow White didn't live with seven dwarves. People simply shrug and say that maybe she lived with six dwarves instead. So what?

Where is this new politics of fake reaction coming from? Like all products, it has a supply side and a demand side. The supply side is the world of media and branding. The Leave campaign was the product, not just of media barons such as Rupert Murdoch and Paul Dacre, but of the Frankensteins they have specialised in creating – chimeras who are half politician and half professional journalistic provocateur.

It says it all that Johnson's first pronouncement on what the campaign he had led actually meant for the lives of UK citizens came, not in a press conference or a public speech, but in his 'exclusive' *Daily Telegraph* column, for which he is paid £275,000 a year.

Johnson and Gove have followed the same path, from the Oxford Union where they learned to argue opposite sides of any case with an equal pretence of conviction, to Murdoch's *Times* to the Tory party and high office. They are, as Nick Cohen put it in the *Observer*, 'the worst journalist politicians you can imagine: pundits who have prospered by treating public life as a game'.

Both are highly practised in a kind of meta-politics, in which commentary and activity, medium and message, are fused into one. In that meta-politics, what the US satirist Stephen Colbert called 'truthiness' – stuff that feels like it should be true – trumps the truth every time.

Trump is even further along this postmodern road, a longtime harbinger of the new world in which you don't make money by creating and selling things, but by being known as a guy who makes money. His real business career is pockmarked with bankruptcies. But he had the genius to understand early on that reality was entirely irrelevant. He went into self-branding. As a *New York Times* investigation of Trump's business career concluded: 'Putting his name on products and services – and collecting fees – was often where his actual involvement began and ended.'

Trump is a performer who acts out the role of mogul: an act perfected and popularised, of course, on *The Apprentice*. In that role, he has learned that political statements may be even more power-ful when they have the same relationship to reality as his mogul brand has to actual business: none whatsoever.

On the demand side of the equation, we know, of course, that this new reactionary politics appeals to something all too real. That is the desperation of people who have been dumped out of the working-class lives of industry and aspiration they once knew and into the humiliating experience of being discarded as human set-aside.

We should not underestimate the extent to which Trump and the Brexiteers feed off the sheer anomie of life in these left-behind communities. Yes, this is a politics that thrives on anger, but it also thrives on boredom.

Working-class communities have been taught by late capital-ism to consume fantasies. They know very well that buying and wearing an acrylic T-shirt with the colours and advertising logos of Manchester United or the Cleveland Browns doesn't really make you one with the multimillionaire sports star whose name is on the back. And they know that cheering for Trump or having a selfie taken with Boris doesn't actually make you one with these entitled scions of the ruling class. But there is a comfort in the illusion: it breaks the boredom of a hopeless existence.

Listening to Trump tell you that he is going to build a wall or to a Brexit leader telling you that there will be no more immigration is like buying a lottery ticket. You don't have to actually believe that you are going to win $100 million or £100 million this week. For even if the chance is one in a billion, it's still a chance: it keeps the boredom at bay by introducing a fantastic possibility.

In this logic, the bigger and more outlandish the political claim (No more Muslims! Your industrial job is coming back!), the more reason there is to buy the ticket. You don't have to actually believe that Trump is telling the truth when he says he will build a wall. You just have to believe that there's a one in a million chance he might. The more desperate you are, the more brightly the prospect of a transformative moment glimmers on the distant horizon of your dreams.

The problem now is that, with Brexit, many of these people think their numbers have actually come up. Brexit, to its leading champions a mere linguistic construct, has become a real-world event. The transformative moment has arrived. And then their leader, Boris Johnson, walks away, tacitly admitting that his successful advocacy of this great upheaval was no more serious than winning a debating competition at the Oxford Union.

He was only playing, after all. But he was playing with fire. The fantasies that he and Trump have pumped into public life are not harmless – these dreams are other people's nightmares.

And these dilettantes may have opened the door for more serious people. It would be entirely in keeping with this weird postmodern drama that the simulacrum could become a reality, that the cod reactionaries could usher in the real ones.

In the fake orgasm scene of *When Harry Met Sally*, Meg Ryan's performance of ecstasy is observed by another customer in the café, who mistakes it for reality and tells the waitress: 'I'll have what she's having.' Now that xenophobia, ruling-class anarchism and self-destruction have been placed on the menu of political stimulants by the reckless fabulists, the rapidly disillusioned millions may be ready to place the same order.

Perhaps another Yeats line will have its day:

'We had fed the heart on fantasies,
The heart's grown brutal from the fare...'

12 July 2016

The Conservative Party leadership contest is continuing,
with the ludicrous Andrea Leadsom as a serious candidate,
as is Trump's rise towards the presidency.

New times require new words. In this spirit, I offer 'hopeitude' and define it as a political discourse in which overwhelming optimism is expressed on no grounds whatsoever. Hopeitude is the language both of Brexit and of Donald Trump.

Real hope has an intimate and serious relationship to despair. Hope and despair are not pure opposites. The great developments of modern civilisation – democracy, universal healthcare, access to education for the masses, recognition of equality between genders, the revolt against prejudice based on race, religion and sexual orientation – have all been driven by both emotions. You have to despair of poverty, ignorance, prejudice, injustice, indignity and patriarchy before you can rise up against them. Out of despair comes the hope that something better must be built. And this hope is concrete: it provides the sense of direction from which realistic maps of the future can be made.

Hopeitude is the political gambler's bluff. You don't have two cents' worth of real hope in your hand, so you put a big pile of hopeitude chips on the table. It's a perfect parallel to the diet of empty calories that late capitalism has devised for the poor – instead of feeding the body politic, it bloats it with corny emotional syrup and cheap rhetorical trans fats.

Consider Andrea Leadsom's ludicrous speech last Thursday, setting out why she should be the next prime minister of the UK, delivered with the weird rictus of a beauty pageant contestant:

'You see, I am an optimist. I truly believe we can be the greatest nation on Earth… I believe we have a great future ahead of us… We are a remarkable people and we have so much more to give.'

Part of Leadsom's rhetoric is a more demure English echo of Trump's carnival barker bombast in which everything is going to be 'huge', 'beautiful' and 'great'. Presumably Leadsom's UK and Trump's USA will go to war to decide who deserves the title of greatest nation on earth. Though, come to think of it, a reality TV contest would be much more apt. (The British have already had their qualifying round: 'I'm an Empire, Get Me Out of Here.')

For much of this rhetoric is pure *X Factor*. Hopeitude resonates in large measure because it chimes with the new religion of the talent show. If you dream hard enough, your wish will come true. If you really, really want it, it will happen. Leadsom actually said this: 'I want to lead a nation where anyone who aims high can achieve their dreams.' This is the politics of reality TV: wanting a job or an education is like wanting to be a star. Believe it and it will happen. In hopeitude, the real-world struggle to achieve dignity is replaced with the fantasy of achieving your dreams.

What's happening here is a Ghost Dance for the twenty-first-century white working class. In the late nineteenth century, when their world had been destroyed, the Plains Indians of the American Midwest looked to the prophecies of the shaman Wovoka. He said that if they did the Ghost Dance, the buffalo would come back, the dead Indians would return and a great natural disaster would make all the white people disappear. Hopeitude is the Ghost Dance at the fag end of a sleazy rave, with privileged politicians selling coke and ecstasy and the promise that if you keep dancing the steel plants will come back to the great plains and the dead hopes of social democracy and the New Deal will return to the earth. The sugar rush of ersatz optimism will wear off soon enough, but it will be followed by an even deeper despair. The questions will get nastier: why is everything not great and beautiful? Why have the immigrants not gone home? Why are we not prospering, as Trump has it, 'bigly'? Why have the buffalo not returned?

21 October 2016

When James Joyce's alter ego Stephen Dedalus claims in *Ulysses* that 'History... is a nightmare from which I am trying to awake', it is surely Irish history he has in mind. But now the Irish have to awake to the living nightmare of British – perhaps we should say English – history. Brexit is disconcerting on so many levels that it is easy to miss one particularly discombobulating shift. For centuries, there has been a potent contrast between the place of history in the two islands: in Britain, history was over; in Ireland it was continuing on its baleful path.

All the mad conflicts over nationhood and identity and constitutional structures had ceased to trouble the essential British settlement. It was the poor bloody Irish who were still roiled and racked by all that dark passion. There was an Irish question and it was a maddening perplexity. But there certainly was no English question.

And now our little archipelago is turned inside out. We have swapped places. Ireland has, or thought it had, a workable settlement, a way of taming and managing its history. It has been awfully hard won, carved slowly out of a big block of human agony.

But then up pops the English question. It seems as if these islands must have a fixed quantum of nationalist fervour, a strict allocation of identity crises and cultural neuroses. When it diminishes in the west, it suddenly wells up in the east. The bad habit of defining 'Us' as 'not Them' finally wanes in Ireland, but just as it does so it waxes again in *England*. Britain's Irish question becomes Ireland's English question.

For Ireland, our English question is every bit as intimate and excruciating as it is for those in Britain who are still wondering how Brexit came to pass. For good and ill, the two islands are stuck together in a marriage that can be sundered neither by death nor divorce. And in a marriage, you suffer badly when your spouse goes off the rails.

Brexit threatens the Northern Ireland peace process, undermining the Belfast Agreement. It poses the real risk of the imposition of an external European Union border across the fields of Fermanagh and Tyrone. It hurts indigenous Irish businesses whose main trade links are with the UK. To misquote W. B. Yeats, we are locked in to the Brexiteers' recklessness and the key is turned on our uncertainty.

The initial Irish reaction to being dragged into the mad antics of English nationalism has been one of fury. It is one thing to be made part of someone else's historic nightmare, but quite another to be given this role by people who seemed not to know or care what Brexit might do to Ireland.

And this applies as much to the Remainers as to the Brexiteers. I've just read Craig Oliver's gripping account of the whole referendum debacle from inside Downing Street. I note that the *Daily Mail* is mentioned fourteen times and the *Daily Telegraph* twenty-two. *Game of Thrones*, *The Godfather* and *The X-Files* all feature. Northern Ireland? Not once. The Republic of Ireland? Zilch. John Bull's Other Island was apparently cut off by a thick mental fog for the duration of the campaign.

The careless rapture of England's identity crisis leaves many of us on the other side of the Irish Sea in a cold rage. Tempers have not been calmed by the patronising vagueness of the reassurances that we shouldn't worry because everything will be all right. It doesn't help either that at the back of these reassurances is an assumption among some Brexiteers – including some of the Unionist leadership in Northern Ireland – that the Republic of Ireland is not really an independent country, and that it will simply have to follow Britain out of the EU. The suggestion that Ireland will operate UK migration controls at its own ports and airports carries with it the same presumptuous air.

But anger is of little use. No one knows better than the Irish the chagrin of having your neighbours adopt a superior tone and tell you to get over your funny historic obsessions – so Ireland shouldn't do that to England now. Instead the Irish government has to do the decent thing for all concerned, which is to try to talk its British friends down from the ledge of a hard Brexit, and to talk its European friends out of pushing Britain off that ledge.

It's not the kind of job that one sovereign government would normally undertake in relation to another. But in the current circumstances, what has normal got to do with anything?

There are signs now that the vanquished Remainers are trying to find a voice. The economic consequences of Brexit are becoming clearer and the ugly tone of the new xenophobia is becoming more repellent to the great British traditions of moderation and tolerance.

There is still time between now and the invocation of Article 50 in March 2017 to galvanise a common effort across all the polities of these islands, and to look for a third way between hard Brexit and no Brexit. While both the Brexiteers and the EU leadership are posing this stark choice between extremes, the mutual interest in achieving a more fluid, ambiguous compromise must not be lost.

Zealots will find this despicable and claim that compromises never work. But the fact is that the Irish question was solved (in the medium term at least) by just such a creative fudge. The 1998 Belfast Agreement, which came from the intimate co-operation of the Irish and British governments, is a masterpiece of ambiguity. It replaces hard certainties about identity and constitutional status with an open, contingent and deliberately slippery compromise.

It works imperfectly, but it does work – precisely because multiple identities and political contradictions are what we all have to live with – in Ireland, Britain and Europe. It is, in this, a fine model for the kind of creative reconciling of opposing impulses that could solve the English question. And remember that it was much harder to achieve than a sensible semi-Brexit may be because it had to be negotiated across a blood-soaked table.

The Irish government needs to forget protocol and set itself up explicitly as the champion of a soft, ambiguous and contingent Brexit that leaves open the possibility of a return ticket. Keeping Britain within the single market is a vital Irish national interest, and some of us are arrogant enough to suggest that it might be no less vital for Britain.

Before the war of words escalates, and positions petrify into irreconcilability, Ireland should make an urgent and coherent effort to plead the virtues of equivocation. If nothing else, Ireland helping England out of a hole would be a historical irony worth savouring.

TIMELINE

17 January 2017:   Prime Minister Theresa May gives her Lancaster House speech, setting out a hard-line interpretation of the meaning of the Brexit referendum result.

26 January 2017:   Government publishes European Union (Notification of Withdrawal) Bill.

2 February 2017:   Government publishes its Brexit white paper, formally setting out its strategy for the UK to leave the EU.

March 2017:   The prime minister triggers Article 50 of the Treaty on European Union, meaning that the UK is to leave at 11 p.m. on 29 March 2019.

18 April 2017:   May calls a general election – to be held on 8 June 2017.

17 January 2017

Elections are held for the Northern Ireland Assembly, following the collapse of the Executive over, among other things, the 'cash for ash' scandal in which DUP ministers allowed a subsidy scheme for renewable energy to run wildly out of control. A strange story of the DUP's role in channelling dark money towards the Leave campaign emerges.

A funny thing happened on the way to the Brexit vote last June and it has important resonances for the Northern Ireland elections.

Two days before the referendum, more than a million people commuting to and around London got their free copy of the *Metro* newspaper.

But it came wrapped in a four-page glossy ad supplement. The front page carried three slogans: 'Vote to leave the EU on Thursday', 'We can be even stronger if we take back control' and (for the slow learners) 'Vote to leave'.

The rest of the content was the usual pro-Brexit propaganda, including the false claim that Turkey and Albania were about to join the EU and the notorious lie that £350 million a week was being paid by the UK to Brussels. (This already-discredited claim was cunningly adjusted to 'the European Union bills us £50 million every single day'.)

But the funny thing is that the wraparound was credited to an entity that must have seemed mysterious to most of those bleary London commuters: DUP. Was that, some might have wondered, short for Don't Understand Politics?

The *Metro* does not circulate in Northern Ireland. The glossy supplement was for voters in the London area only. It was undoubtedly very expensive – newspapers, even freesheets, don't like to hide themselves inside someone else's ad so they charge a very heavy price for this kind of thing. It is safe to assume that this was the most expensive single piece of propaganda ever issued by an Irish political party. Yet we have no idea who paid for it: Northern Ireland, charmingly, is exempt from British laws on the disclosure of political donations.

At the time, the Democratic Unionist Party's Mervyn Storey would say only that whatever the cost, it was a 'price worth paying' to establish the DUP as a key player in the Brexit campaign, not in Northern Ireland but in the UK as a whole.

There is a lot we don't know about the funding of the DUP's pro-Brexit campaign: the right-wing English businessman Arron Banks claims the DUP asked him for £30,000 a week to join his Leave.eu campaign but the DUP vehemently denies this.

What is absolutely clear, however, is that the DUP willingly allowed itself to be sucked in to the murkier side of the Brexit movement.

It wanted to express an ultra-British identity (which it is fully entitled to do) but it did so through opaque funding and fake claims. And, more importantly, it did so in a way that was breathtakingly irresponsible.

Arlene Foster and her colleagues knew with complete certainty that a large majority of voters in Northern Ireland wished to stay in the EU. Foster as first minister had a duty to represent, not the DUP, but the whole of Northern Ireland. She and her colleagues abandoned that duty. They decided it was far more important for the DUP to cosy up to English nationalism than it was to set out a coherent analysis of the interests of the people of Northern Ireland. And this is why Foster should not be first minister and why the DUP should be turfed out of office.

Without diminishing the importance of the 'cash for ash' scandal, the cash used for the purpose of politically trashing Northern Ireland's vital interests is a much bigger question.

Sinn Féin has its own agenda in its war with the DUP, but there is a much bigger agenda: the democratic wishes of the majority of the people of Northern Ireland and the DUP's open determination to thwart those desires.

The assembly elections may be unwanted but they do provide a fortuitous opportunity to make a clear statement: Northern Ireland wishes to remain in the EU and it is not, as the DUP keep insisting, just another part of the UK. But to make that statement, something big has to happen. For the first time, there has to be a non-sectarian alliance. The three main Opposition parties, the Ulster Unionists, the SDLP and Alliance, agree on many things, and by far the most important of them is Brexit. They each opposed it.

And they have a very strong case to make: Northern Ireland needs a government that is committed solely to getting the best deal for its own people. A DUP-led government is entirely unable to offer that commitment because the DUP is deeply compromised on the whole question. It chose to be part of the heedless and headless adventurism that has created this crisis for Northern Ireland. Even if it wished to do so, it cannot disentangle itself from the Brexiteers in London.

And Northern Ireland patently needs a government that is willing and able to fight its own corner. So make Brexit the issue. The UUP, SDLP and Alliance have a real proposition to put to voters: the DUP which blithely led us into this crisis cannot get us out of it. And it is also a positive proposal: we can offer an alternative government that is not compromised on the biggest question facing us, one that will shape all our futures. It offers a way forward, beyond the usual sectarian head-count. And it could do what elections, at their most basic, must do – punish arrogant and incompetent governments.

23 February 2017

*The EU Withdrawal Bill passed its third stage in the House
of Commons on 8 February by 494 votes to 122. But there
is no sense that Britain has yet seriously considered
what will happen in Ireland after Brexit.*

One thing the Brexiteers did not lie about was their emphatic assurance that the island of Ireland would experience, as Theresa May continues to insist, 'no return to the borders of the past'. What they did not say was that there will be a whole new frontier – welcome to the borders of the future.

We are not going back to the way things used to be before the UK and Ireland joined the European Economic Community in 1973. We are going forward, accidentally and haphazardly, into a division of the island that could be more profound than it has ever been. At best, it will be a border between the UK and the European Union itself. But, at worst, it could even be a border between a new Trumpian world order and a Europe struggling to hold on to a notion of transnational democracy. Yet nobody seems to be thinking much about these possibilities.

Politics are in turmoil in both Irish jurisdictions. In the Republic, Enda Kenny is being shooed towards the exit door because of the failure of his government to deal with an extraordinary scandal over the alleged smearing of a police whistleblower, Maurice McCabe. In Northern Ireland, there is an election brought about by the almost equally extraordinary scandal of a breathtakingly expensive renewable heating initiative.

Both issues are important. But neither is of the scale of what Brexit is threatening to do to Ireland. What is at stake is quite literally Ireland's place in the world. An island that has been bedevilled by great uncertainties of belonging is being forced to think again about where it belongs in an even more uncertain geopolitical context.

Assurances that there would be no hard border between north and south when Northern Ireland is hauled out of the EU against its will were always lazy and reckless. At heart, they were based on an arrogant assumption by many Brexiteers and some unionists that the Republic is really still no more than an eccentric adjunct of the UK. It wasn't necessary to think the thing through in detail because the Irish would quickly realise that their best bet was to follow Britain's lead out of the EU and into the new Isles of the Blest that would emerge in the Atlantic. And even if they didn't, the Irish authorities would obediently agree to operate British border controls at Irish ports and airports.

As Brexit moves from airy fantasy into messy reality, only the most deluded still think any of this. Ireland will remain in the EU, and because it is part of the EU, the Irish border will be an external EU border. Even if the implications of this fact for migration can be fudged, the border will be inescapably present. The new line from May is that it will be 'as fluid and frictionless' as possible – not so much a UK border, perhaps, as a KY border. But no amount of verbal lubrication can ease the reality that the UK (and thus Northern Ireland) will be in an entirely different customs regime to the Republic.

The need for a quick deal will suck the UK into the gravitational field of Trump's assault on liberal democracy. So when the UK does its 'fabulous' trade deals with Donald Trump's US, what happens to the KY border? The Oxford-based economic historian Kevin O'Rourke has cited the simple example of one of the things that Trump would undoubtedly want in such a deal: duty-free access to the UK market for cheap, hormone-enhanced American beef. The EU, including the Republic, will keep a 15 per cent tariff on this beef. Without rigorous border controls, clever importers in, say, Newry, could bring in that US beef without paying duty and send it across to Dundalk and thence into the whole EU. And the same could go for cars or steel or anything else that Trump would love to boast about exporting in order to save American jobs. The EU's own customs union would become a nonsense. Why on earth would it allow that to happen? It won't – customs checks, with all the economic cost and all the psychological irritation, are inevitable.

But there's something even larger at stake now. The consequences of Britain's need to replace EU markets are not just economic. The tectonic plates that underlie the current political architecture are shifting. When reality bites and Britain realises that the EU is not going to give the UK back all the cake it has eaten, there will most probably be a ramping up of nationalist and anti-European rhetoric in England. And the need for a quick trade deal with the US will suck the UK as a whole into the gravitational field of Trump's reactionary assault on transnational institutions and regulations. If that happens, the Irish border will become not just an economic, migration and political frontier. It will become an ideological boundary.

None of this is inevitable – and in truth none of us has a clue where the Trump escapade will lead – but it is a live possibility. We have to consider a grotesque absurdity: that the road between Newry and Dundalk or Lifford and Strabane leads from one geopolitical zone to another. On the one side there is the neo-nationalist world order; on the other the rather isolated edge of an embattled, transnational EU. This would make the 'borders of the past' seem like garden paths strewn with rose petals.

Even in the most benign scenario, where post-Brexit Britain somehow escapes the clutches of a reactionary nationalism and does not fall into Trump's orbit, Ireland has to deal with a profound question of belonging. It has long enjoyed the luxury of not having to choose between being part of the EU on the one hand and being closely intertwined – culturally and economically – with the Anglo-American world. But as these two spheres drift apart, Ireland risks being pulled asunder if it tries to stay with both. It will have to think of itself, politically and psychologically, as a more European country. Which would be all very well if part of the island were not being forced to define itself as much less European.

There is only one way to avoid this and that is, of course, for Northern Ireland to remain effectively within the EU as a special zone whose recent history justifies its status as an exceptional place – a part of the EU in the UK and a part of the UK in the EU. That, we will be told, is too great a stretch of the imagination. But it is not nearly so big a stretch as the crazy divisions that the Brexit zealots are imposing on a small island that was trying hard to escape from the legacy of the narrow nationalism they are embracing.

21 March 2017

*The EU Withdrawal Act became law on 16 March 2017.
This should have been a moment of triumph for those who
believed in Brexit. But it is already clear that Brexit will never
be what those who voted for it were promised. Brexit thus
has a toxic by-product – betrayal – and it is already in
the bloodstream of British politics.*

The fate of progressive democracy over the next few years may be determined by the struggle to control a single word: betrayal.

We can be certain that the people who voted for Brexit and Donald Trump will be betrayed. The great uncertainty is who gets to define that treachery. The answer will determine whether the current crisis comes to be seen as a warning that produced a healthy response – or as a prelude to a far deeper shift away from democratic values.

Brexit and Trump's victory are complex phenomena. But there is considerable truth to the idea that both were driven by the anger of people who feel left behind by economic globalisation. Theresa May's JAMs (people who are 'just about managing') and Trump's 'forgotten men and women' do actually exist.

They are not necessarily the people at the bottom of the pile – they are those who have something but are terrified of losing it. They have images in their heads of a former world (part real, part imagined) in which there were enough good, unionised industrial jobs to keep their communities thriving and enough access to education to make it possible for their kids to have better prospects.

Brexit and Trump gave these people opportunities to signal their distress in the most dramatic ways, by kicking political elites who seemed not to care about their lives.

This revenge has its immediate satisfactions. But after a good kicking has been delivered, what are these people left with? A phoney populism, an anti-elitist cover worn by elites who are 'of the people' in the way a sad oul' lad's comb over is on his head. Using the Conservative and Republican parties as vehicles for revolutionary social protest is putting diesel in a petrol car: it will go for a while, but breakdown is inevitable.

Neither of these parties has the slightest intention of seriously tackling the economic inequality at the root of the anger they have exploited – they exist primarily to do the opposite. And it has therefore always been a certainty that they will sell out their core supporters, that the forgotten men and women will be forgotten once again.

It was, admittedly, harder to predict just how fast and total Trump's betrayal of his own fans would be. The healthcare 'reform' he is championing is quite breathtaking in its assault on his own base. If it were actually designed by a vengeful God to punish those people marked for destruction by their red trucker caps, it would look exactly as it does. It devastates older, poorer, unhealthier people in rural areas – precisely the most enthusiastic Trump voters. And it benefits younger, healthier, better-off people in cities – most of whom voted for Hillary Clinton.

If this is populist, tattoo a gorilla on my chest and call me Conor McGregor. The truth, of course, is that the Trump administration's policies of transferring unprecedented amounts of money and power from the poor to the ultra-rich are so elitist they make *Downton Abbey* look like *Shameless*.

Exactly how Brexit will play out is less obvious for now. But there is little doubt that, when the dust settles, many of the JAMs will not be managing at all. Economic insecurity and inequality will rise still further. The nonpartisan Institute for Fiscal Studies reckons real median incomes will not grow at all in the next two years. Average real incomes (after housing costs) for the poorest 15 per cent are actually set to fall. Income inequality will rise as Brexit-fuelled inflation erodes the value of benefits for the poorest people.

For all Theresa May's rhetoric, there is no evidence at all that the Tories will do anything much to improve the economic lot of the disgruntled outsiders – and there is every chance that Brexit will change it for the worse.

So, in the next few years there will be a hard rain of metal as all the pennies start to drop. People may have been stupefied, but they are not stupid. They will see that they have been lied to and taken for fools. Hence the crucial question: who manages to give that sense of betrayal 'a local habitation and a name'? Who does the best job of explaining why people have been sold out and what they can do about it?

Going by history, you'd have to give a pessimistic answer – authoritarian nationalist movements are much better than progressive democrats at wielding treachery as a weapon against their enemies. The 'stab in the back' has been a central motif of Nazism, Stalinism and all the most virulent forms of reactionary nationalism.

And precisely because progressives know this history, they have a proper distaste for cries of treachery. They don't like handling this most radioactive of political materials. They are too decent to set up this dangerous cry.

They will have to overcome their distaste very fast. There really is a great betrayal going on, and the far right has ready-made traitors to blame for the inevitable failure of phoney populism. Progressives need to get in first, talk to those who are being betrayed and put the blame where it really lies.

28 March 2017

*The day before the glorious date on which Article 50 was
triggered, I wondered whether Britain could produce
a political leader capable of leading the climbdown.*

Brexit is England's Easter Rising – an unlikely event that allows
a zealous minority to change the course of a nation's history.
But who, then, will be England's Michael Collins? The grand
gesture of national self-assertion must be followed, eventually, by
a painful reconciliation with reality. After the rapture comes the
reckoning. After their glorious resurrections, nation states do not
actually ascend into heaven – they come back to earth. Guiding
that descent is the greatest test of political skill, of moral courage
and of genuine patriotism. England's tragedy is that there is no
sign that anyone in power has those qualities.

On the face of it, the English nationalist revolution (which is
what Brexit really is) should have a relatively easy comedown
from the euphoria of that extraordinary night last June to the
long, hungover dawn of messy compromise. By the standards of
nationalist revolutions – standards we know very well in Ireland –
the English have one enormous boon. The Brexiteers do not have
blood in the game. The thing that usually makes the ultimate
concession to reality so bitter is that people have killed and died
for the idealist cause. As Patrick Pearse understood so well in 1916,
the blood sacrifice is also a kind of historical blackmail. It forces
those who come after to either match the intensity of its zeal or
be guilty of betraying the martyred dead.

The only person whose blood was shed in Brexit was a Remainer,
the murdered Labour MP Jo Cox. The people who are now driving

Britain towards the cliff – Theresa May, Boris Johnson, David Davis – risked nothing at all. Brexit has been a great career move for them: May, who sat on the fence with a lukewarm endorsement of Remain and a wink at Leave, got to be prime minister. For people like Johnson, the whole thing is a jolly escapade, a thrilling game in which, as it turned out, he couldn't lose. There are genuine zealots, of course, but the people who have made a hard Brexit inevitable are phoney enthusiasts. Their nationalist bliss is all an act. The politics of the fake orgasm are not the politics of the blood sacrifice.

The other thing that should, in theory, make an eventual climbdown easier is that Brexit, as it was actually framed in the referendum, was a vague proposition. Its most tangible promises – such as the infamous £350 million a week for the National Health Service – were such patent lies that they were immediately abandoned after victory. That sell-out is already a done deal. On the substantial question of Britain's relationship with the European Union, there was no coherent proposal at all. The basic pitch to voters was Johnson's 'having your cake and eating it': Britain would enjoy all the benefits of EU membership – including unfettered access to the single market – while bearing none of the costs. When your come-on is so self-evidently fantastical, it should not be hard to admit that the eventual outcome will not be quite as advertised. After all, politicians do this all the time – they campaign in poetry and govern in prose.

And yet, instead of preparing its electorate for compromise, the Brexit government has taken the bad poetry of the campaign and turned it into ludicrous heroic verse. It has gone harder, noisier, more absolutist. Instead of dealing with the hangover, it is sniffing more lines of white nationalist marching powder and relishing the drug-induced delusion of omnipotence.

Let's be optimistic for a moment and assume that, for May herself, this posturing is a negotiating tactic: start with the extreme so you end up with a somewhat better final bargain. Does she then know how much this will demand of her? Does she realise that the more inflated the position she is starting with, the more air she is going to have let out of it when the time comes to make the deal? Is she ready for the screams of treason that will now accompany any possible compromise? Will she have the guts to tell the obvious truth: that if Britain wants a deal it will have to accept the bulk of EU regulations and continue to pay into the EU budget?

Michael Collins had to come down from the mountaintop of nationalist fervour and say: sorry, but this is the best deal we can get in the real world. He had to face down men with guns who could – and did – kill him. Theresa May merely has to face down the *Daily Mail*. But nothing so far suggests that she or anyone who might replace her has the courage to do even that. England has placed itself in one of those strange historical moments when the road to self-harm is also the path of least resistance. The stroll to the cliff edge is strewn with daisies; to veer away from it is to wade through thorns. Long-term madness is short-term careerist calculation. The current logic of English politics is that logic must be abandoned. Heroic failure beats down courageous realism. In this imaginary replay of the Battle of Britain, it is easier to be shot down in flames than to bring the country to a safe emergency landing.

18 April 2017

*For decades, I had argued against Ireland's habit of
defining itself as whatever England is not. Suddenly,
this did not seem such a bad idea after all.*

Karl Marx famously wrote that everything in history happens twice: the first time as tragedy, the second as farce. But in Ireland's current predicament, we might well think of one part of our modern history happening twice: the first time as tragedy, the second as a smart political drama. The part of history I'm thinking about is the notion of Ireland as the anti-England. It was a bad idea that might now be a good idea.

Being anti-England is not about being anti-English. Irish Anglophobia is dead and if it ever stirs again we should place another stake through its heart, just in case. What's at play is something different: a way of thinking about Irish identity that was summed up with typical pithiness by Samuel Beckett when he was asked 'Vous êtes anglais?': 'Au contraire.' Irishness, in one deep stream of thought and feeling, was the opposite of Englishness.

Identities are often defined by what they are not, and this form of negative self-identification came naturally to an Irish nationalism struggling to break the link with a country that dominated not just us but much of the world. In our dictionary, 'Us' could be defined simply as 'not Them'.

It worked in so many ways. England was Protestant; so Catholicism had to be the essence of Irish identity. England was industrial; so Ireland had to make a virtue of its underdeveloped and deindustrialised economy. England was urban; so Ireland had to create an image of itself that was exclusively rustic. The English were scientific rationalists; so we had to be the mystical dreamers of dreams. They were Anglo-Saxons; we were Celts. They had a monarchy, so we had to have a republic. They developed a welfare state; so we relied on the tender mercies of charity.

Most of this was nonsense, of course. Actual Irish people quietly chose to live in urban, industrial, welfare-state England. But nonsense can be powerful. The idea of being the anti-England hung around like a bad smell long after it had ceased to have any purpose.

It locked Ireland for far too long into a sectarianism that equated Irishness with Catholicism and into the lie that the misery of rural poverty was really a mark of national nobility. It allowed us to devalue science and exalt the irrational. It convinced us that we actually had a republic merely because we didn't bow before the English throne. It excused the slow and inadequate development of a state that places public welfare at its heart.

The gradual demise of the mentality in which Ireland was merely the opposite of England has done us nothing but good, even though it could be argued that we've never managed to replace this negative identity with a fully positive one. So why the hell would we want any part of it back? Because, of course, Brexit and the English nationalism that underlies it are redefining England for the rest of the world as an angry, hostile, unlovable place. And it's vital for Ireland that we are clearly distinguished from that new English identity.

This – to stress again – has nothing to do with hostility to England or the English. Geography, history, economics, politics, family, friendship and common decency all give Ireland an overwhelming interest in England's prosperity. There is no satisfaction in seeing our neighbours harm themselves by adopting forms of national self-assertion that we know from our own experience to be self-destructive. Ireland should and will do everything it can to keep England as close as possible to the European Union and as alert as possible to the dangers and delusions of reactionary nationalism.

But this goodwill on our part may have very few practical consequences. Brexit may well prove to be unstoppable and we have to react it to it by thinking again about how we want to be seen in the world. The state has, so far, reacted by making the world, and especially our fellow EU members, acutely aware of how closely our fate is tied to England's, how much their decisions are our destiny.

This is quite right, not least because it's obviously true. In the longer term, however, we also have to do something else. We have to define ourselves for the rest of the world as not-England. This is not just about being a separate space; it is about being an opposing kind of space. We have to write '*Au contraire*' on our banners again.

But this time the words, ironically enough, must themselves have a contrary meaning. They have to imply the opposite of what they used to suggest – not that Ireland is enclosed but that it is open; not that we have a monolithic religious and ethnic identity but that we are enthusiastically pluralist; not that we look inwards but that we look outwards; not that we think we can revert to a nineteenth-century nationalism but that we assert our national independence through solidarity and co-operation; not that we are in thrall to dreams but that we understand our own and the world's realities. It is as absurd as it is sad that we've reached a point where these qualities would make Ireland so radically unEnglish.

6 June 2017

The British election – or at least the English election – is saturated with nostalgia. Both Theresa May and Jeremy Corbyn are appealing to notions of how things used to be. Corbyn has had a better election than May because his version of the past has more reality, and more nobility, than hers. The centrality of nostalgia is not hard to understand. General elections are usually about the short- to medium-term future: here's what we say we will do in the next four or five years. But between Britain now and Britain in 2022 there lie the uncharted shoals and reefs of Brexit, and no one is even plotting a course. The medium term is a great unknown.

And for different reasons, the Tories and Labour don't really want to talk about it. The Tories, whose reckless private games created the whole mess, still don't have a clue about what Brexit will really look like. Labour is terrified of losing its traditional voters in the north of England who defied the party's advice and backed Brexit. Hence the weirdness of the election: never mind that iceberg, let's argue about what we should do when the *Titanic* docks in New York.

In a sense, of course, this makes the election itself nostalgic. It is the last of its kind, a valediction to the brief era of a European-centred British democracy. We shall not see its like again – unless Brexit falls apart very quickly, the next election will take place in a very different Britain. It is even conceivable – though unlikely – that this could be the last general election ever to take place in the current United Kingdom. It has the bittersweet quality of a last late autumn day when you can convince yourself that winter is not coming.

It is perhaps inevitable that an election with such a nostalgic form should acquire nostalgic content, too. It is striking nonetheless that on both sides the soundtrack is so wistful. Corbyn's Labour has been characterised by the overwhelmingly Tory press as a throwback to the early 1970s and there is some truth in the accusation. In fact, May is much more deeply involved in a yearning for an imagined past. Strip away the ruthless opportunism that is her only real political skill, and what you find is a devotion to a static fantasy of Englishness that harks back, not to the 1970s, but to the 1950s.

It was always foolish for the Conservatives to try to create a cult of personality around a woman who doesn't have one. They are selling, not just May, but her childhood. She does this herself on a literal level, constantly reminding voters that her values are entirely rooted in her upbringing: 'values that I learned in my own childhood, growing up in a vicarage.' A vicarage in Oxfordshire is as valid a place to grow up as anywhere else, but in May's world view it is another Eden, a centre from which high church Toryism radiated benevolence and decency and everyone was enfolded in its paternalistic embrace. All was right with England – and therefore with the world. And it will be so again, when England reasserts its greatness outside the EU, immigrants are kept away and grammar schools return.

It is striking, though, that for all her harping on values, only 30 per cent of voters tell pollsters they believe that May shares theirs. They sense the essential phoniness at the heart of her vision of the past.

And, yes, Corbyn's Labour is nostalgic, too. But it at least has a yen for something more real and less romantic. Its manifesto yearns for tangible things that were once possible for tens of millions of British people: access to public housing; a safe national health system; unionised jobs where workers had some bargaining power; free education up to and including third level; a rational expectation that your kids would have a better life than you do.

This imagined past matters. It shapes a nation's sense of what is possible – if these things were done before in much worse circumstances, they can be done again. And if ordinary people do not believe in concrete possibilities for a better life, their hopes sour into resentments. We know what this looks like and what it means for democracy.

Corbyn is a highly problematic leader, not least in his inability to think about how to create a majority in England for this radical social democratic vision. But he is much less of a fantasist than the supposedly hard-headed May. Every objective analysis shows that a hard Brexit will be followed by greater poverty, rising inequality and at best stagnant earnings for most ordinary workers.

May's air of regal authority vanished because she has nothing much to say about these realities. It became very clear that she does not even believe her own rhetoric of a liberated and united country striding confidently forward to its golden future.

The most unrealistic proposition in contemporary politics is that 'strong and stable' democracies can coexist with inequality, insecurity and hopelessness. Corbyn will not win the election, but he has won the campaign by showing that he understands this far better than May does.

9 June 2017

May and Corbyn both lost the election. The result –
a hung parliament – seems to bear out the feeling that
the Brexit referendum had undermined the stability
of Britain's political institutions.

So there's only one queen in England after all.

The coronation of Queen Theresa is much more likely to be a decapitation. And the remarkable result of the election she called in the expectation of a triumphal procession raises the most fundamental question that can be asked in any state: who's in charge here?

It's not Theresa May, and it's not anybody else either.

To understand what has happened you have to put together the slogans of the Sex Pistols and the royal family. The Pistols gave us anarchy in the UK. The royals' motto is *Nemo me impune lacessit*, which roughly translates as 'Don't mess about or there will be consequences'. The British political class messed about with the Brexit referendum, and the consequence is, if not quite anarchy in the UK, a crisis of authority that has profound implications for Brexit itself.

The prime minister's robotically repeated promise of 'strong and stable' leadership raised two obvious questions: can you have strong and stable leadership in a country that has just thrown its entire institutional framework into disarray?

And, in particular, can a Conservative Party that has shown itself to be flakier than a snowstorm and more panicky than an enervated chicken credibly present itself as firm and steady? On both counts the clear answer from voters is no.

May was attempting to trade on the tried-and-trusted Tory brand of good government and pragmatic economics. But it's a brand that has been trashed three times in two years by the Tories themselves.

David Cameron took a hammer to it when he called the Brexit referendum in the first place. May gave it another kick when she decided, entirely spuriously, that the vote in that referendum was a mandate for an extreme form of Brexit. Then she finished it off by calling an unnecessary general election. The Tories have been as stable as a kid trying to ride a bike for the first time.

And in all of this panic there has been a deep undermining of the idea of political authority. Modern British history is all about the establishment of a bedrock political principle: authority comes from parliament. In its long nervous breakdown the Conservative Party has cut itself adrift from this principle.

In the Brexit debacle authority has come from two sources: 'the people' imagined as the all-sovereign 52 per cent who voted to leave the EU, and the *Daily Mail*, whose far-right rantings have been May's gospel. A constitution based on crude majoritarianism and fascistic denunciations of 'saboteurs' and 'enemies of the people' is not a recipe for stability. Both of these impulses have been firmly rejected. The British looked at the prospect of a virtual Tory one-party state and recoiled from it. And the hysterical smearing of Jeremy Corbyn and his Labour allies by the *Mail* and the rest of the Tory press failed.

Corbyn, the 'unelectable', terrorist-loving loony, garnered more votes for Labour than Tony Blair did in two of his three election victories. The idea that Labour can be a force only if it abandons its social-democratic roots has been overturned. A radical social-democratic manifesto transformed the election and gave the young and the marginalised a reason to vote.

But if it's not 'the people' conceived as a populist mass, and it's not the propagandist press, who *is* in charge? More immediately, who has the authority to negotiate Brexit? In effect, no one at all.

May is a beaten docket: she asked for a mandate to be a 'bloody difficult' champion for a Britain going into battle with Europe. She emerged instead as a pitiful figure: weak and wobbly, cowardly and indecisive. But even when the Tories replace her, her successor will have no electoral mandate at all.

And this means that there is emphatically no mandate for a hard Brexit. A very close referendum result, won by the Brexiteers with flagrant lies and promises that the UK would stay in the single market, was hijacked to claim total democratic authority for an extremist coup. That operation has failed: the claim that 'the people' are unified behind an absolutist Brexit cannot be sustained even by the most shameless of its propagandists.

What Britain will have is a renewed and invigorated parliament with a Labour Party that does have a mandate from its voters for a radically different vision of Britain. Labour has found its voice on social justice, public services and fair taxation. It needs to find its voice on Europe, to say clearly that a hard Brexit will be a disaster for workers, for the poor and for the young people who flocked to its banner.

If it does so it can also begin to return authority to the parliament that has just been elected. That authority must extend to the Brexit negotiations themselves. Parliament must take back control.

Brexit itself is thus not a fait accompli. It has been entirely based on a single strategy: grab an ambiguous referendum and transform it into an unambiguous authority for fanaticism. Plan A has decisively failed. To win an election you have to have a convincing narrative. May's story had a huge Brexit-shaped hole. She lost because she lost the plot. But who can invent a new one?

10 June 2017

To understand the sensational outcome of the British election, one must ask a basic question. What happens when phoney populism collides with the real thing?

Last year's triumph for Brexit has often been paired with the rise of Donald Trump as evidence of a populist surge. But most of those joining in with the ecstasies of English nationalist self-assertion were imposters. Brexit is an elite project dressed up in rough attire. When its Oxbridge-educated champions coined the appealing slogan 'Take back control', they cleverly neglected to add that they really meant control by and for the elite. The problem is that, as the elections showed, too many voters thought the control should belong to themselves.

Theresa May is a classic phoney Brexiteer. She didn't support it in last year's referendum and there is no reason to think that, in private, she has ever changed her mind. But she saw that the path to power led towards the cliff edge, from which Britain will take its leap into an unknown future entirely outside the European Union. Her strategy was one of appeasement – of the nationalist zealots in her own party, of the voters who had backed the hard-right UK Independence Party (UKIP), and of the hysterically jingoistic Tory press, especially the *Daily Mail*.

The actual result of the referendum last year was narrow and ambiguous. Fifty-two per cent of voters backed Brexit but we know that many of them did so because they were reassured by Boris Johnson's promise that, when it came to Europe, Britain could 'have its cake and eat it'. It could both leave the EU and continue to enjoy all the benefits of membership. Britons could still trade freely with the EU and would be free to live, work and study in

63

any EU country just as before. This is, of course, a childish fantasy, and it is unlikely that Johnson himself really believed a word of it. It was just part of the game, a smart line that might win a debate at the Oxford Union.

But what do you do when your crowd-pleasing applause lines have to become public policy? The twenty-seven remaining member states of the EU have to try to extract a rational outcome from an essentially irrational process. They have to ask the simple question: what do you Brits actually want? And the answer is that the Brits want what they can't possibly have. They want everything to change and everything to go as before. They want an end to immigration – except for all the immigrants they need to run their economy and health service. They want it to be 1900, when Britain was a superpower and didn't have to make messy compromises with foreigners.

To take power, May had to pretend that she, too, dreams these impossible dreams. And that led her to embrace a phoney populism in which the narrow and ambiguous majority who voted for Brexit under false pretences are to be reimagined as 'the people'.

This is not conservatism – it is pure Rousseau. The popular will had been established on that sacred referendum day. And it must not be defied or questioned. Hence, Theresa May's allies in the *Daily Mail* using the language of the French revolutionary terror, characterising recalcitrant judges and parliamentarians as 'enemies of the people' and 'saboteurs'.

This is why May called an election. Her decision to do so – when she had a working majority in parliament – has been seen by some as pure vanity. But it was the inevitable result of the *völkisch* rhetoric she had adopted. A working majority was not enough – the unified people must have a unified parliament and a single, uncontested leader: one people, one parliament, one Queen Theresa to stand on the cliffs of Dover and shake her spear of sovereignty at the damn continentals.

And the funny thing is that this seemed possible. As recently as late April, with the Labour Party in disarray and its leftist leader

Jeremy Corbyn deemed unelectable, the polls were putting the Tories twenty points ahead and telling May that her coronation was inevitable. All she had to do was repeat the words 'strong and stable' over and over and Labour would be crushed forever. The opposition would be reduced to a token smattering of old socialist cranks and self-evidently traitorous Scots. Britain would become in effect a one-party Tory state. An overawed Europe would bow before this display of British staunchness and concede a Brexit deal in which supplies of cake would be infinitely renewed.

There were three problems. Firstly, May demanded her enormous majority so that she could ride out into the Brexit battle without having to worry about mutterings in the ranks behind her. But she has no clue what the battle is supposed to be for. Because May doesn't actually believe in Brexit, she's improvising a way forward very roughly sketched out by other people. She's a terrible actor mouthing a script in which there is no plot and no credible ending that is not an anti-climax. Brexit is a back-of-the-envelope proposition. Strip away the post-imperial make-believe and the Little England nostalgia, and there's almost nothing there, no clear sense of how a middling European country with little native industry can hope to thrive by cutting itself off from its biggest trading partner and most important political alliance.

May demanded a mandate to negotiate – but negotiate what exactly? She literally could not say. All she could articulate were two slogans: 'Brexit means Brexit' and 'No deal is better than a bad deal'. The first collapses ideology into tautology. The second is a patent absurdity: with 'no deal' there is no trade, the planes won't fly and all the supply chains snap. To win an election, you need a convincing narrative but May herself doesn't know what the Brexit story is.

Secondly, if you're going to try the *uno duce, una voce* trick, you need a charismatic leader with a strong voice. The Tories tried to build a personality cult around a woman who doesn't have much of a personality. May is a common or garden Home Counties conservative politician. Her stock in trade is prudence, caution and stubbornness. The vicar's daughter was woefully miscast as the Robespierre of the Brexit revolution, the embodiment of the British popular will sending saboteurs to the guillotine. She is awkward, wooden, and, as it turned out, prone to panic and indecision under pressure.

But to be fair to May, her wavering embodied a much deeper set of contradictions. Those words she repeated so robotically, 'strong and stable', would ring just as hollow in the mouth of any other Conservative politician. This is a party that has plunged its country into an existential crisis because it was too weak to stand up to a minority of nationalist zealots and tabloid press barons. It is as strong as a jellyfish and as stable as a flea.

Thirdly, the idea of a single British people united by the Brexit vote is ludicrous. Not only do Scotland, Northern Ireland and London have large anti-Brexit majorities, but many of those who did vote for Brexit are deeply unhappy about the effects of the Conservative government's austerity policies on healthcare, education and other public services. (One of these services is policing, and May's direct responsibility for a reduction in police numbers neutralised any potential swing towards the Conservatives as a result of the terrorist attacks in Manchester and London.)

This unrest found a voice in Corbyn's unabashedly left-wing Labour manifesto, with its clear promises to end austerity and fund better public services by taxing corporations and the very wealthy. May's appeal to 'the people' as a mystic entity came up against Corbyn's appeal to real people in their daily lives, longing not for a date with national destiny but for a good school, a functioning National Health Service and decent public transport. Phoney populism came up against a more genuine brand of anti-establishment radicalism that convinced the young and the marginalised that they had something to come out and vote for.

In electoral terms, of course, the two forces have pretty much cancelled each other out. May will form a government with the support of the Protestant fundamentalist Democratic Unionist Party from Northern Ireland. That government will be weak and unstable and it will have no real authority to negotiate a potentially momentous agreement with the European Union. Brexit is thus far from being a done deal: it can't be done without a reliable partner for the EU to negotiate with. There isn't one now and there may not be one for quite some time – at least until after another election, but quite probably not even then. The reliance on a spurious notion of the 'popular will' has left Britain with no clear notion of who 'the people' are and what they really want.

13 June 2017

Theresa May does a deal with the Democratic Unionist Party to allow her to form a minority government.

Clio, the muse of history, has a wicked sense of humour. You can hear her cackling to herself these last few days: 'What can I do to make the Brexit fantasia even nuttier? Ah yes – the return of the repressed! They recklessly ignored Ireland. Wouldn't it be such a laugh to leave their whole mad project at the mercy of a weird Irish party? What's this they're called? Hup, mup, dup?' The internet exploded in the early hours of Saturday morning with anxious Brits frantically googling 'Where is Northern Ireland?', 'What does DUP stand for?' and 'Do they still believe in witchcraft over there?'

And it serves them right. Watching the Brexit campaigns last year, it was as if no one had heard of the Belfast Agreement. Ireland might as well have been Albania for all it seemed to matter. When the trade union leader Frances O'Grady raised it, the poor woman was obviously losing the plot – everyone quickly got back to serious questions like how to have one's cake and eat it.

So there is something delicious about the Brexit train having as its co-driver a party that hitched its wagon to it at least in part because of the lure of dark money channelled through sources with links to the Saudi government. And there is every chance that, if the DUP does manage to shore up Theresa May, it will drive the whole project off the rails. This would be no bad thing: Clio may have chosen a suitably crazy way to stop a crazy misadventure.

The European Union has made clear its three priorities in the Brexit negotiations that will start next week: people, money and

Ireland. People means the mutual recognition of the rights of EU citizens currently resident in the UK and Brits resident in the EU. It's doable. Money means sorting out the divorce settlement and how much the UK will pay to meet its existing commitments to the EU budget. It will be a very bitter negotiation, but it is doable. Ireland means finding a way to honour the Belfast Agreement and prevent the recreation of a hard border. It is not doable – with the DUP dictating terms on the British side of the table, it is an impossibility.

The DUP's bottom line has the virtue of clarity. Nigel Dodds spelled it out: the DUP will block any attempt to avoid a hard border by giving Northern Ireland a 'special status' within the EU. But to think that a hard border can be avoided without a special status for Northern Ireland one must, to misquote the Queen in *Through the Looking-Glass*, be prepared to believe three impossible things before breakfast.

The first impossibility is the idea that a soft border can be achieved while Northern Ireland leaves the single market and the customs union. It is purest fantasy. The frictionless, fully lubricated border, guaranteed to be free of chafing, rasping and abrasion, is an advertising slogan. It is not an actual proposition. If and when the UK leaves the single market and does its own trade deals with other countries, the EU and the UK will exist in radically different trading and regulatory regimes. No amount of technological wizardry or wishful thinking can make that reality disappear.

But the second impossibility is a hard border. There is no default option of creating a standard international frontier. This is a matter of fact, not of opinion – a hard border could not be created during the Troubles with watchtowers, troops and helicopters. It is certainly not going to be achieved with polite customs officers.

And in any case, the creation of this kind of border requires co-ordination on both sides. So let's be clear in return: no Irish government will ever agree to its creation – and if the Irish government does not agree to it, the EU as a whole cannot do so either. No conventional EU frontier will be created on the island of Ireland because any Irish government has to stop it happening.

The third impossibility is that the Belfast Agreement be torn up. The biggest problem with the DUP's insistence that Northern Ireland must not have special status is that it already does. The Belfast Agreement gives everyone in Northern Ireland an absolute right to Irish – and thus to EU – citizenship. This is a special status. And the EU has followed this logic by offering Northern Ireland a special Brexit. Unlike the rest of the UK, it has a return ticket – it can re-enter the EU unconditionally if it chooses to join with the Republic.

Now, in principle, Britain could simply withdraw from the Belfast Agreement and this is certainly the logic of the DUP's position. But if it unilaterally tears up the most important bilateral treaty in its post-war history, a treaty registered with the United Nations and guaranteed by the EU and the United States, what country in its right mind would enter the kind of bilateral trade deal on which Britain's post-Brexit future is predicated?

Cackling Clio has placed an Irish obstacle on the Brexit tracks. The choice has narrowed – all aboard for the train wreck, or stop and think about taking a different line.

17 June 2017

*It seemed to me that there was nothing surer than that
the Conservatives would betray the DUP eventually –
though the DUP never saw it coming.*

Dante and Beatrice. Quasimodo and Esmeralda. Cyrano and Roxane. Don Quixote and Dulcinea. These unrequited loves have great poignancy. But they've nothing on the tenderest, most poignant tale of unrequited love in our times, the tragically one-sided crush the DUP has on Britain.

It is one thing to be infatuated with someone who just ignores you. The unfulfilled love retains its bittersweet purity, its dreamy half-life of pure possibility. But the true tragedy occurs when your love is apparently consummated at last and you find that the loved one really despises you. The DUP has long dreamed of being wrapped fully in the warm embrace of the Tory world with which it strives so hard to identify. And now, miraculously, its moment has come. But the loved one is thinking of England, sneaking glances at her watch and praying 'Oh God! When will this be over?'

The DUP used to be unionist but not really British. Ian Paisley was many things but no one could ever seriously think of him as a Brit. His touchstones were fundamentalist Presbyterian dissent and the place he called Ulster. Its hinterland was Calvinist Scotland, not Westminster.

The aphrodisiac that got the DUP all hot on Britishness was, of course, Brexit. David Cameron's referendum gave the DUP a chance to indulge in a fantasy of ultra-Britishness. It had been forced, in its slow and reluctant acceptance of the Belfast Agreement, to come to terms with the complicated reality of its world, which is the island of Ireland in all its ambiguities of belonging. For the DUP, Brexit was a kind of holiday from this messy, compromised reality, a mental sojourn in a sunny Playa del Inglés where all the cafés fly the Union flag and serve fish and chips.

The problem, of course, is that the holiday turned out to be a semi-permanent relocation. The DUP was surely as perplexed as Boris Johnson was when the jolly jaunt to imperial nostalgia turned into a moment of destiny. The day trippers to Little Britain found out that there was no return train and that they were stranded on a beach far from reality with the tide of bad news slowly but relentlessly coming in. That's not 'Land of Hope and Glory' playing on the tannoy – it's 'Hotel California'.

The other problem is that Northern Ireland, Paisley's beloved Ulster, voted emphatically against Brexit. And this, paradoxically, has forced the DUP to double down on its besotted Britishness. It can justify ignoring the democratic wishes of the polity it actually leads only by reviving a notorious line from Margaret Thatcher. She said in 1981 that Northern Ireland is as British as her own constituency of Finchley. The DUP has to claim that Northern Ireland is as British as Lambeth or Edinburgh – it doesn't matter that they all voted Remain because they are merely parts of the greater British whole.

This is nonsense, of course. Northern Ireland is not as British as Finchley and Brexit dramatises the difference: it is not the absolute right of the residents of Finchley to remain citizens of the European Union after Brexit. But it is, for the DUP, a necessary nonsense. It has to remain frozen in an absurd ultra-British posture that even Thatcher abandoned when she signed the Anglo-Irish Agreement in 1985.

The infatuation mires the DUP in a hopeless contradiction. Because it wants to be super-British, its manifesto in the Westminster election commits it to a hard Brexit, including exit from the customs union. But because it is actually an Irish political party, it really wants a soft border. And these two desires are utterly incompatible. You can leave a customs union or you can remain within an arrangement where no customs barriers apply. You can't do both.

The fortunes of electoral arithmetic have now given the DUP's pretence a weird moment of apparent validation. It is, at last, a British political party, a key player in the Westminster game. Its hour has come. But does it notice that, even as the Tory party clasps it to its bosom, the lack of enthusiasm would be scarcely less evident if the Tories were wearing rubber gloves and surgical masks? They are not swooning with love, they are fainting with revulsion. The DUP may think it is coming home; most Tories think the mad woman has come out of the attic of an old hyper-Protestant British identity and is sitting in the parlour demanding tea and scones with lots of jam and a bucket of clotted cream. She has to be humoured for now, but only until there is some way to get rid of her.

The tragic truth behind the DUP's mooning infatuation is that for the British establishment Northern Ireland is not a place but two places: out of sight and out of mind. And the DUP, to them, is Northern Ireland writ large, a thing from the swamp of bad history. They don't like it and they dread having to pretend to love it. It is a frog that must be kissed but it is never going to turn into a prince. The Tories will endure the DUP while they must and betray it when they can.

8 July 2017

*Formal negotiations on a withdrawal agreement have begun
in Brussels between the EU, led by Michel Barnier and the
British government, led by the Brexit secretary David Davis.
It is quite clear that the EU has the upper hand – but will the
Brexit mess encourage a complacency it can ill afford?*

When the alarm clock goes off you can do one of two things. You can get angry at the clock, throw it across the room, turn over and go back to sleep. Or you can wake up and face the day. Brexit is the European Union's alarm clock, and it is not yet clear which of the two reactions will take hold. On this choice may well depend the future of the EU itself. If the response to the departure of one if its largest members is simply a blithe 'good riddance', the EU may sleepwalk towards its own destruction. If it is a more rueful 'there but for the grace of God', the union may be stirred into facing the hard work of saving itself.

Brexit arises from political and historical forces specific to the United Kingdom. But shocks of a similar order could have happened in one of the EU's core founding members, France or Italy, last year. The extraordinary rise of the proudly pro-EU Emmanuel Macron in France obscures the reality that in the first round of the presidential elections, in April, a clear majority of voters backed either the anti-EU Marine Le Pen and Jean-Luc Mélenchon or the heavily Eurosceptical François Fillon. In Italy three of the four major parties are hostile, if not to the EU itself, then at least to membership of the eurozone. If there had been referendums in France or Italy last year, when the wave of anti-establishment anger was at its height, there is every possibility that the EU could now be facing an existential crisis of much greater import than Brexit itself.

Yet there is a strong impulse to simply forget this. Last week schoolchildren in France received an educational guide to the EU. Already it is a union of '27 pays' – the UK has disappeared from the map. It's over – and the EU, the not-so-subtle message suggests, is moving on. This message is being inadvertently reinforced by the chaotic mess that is Brexit itself. The British government has been performing an accidental morality play for the citizens of other countries: if you think the EU is bad, just consider what leaving it looks like.

In this way the tragicomedy of Brexit paradoxically reinforces some of the smug habits of mind that contribute to popular distrust of the EU: if the only alternative to technocracy is setting your own hair on fire, technocracy must be doing okay.

But 'stick to nurse for fear of something worse' is not a programme for the long-term survival of the most innovative political experiment in modern history.

The EU is currently caught in a maze of contradictions. It has created, especially with the adoption of the euro, a huge technocratic infrastructure (most obviously in the European Central Bank) without creating the mechanisms of democratic accountability to keep it in line. It has acquired many of the characteristics of a state without having the deep sense of identity and allegiance a state requires. It has created expectations that it should be able to solve problems collectively, but when faced with crises like the vast influx of refugees it lacks the power (and apparently the will) to do so.

It has created (as the eurozone crisis showed) the need to build federal institutions with formidable economic powers, but it has not created an appetite among most of its citizens for those powers to be ceded to the European centre. It can neither move forward to a federalised future nor retreat to the more minimal status of a trading bloc.

At the core of these problems is an ideological crisis. The EU has to root itself in ideas and values because it can't root itself in anything else. It can't be built on the foundations of the nineteenth-century nationalism from which most of its member states draw their sense of identity: the narratives of blood, soil and belonging, or even affiliation to a common language.

The United States of America, to which it is often compared, struggled to create a common identity even within a dominant white, Christian, anglophone capitalist ethic. The EU can't – and certainly shouldn't try to – bind itself together in the way the US did, through aggressively violent expansion and a cult of military greatness.

So what has it got instead? Fear. Historically fear is almost always politically toxic. The EU is one of the very few examples of a political project built on fear that is positive and inclusive. It came about because of fear of fascism and communism on a continent that had been torn apart by one and split in two by a totalitarian form of the second.

The fundamental perception that gave it life was that in order to avoid a resurgence of fascism, and to compete ideologically with communism, structures had to be built in which all citizens could enjoy at least a basic level of security and dignity.

The EU was built on an alliance of social-democratic and Christian-democratic parties, differing in many ways but held together by the belief that capitalism must be heavily moderated if it is not to destroy itself and take down whole societies with it.

But that fear dissipated. The generation scarred by fascism passed on. The Berlin Wall fell and communism ceased to be a threat, either internally or externally. Without this fear the social-democratic parties lost both their radicalism and their relevance and the Christian-democratic parties became cheerleaders for neoliberalism. The consequence is the biggest contradiction of all: while the EU sells itself to its citizens as the motor that drives economic and political 'convergence', the reality is one of fatal social divergence.

In the 1980s the average income of the richest 10 per cent of

Europeans was seven times higher than that of the poorest 10 per cent; today it is about 9.5 times higher. The long-term trend is towards increasing inequality in both income and wealth. The poorest 40 per cent now own just 3 per cent of wealth.

And since the young have now replaced the elderly as the age group most at risk of poverty, this inequality is being cemented into the foundations of Europe's future.

Those foundations simply cannot be secure. Growing inequality is fundamentally incompatible with either economic or political stability. People who feel that their political institutions are not only not protecting them from the ravages of hypercapitalism but are actually dismantling the protections they did have will be angry and volatile.

And this is the fear that the EU has to use to motivate itself, just as the dread of dictatorship and war got it moving in the first place. It should hear the alarms going off and take fright at the inevitable consequences of growing inequality.

When it came into being, the case for the EU could be explained to every citizen in a single, comprehensible sentence: 'The union exists because we must never go to war with each other again.' Now it has to be able to express its reason for being in a similarly compelling sentence: 'The union exists because citizens in a globalised economy need a transnational power to protect them from a feral capitalism that would destroy their environment, their social services, their rights as workers and their belief that their children can have better lives than they do.'

The EU's double bind is that in order to do this job of protecting its citizens it needs to be more powerful. But in order to become more powerful it needs to convince those citizens that it actually does exist to protect them. For far too many of those citizens, especially in the wake of EU-led austerity programmes, that conviction is hard to come by.

There is a very strong case for an EU that moves forward to become something much more like a federal state, with powerful democratic institutions and the power to redistribute wealth from its richest to its poorest citizens. But that case is weakened by the existence of an EU that is neither democratic enough nor sufficiently committed to economic equality.

It may be that by the end of 2017 we will be able to say that the EU has had a lucky escape, that a year in which its effective demise was conceivable has passed and left it more or less intact. But if relief gives way to complacency this will be a mere stay of execution. Samuel Johnson claimed that nothing concentrates the mind like the thought of being hanged in the morning. The EU should not need the prospect of its own imminent demise in order to concentrate its mind on the inequalities that will kill it more slowly.

8 August 2017

As it becomes clear that Britain will have to seek a transition period after March 2019, it is also clear that something extraordinary is unfolding: in the Brexit negotiations, Ireland has more power than Britain. This has never happened before.

Yes, those really are vague pink glimmers in the early morning sky. Reality is dawning on the Brexiteers. Once, they were going to walk away from the European Union in March 2019, whistling 'Rule, Britannia' and greeting queues of foreign supplicants begging for trade deals. Now, they are hoping to cling on until June 2022. They know they are going over a cliff and realise that it is better to climb down slowly than to plunge off the top.

But this climbdown also creates a crucial weakness – one that explains why the Irish government's tone has changed so radically. To understand this new weakness, we have to recall that there were two possible scenarios in which the Irish government had very little power. One was that the UK would simply walk away from the EU without any deal, the car-crash Brexit for which British prime minister Theresa May's old mantra, 'No deal is better than a bad deal', was meant to be the overture. If that happened, Ireland was completely impotent.

The other possible scenario was the straightforward one set out in Article 50 of the Lisbon Treaty. The UK and the EU would negotiate a full exit deal by March 2019. In this case, Ireland would have very little power either. Even if the deal was a betrayal of our interests, we could not veto it.

The deal would have to be ratified by the European Parliament and then by the European Council. But, crucially, the council has to accept the deal only by a qualified majority. In both bodies, therefore, Ireland could easily be outvoted.

We could exert moral pressure but, as we've seen in our recent past, moral pressure from small member states can count for very little in European realpolitik. For all the fine words and assurances, Ireland would be relying on the kindness of strangers.

Not any more. If there is a new assertiveness in the pronouncements on Brexit of Taoiseach Leo Varadkar and Minister for Foreign Affairs Simon Coveney, it is because the balance of power has shifted in Ireland's favour. The two scenarios in which Ireland has no real muscle are effectively off the table.

The 'no deal' mantra has been exposed for the hollow nonsense it always was. But, equally, because the British have wasted so much time and energy on ludicrous posturing and internal warfare, there is no chance of a clean, negotiated settlement coming into effect in March 2019.

Staggering as it seems, the British government is only now beginning to think about basic realities like the needs of its industries for immigration, how the planes will continue to fly and the regulation of nuclear materials. Hence its requirement for a long transitional period: even 2022, as mooted by UK chancellor Philip Hammond, may even be highly optimistic.

But – from an Irish perspective – this changes everything. Under Article 50, it is indeed possible for the member state that is exiting to seek to extend the remit of the EU treaties beyond the stipulated two years. This is what a transitional period would have to mean. But – and here's the rub – this can be done only with the unanimous consent of every other member state. In other words, Ireland has a veto.

We can now block the implementation of a transitional deal even if Germany and France and every other member state wants it to happen. The chaotic foolishness of the Brexiteers has, to coin a phrase, allowed us to take back control.

The Brexiteers don't know this, of course – they haven't given Ireland a moment's thought. More remarkably, the Democratic

Unionist Party seems not to know it either, hence the idiotic twittering from Ian Paisley Jnr about how Ireland will either have to accept a 'very hard border' or 'wise up and leave the EU'. But the Irish government knows it. The dramatic shift in tone in the last two weeks is not accidental. It is the voice of the newly empowered.

Let's be frank: there is a conflict unfolding on this island and one side has just acquired a formidable weapon. The conflict is between two incompatible imperatives. On one side is the DUP's need to cover up its own foolishness by getting everybody to go along with the pretence that there is no real border problem at all.

On the other is the Irish government's absolute need (and the need of the people of Northern Ireland) to avoid a hard border on the island of Ireland. These desires are mutually exclusive.

The DUP's new religious faith in the power of technological miracles to make the problems go away is touching, but the 'frictionless' border remains a fantasy.

So we now have two Irish vetoes. The DUP's consists in having ten Westminster votes to dangle in front of a weak, divided and unstable Tory government. The Irish government's consists in an absolute power under EU law to derail the whole Brexit process.

It reminds me of the scene in George Bernard Shaw's *Arms and the Man* in which Bluntschli replies to Sergius's challenge to a duel with sabres: 'That's a cavalry man's proposal. I'm in the artillery; and I have the choice of weapons. If I go, I shall take a machine gun.'

81

15 August 2017

The disarray in the United Kingdom makes a united Ireland seem like an obvious and easy solution. But it isn't.

Among the many madnesses of Brexit is the licence it gives for loose talk about a united Ireland. As, for example, in a recent letter to the *Irish Times* from Sinn Féin president Gerry Adams: 'the Good Friday Agreement... allows for Irish reunification in the context of a democratic vote: 50 per cent +1. I believe we can secure a greater margin, but ultimately that will be for the electorate. That's what democracy is about.' There's a remarkable blitheness to this, but the Brexiteers have given some apparent substance to such insouciance. The simplest way to avoid a hard border, after all, is to have no border at all. And the European Union has quite explicitly – and quite remarkably – stated that Northern Ireland can automatically rejoin the EU at any time after Brexit takes effect if it agrees to a united Ireland.

But we need to slow down here. Yes, Brexit and the upsurge of English nationalism that drives it have created a deep existential crisis for the United Kingdom that will unfold over the next twenty years. And over that time frame Irish unity is now much more likely than it was before. Northern Ireland voted against Brexit and will be very deeply and adversely affected by it. The crisis of authority that is already so evident in London is likely to become even more acute: any conceivable deal with the EU will reignite the uncivil wars in English politics. Scotland's resentment will deepen if an economic crisis results from a revolutionary change it emphatically rejected. Any sensible unionist would be looking across the Irish Sea and asking – what the hell is it we are supposed to be united to?

I will be sixty next year, and before the Brexit vote I would not have put any money on my chances of seeing a united Ireland in my lifetime. But after that vote, I'd be glad to take a flutter. In some form, it now seems more likely than not, thanks in part to the Democratic Unionist Party. But it is an odd kind of likelihood, one that is simultaneously of great significance and scarcely worth talking about yet.

In Adams's formula, it is all so simple. The Belfast Agreement allows for a border poll; the poll is called and the nationalists beat the unionists by one vote. *Voilà!*

The first problem with this is that Adams is actually wrong about the formula. It is not 50 per cent + 1 = a united Ireland. It is in fact 2x (50 per cent + 1) = a united Ireland. He likes to forget that there are two parties to this potential marriage. The citizens of the twenty-six counties have as much of a say in the matter as those of the six counties. The Irish constitution, as amended specifically in the context of the Belfast Agreement in 1998, is explicit on the subject: 'a united Ireland shall be brought about only by peaceful means with the consent of a majority of the people, democratically expressed, in both jurisdictions in the island'.

The second problem arises directly from this need for a referendum south of the border. It has always been a mistake to assume that the consent of the Republic's population to the creation of a new state can be taken for granted. Enthusiasm for Irish unity tends to increase the further into the future its achievement is postulated. (Make us whole, O Lord, but not yet.) That enthusiasm, moreover, is not unconditional. To put it bluntly (as no one ever does) southerners have no interest in inheriting a political wreck, or becoming direct participants in a gory sequel, 'Troubles III: The Orange Strikes Back'. They will not vote for a form of unity that merely creates an angry and alienated Protestant minority within a bitterly contested new state.

And this in turn brings us to the third problem. In the context of Ireland's future, 50 per cent + 1 is not, as Adams claims, 'what democracy is about'. That kind of crude, tribal majoritarianism is precisely what the Belfast Agreement is meant to finish off. Again, the new article 3 of the constitution is a good guide: 'It is the firm will of the Irish nation, in harmony and friendship, to unite all the people who share the territory of the island of Ireland, in all the diversity of their identities and traditions.' Harmony, friendship, diversity, multiplicity, a unity not of territory but of people – not: 'We beat you by one vote so suck it up and welcome to our nation.' Irish democracy has to be 'about' the creation of a common polity in which minorities of different kinds can feel fully at home. We're not remotely there yet – on either side of the border.

Pushing for a border poll in which a majority of one vote would solve all our historic problems is as pointless as it is delusional. The ultimate cause of Irish unity is being very well served as things stand – by its sworn enemies. Its friends can serve it best by working to create a republic of equals that might be worth joining.

16 August 2017

The British government publishes its position paper on the border question. It promises there will be no physical infrastructure but has no realistic suggestion as to how this can be possible if Northern Ireland leaves the EU single market and customs union.

Sweet nothings are lovely while they're being whispered in your ear. The problem is that a sweet nothing is still nothing. The British government's long-awaited position paper on the Irish border after Brexit is really rather lovely. It tells Irish people of all political persuasions exactly what they want to hear: that there will be no physical border of any kind across the island and that free movement will go on as if nothing had happened. But behind all of these delightful reassurances, there is sweet FA.

The British government has a lot of seducing to do. By October, it has to have persuaded all the EU member states that 'sufficient progress' has been made on the three big preliminary issues: the monetary divorce bill; the mutual rights of British citizens living in the EU and vice versa; and Ireland. To put this more bluntly, if the Irish government is not persuaded that Britain has a serious plan for the avoidance of a hard border on what will be its only land frontier with the European Union, the talks on a post-Brexit final status are going nowhere. This reality seems to have dawned at last – hence a position paper that could not be more emollient if it came dripping with honey.

But to understand how this seems to the Irish government and to most people on the island, imagine you are in a decent job. It is reasonably paid, apparently secure and the working environment is quite amicable. Your neighbour, who you like but do not quite trust (there's a bit of history there) comes to you with a proposition. She's establishing an extremely risky start-up venture with a high probability of catastrophic failure. Will you join her? Well, you ask, what are the possible rewards? Ah, she says, if – against the odds – everything goes splendidly, you'll get the same pay and conditions you have now.

This is, in essence, what the British government is offering Ireland. If everything goes fantastically well, you'll end up with, um, the status quo. Trade will 'operate largely in the same way it does today'. The position paper is effectively a hymn to the way things are now. We don't have a hard border, and we won't after Brexit. We do have a common travel area that works remarkably well, and it will continue to go splendidly. The position paper takes existing realities and repositions them as a distant mirage, a fantastical possibility: less emerald isle, more Emerald City.

As with the whole Brexit project, the proposals for Ireland are credible only if you accept two mutually incompatible propositions: a) The UK is creating the biggest political and economic revolution since 1973; b) pretty much everything will stay the same. It fully concedes that the changes most of us fear from Brexit – the reimposition of a political and economic border and the reversal of so much of the progress made since the Good Friday Agreement of 1998 – would be terrible. Indeed, it goes even further and characterises these changes as unacceptable. But it then goes on to suggest, in effect, that these utterly unacceptable things will not happen only if the EU gives the UK all the benefits of the customs union and the single market with none of the costs or restrictions.

The one really bold move in the paper is its rejection of the technological utopianism of the more enthusiastic Brexiteers, especially in the Democratic Unionist Party. The commitment to 'avoid any physical border infrastructure' means that there can be no CCTV cameras or registration-plate recognition systems. Magical machines are not going to take the place of human customs officers.

This is a welcome concession to reality, but it is predicated on an even bigger unreality: the assumption that the EU will agree to something quite extraordinary: that a 500-kilometre external EU border with more than 200 crossing points will be effectively unpoliced. People and goods will pass over it without let or hindrance. Smugglers, people traffickers and terrorists will go on their merry way unmolested. Small companies will not have to do customs checks at all; large ones will operate a charming honour system in which they retrospectively declare the goods they have moved and pay their duties.

The absurdity of the proposition becomes clear when we think about all the new trade deals that post-Brexit Britain is going to make. With no Irish border controls, US beef, Australian lamb, Chinese steel and Indian cars can be imported into Belfast, sent an hour down the road to Dundalk and exported tariff-free to France, Germany or any other EU country. The only way to stop this happening would be in effect to make Ireland itself a semi-detached member of the EU with all Irish exports subjected to customs controls at EU ports. And this is simply not going to happen – why on earth would any Irish government ever agree to it?

This is why the position paper, for all its nice words, feels less like a serious attempt to find solutions and more like an early move in the blame game that will unfold when those solutions have not been found. It claims the moral high ground: Britain is utterly opposed to a hard border. Thus, when the EU responds by saying that a hard border follows inevitably from a decision to leave the customs union, it will be the EU's fault. But this is not a blame game or any other kind of game. It is deadly serious. Britain has enormous political and moral responsibilities in Ireland. The position paper tells us what fulfilling those responsibilities would look like in practice – and it looks very like preserving the status quo. The minimum necessary for that to be a credible proposition would be for Britain to stay in the customs union. If it is not willing to do that, it cannot claim to be taking its responsibilities seriously.

29 August 2017

The council of the European Union is due to meet on 19 and 20 October to decide whether 'sufficient progress' has been made in talks on the withdrawal agreement to allow negotiations on Britain's post-Brexit trade relations with the EU to begin.

People, money, Ireland. These are the three big questions on which the immediate future of the Brexit project hinges. When European Union leaders meet in October, they will decide whether 'sufficient progress' has been made in talks with the British to allow for the opening of substantive negotiations to determine the United Kingdom's relationship with the EU after it leaves in March 2019. As the EU's lead negotiator Michel Barnier put it last May: 'I... made very clear that the [Irish] border issue will be one of my three priorities for the first phase of the negotiation. Together with citizens' rights and the financial settlement. We first must make sufficient progress on these points, before we start discussing the future of our relationship with the UK.'

By the border issue he means the question of whether a hard customs and immigration border is to be imposed between Northern Ireland and the Irish Republic.

And so the Irish question rises yet again, looming on the road to Brexit like the Sphinx on the road to Thebes. It threatens to devour those who cannot solve its great riddle: how do you impose an EU frontier across a small island without utterly unsettling the complex compromises that have ended a thirty-year conflict? The 'people' part of the preliminary Brexit negotiations concerns the mutual recognition of the rights of EU citizens living in the UK and vice versa. The 'money' part concerns Britain's outstanding obligations to the EU budget and the calculation of the final divorce bill. Both are awkward and politically divisive issues, but it should be perfectly possible to reach a settlement.

Ireland, however, is quite another matter. Winston Churchill famously surveyed the dramatically altered landscape of Europe after the Great War and claimed that 'as the deluge subsides and the waters fall short, we see the dreary steeples of Fermanagh and Tyrone emerging once again'. The Brexiteers forgot the dreary steeples of Fermanagh and Tyrone as they waged their glorious European war in last year's referendum. But as the deluge of euphoria subsides, their bells are sounding a wake-up call.

The European Union's guidelines for its negotiations with the British, published last April, implicitly acknowledge the ferocious difficulty of the riddle: 'In view of the unique circumstances on the island of Ireland, flexible and imaginative solutions will be required.' That is a diplomatic way of saying: 'We don't know how this thing is going to be solved.' And it is hard to blame the European leaders. For, at its heart, this is not really a technocratic problem of borders and customs, of tariffs and passports. Running beneath it is a problem of national identity – how it is to be conceived and expressed, how it is to be given political and institutional form. It is not a problem on which the two sides in the negotiations can simply set their masters and mistresses of the arcana and minutiae of the laws of trade. It is a large-scale conceptual clash. To put it bluntly, Ireland has evolved a complex and fluid sense of what it means to have a national identity while England has reverted to a simplistic and static one. This fault line opens a crack into which the whole Brexit project may stumble.

The simplest way to understand how radically Irish identity has changed is to consider the country's new prime minister, Leo Varadkar. He is thirty-eight and in many ways a typical politician of the European centre-right. He is also part Indian – his father Ashok is originally from Mumbai. And he is gay. When Varadkar was born in 1979, over 93 per cent of the population of the Republic of Ireland was born there and most of the rest were born in Northern

Ireland or in Britain (often as children of Irish emigrants). Ethnic minorities were scarcely visible – just 1 per cent of the population was born in what the official figures charmingly described as 'Elsewhere'. Now Varadkar leads an Ireland in which over 17 per cent of the population was born Elsewhere. The ultra-globalised Irish economy sucks in migrants from all over the world, notably Poland, Romania, the Baltic states and Nigeria.

And in 1979, when Varadkar was born, Ireland retained the laws against acts of 'gross indecency' between consenting adult men under which one of its most famous sons, Oscar Wilde, had been prosecuted in 1895. As late as 1983, when Varadkar was four years old, the Irish Supreme Court upheld that repressive law 'on the ground of the Christian nature of our State and on the grounds that the deliberate practice of homosexuality is morally wrong, that it is damaging to the health both of individuals and the public and, finally, that it is potentially harmful to the institution of marriage'.

The law was repealed only in 1993, under pressure from the European Court of Human Rights. Yet in 2015 Ireland became the first country to introduce same-sex marriage by referendum – 62 per cent voted in favor. It was in the run-up to that vote that Varadkar, already a senior government minister, came out as gay. The public reaction was overwhelmingly supportive.

The Republic of Ireland was one of the most ethnically and religiously monolithic societies in the developed world. Its official ideology was a fusion of Catholicism and nationalism. The anti-homosexuality laws reflected the dominance of the Catholic Church, which was also manifest in extreme restrictions on contraception, divorce and abortion. While the vast majority of its population was repelled by the savage violence of the Irish Republican Army's armed campaign against British rule across the border in Northern Ireland, most agreed with the IRA's basic aim of ending the partition of the island and bringing about what the Irish constitution called 'the reintegration of the national territory.'

But the Irish radically revised their nationalism. Three big things changed. The power of the Catholic Church collapsed in the 1990s, partly because of its dreadful response to revelations of its facilitation of sexual abuse of children by clergy. The Irish economy, home to the European headquarters of many of the major multinational IT and pharmaceutical corporations, became a poster child for globalisation. And the search for peace in Northern Ireland forced a dramatic rethinking of ideas about identity, sovereignty and nationality.

These very questions had tormented Ireland for centuries and were at the heart of the vicious, low-level, but apparently interminable conflict that reignited in Northern Ireland in 1968 and wound down thirty years later. If that conflict was to be resolved, there was no choice but to be radical. Things that nation states do not like – ambiguity, contingency, multiplicity – would have to be lived with and perhaps even embraced. Irish people, for the most part, have come to terms with this necessity. The English, as the Brexit referendum suggested, have not. This is why the Irish border has such profound implications for Brexit – it is a physical token of a mental frontier that divides not just territories but ideas of what a national identity means in the twenty-first century.

In retrospect, there is some irony in the fact that the Conservative Party in Britain, now the driving force behind Brexit, was crucial to the conceptual revolution that led to the Belfast Agreement (colloquially called the Good Friday Agreement) of 1998. Traditionally, the Conservative and Unionist Party (to give it its full title) held to the line succinctly summed up by Margaret Thatcher in 1981: 'Northern Ireland is part of the United Kingdom – as much as my constituency is.' But by 1990, the Conservatives were articulating a position in which Northern Ireland was very different from Thatcher's English constituency of Finchley. It was (and is) inconceivable that any British government would state that Finchley was free to go its own way and join, for example, France. In 1990, however, the then secretary of state for Northern Ireland, Peter Brooke, announced, in a carefully crafted phrase, that 'the British government has no selfish strategic or economic interest in Northern Ireland'.

This phrase, since embedded in international law through the Belfast Agreement, is remarkable in itself: sovereign governments are not in the business of declaring themselves neutral and disinterested on the question of whether a part of their own state should ultimately cease to be so. Even more remarkable, however, is that this fundamental shift in British thinking was mirrored in a similar shift in the Irish position. Since Ireland became independent in 1922, its governments had always looked on Northern Ireland as a part of its national territory unjustly and temporarily amputated by the partition of the island. Now, Ireland too withdrew its territorial claim – in 1998 its people voted overwhelmingly to drop it from their constitution and replace it with a stated desire 'in harmony and friendship, to unite all the people who share the territory of the island of Ireland, in all the diversity of their identities and traditions'. Those plurals resonate.

This reciprocal withdrawal of territorial claims has recreated Northern Ireland as a new kind of political space – one that is claimed by nobody. It is not, in effect, a territory at all. Its sovereignty is a matter not of the land but of the mind: it will be whatever its people can agree to make it. And within this space, national identity is to be understood in a radically new way. In its most startling paragraph the Belfast Agreement recognises 'the birthright of all the people of Northern Ireland to identify themselves and be accepted as Irish or British, or both, as they may so choose'. It accepts, in other words, that national identity (and the citizenship that flows from it) is a matter of choice. Even more profoundly, it accepts that this choice is not binary. If you're born in Northern Ireland, you have an unqualified right to hold an Irish passport, a British passport, or each of the two. Those lovely little words 'or both' stand as a rebuke to all absolutist ideas of nationalism. Identities are fluid, contingent and multiple.

When these ideas were framed and overwhelmingly endorsed in referendums on both sides of the Irish border, there was an assumption that there would always be a third identity that was neither Irish nor British but that could be equally shared:

membership of the European Union. In the preamble to the agreement, the British and Irish governments evoked 'the close co-operation between their countries as friendly neighbours and as partners in the European Union'. The two countries joined the EU together in 1973 and their experience of working within it as equals was crucial in overcoming centuries of animosity.

Particularly after the creation in 1993 of a single EU market with free movement of goods, services, capital and labour, the Irish border had itself become much less of an irritant. The peace process allowed the British to demilitarise the border region to such an extent that today travellers are generally unaware of when they are crossing it. The idea of a common European citizenship has real substance, and it has made it much easier for people to feel comfortable with the notion that a national identity can have many different dimensions.

What no one really thought about when all of this was being done was the emergence of another force: English nationalism. There were two nationalisms, Irish and 'British', and they had been reconciled in a creative and civilised way. But the United Kingdom contained (in every sense) other national identities: Scottish, Welsh and English. Scotland and Wales were asserting a sense of difference in devolved parliaments and, in the Scottish case, in growing demands for independence. What could not be predicted, though, was that the decisive nationalist revolution would occur not in Scotland or Wales, but in England. Brexit is a peaceful revolution but it is unmistakably a nationalist revolt. It is England's insurrection against the very ideas that animated the Belfast Agreement: the belief that contemporary nationality must be fluid, open and many-layered.

Brexit is, in a sense, a misnomer. There are five distinct parts of the UK: Scotland, Wales, Northern Ireland, the global metropolis that is Greater London and what the veteran campaigner for democratic reform Anthony Barnett, in his excellent new book *The Lure of Greatness*, calls England-without-London. In three of these parts – Scotland, Northern Ireland and London – Brexit was soundly rejected in last year's referendum. Wales voted narrowly in favour of Brexit. But in England-without-London Brexit was triumphant, winning by almost 11 per cent. It was, moreover, a classic nationalist revolt in that the support for Brexit in non-metropolitan England cut across the supposedly rigid divides of north and south, rich and poor. Every single region of England-without-London voted to leave the EU, from the Cotswolds to Cumbria, from the green and pleasant hills to the scarred old mining valleys. This was a genuine nationalist uprising, a nation transcending social class and geographical divisions to rally behind the cry of 'Take back control'. But the nation in question is not Britain, it is England.

The problem with this English nationalism is not that it exists. It has a very long history (one has only to read Shakespeare) and indeed England can be seen as one of the first movers in the formation of the modern nation state. The English have as much right to a collective political identity as the Irish or the Scots (and indeed as the Germans or the French) have. But for centuries, English nationalism has been buried in two larger constructs: the United Kingdom and the British empire. These interments were entirely voluntary. The gradual construction of the UK, with the inclusion first of Scotland and then of Ireland, gave England stability and control in its own part of the world and allowed it to dominate much of the rest of the world through the empire. Britishness didn't threaten Englishness; it amplified it.

Now, the empire is gone and the UK is slipping out of England's control. Britain's pretensions to be a global military power petered out in the sands of Iraq and Afghanistan: the British army was effectively defeated in both Basra and Helmand and had to be rescued by its American allies. The claim on Northern Ireland has been ceded, and Scotland, though not yet ready for independence, increasingly looks and sounds like another country. In retrospect, it is not surprising that the reaction to these developments has created a reversion to an English, rather than a British, allegiance. In the 2011 census, 32.4 million people (57.7 per cent of the population of England and Wales) chose 'English' as their sole identity, while just 10.7 million people (19.1 per cent) associated themselves with a British identity only.

What do you do with this renewed sense of Englishness? It is not surprising that it should be drawn towards anxieties about sovereignty: there is no English parliament and indeed there are very few English national institutions of any kind. The desire that was ultimately captured by the Brexiteers' brilliant slogan – 'Take Back Control' – was not in itself reprehensible. England, after all, has fine traditions of democratic egalitarianism to draw on. It was not inevitable that the desire to restate English sovereignty would be channelled into chauvinism, anti-immigrant sentiment and a misplaced conviction that if you share sovereignty in a complex arrangement like the EU, you lose it. But without a more positive articulation of Englishness, the country that is struggling to emerge has ended up with a nationalism that is both incoherent and oddly naive.

Crudely, passionate nationalism has taken two forms. There is an imperial nationalism and an anti-imperial nationalism: one sets out to dominate the world, the other to throw off such dominance. The incoherence of the new English nationalism is that it wants to be both. On the one hand, Brexit is fuelled by fantasies of 'Empire 2.0', a reconstructed global trading empire in which the old colonies will be reconnected to the mother country. On the other, it is an insurgency and therefore needs an oppressor to revolt against. Since England doesn't actually have an oppressor, it was necessary to invent one. Decades of demonisation by Rupert Murdoch's newspapers and by the enormously influential *Daily Mail* made the European Union a natural fit for the job.

English nationalism is also naive. Wrapped up for so long in the protective blankets of Britishness and empire, it has not had to test itself in the real conditions of twenty-first-century life for a middle-sized global economy. Unlike Irish nationalism, it has not been forced to rethink itself and imagine how it might work in a world where collective identities have to be complex, ambiguous, fluid and contingent. It does not know how to articulate itself without falling back on nostalgic notions of Britishness that no longer function. And since it is not sure what it is, it is not good at adding those crucial words 'or both' and becoming comfortable with an identity that is European as well as English. It gives the most simplistic nationalist definition of 'Us' – we're not Them.

The question of the Irish border is thus as much about mentalities as it is about practicalities, even though the practicalities are formidable enough. It meanders for 310 miles, and it is not a natural boundary. It was never planned as a logical dividing line, still less as the outer edge of a vast twenty-seven-state union. It is simply composed of the squiggly boundaries of the six Irish counties that had, or could be adjusted to contain, Protestant majorities in 1921. And it cannot be securely policed. We know this because during the Troubles it was heavily militarised, studded with giant army watchtowers, overseen by helicopters and saturated with troops – and it still proved to be highly porous. It is an impossible frontier. At best, attempts to reimpose it will create a lawless zone for the smuggling of goods and people. At worst, border posts will be magnets for the violence of fringe militant groups who will delight in having such powerfully symbolic targets.

The British position paper for the negotiations with the EU, published in August, merely evaded all of these problems by suggesting that in the wonderful free-trading Utopia that will emerge after Brexit there will be no need for a physical border at all. This is not so much a serious proposition as a way of shifting the blame: if and when there is a hard border it will be the EU's fault for not giving Britain free access to the market it is leaving.

Even if these practical problems can be solved, however, the larger question remains. Must the great Irish experiment in new, more open forms of national identity be undermined by the resurgence on the neighbouring island of nationalism in an older and cruder form? The only way to answer that question in the negative is to double down on the double identity of Northern Ireland. It is, under the Belfast Agreement, both Irish and British, which means that it must, after Brexit, be both inside and outside the European Union. Its people have an irrevocable right under the agreement to be Irish, which now means that they have an irrevocable right to be citizens of the European Union – even after the UK, of which they are also part, leaves.

When the EU negotiators talk of the need for 'flexible and imaginative solutions', they are certainly not exaggerating. It is apparently insoluble riddles that create the most imaginative solutions: the radical shifts in Irish identity happened, after all, because there was no alternative. The Brexiteers will surely find that, if their project is not to be derailed, they too will have no alternative but to accede to those little words they are most afraid of: *or both*.

29 August 2017

f you write about Northern Ireland, you face heavy fines if you fail to refer regularly to Winston Churchill's great rhetorical evocation of 'the dreary steeples of Fermanagh and Tyrone' emerging from the deluge of the Great War with 'the integrity of their quarrel' unaffected by the cataclysms of Europe. But almost nobody remembers that Churchill was not talking in general terms about the sectarian divisions of Ulster. He was being much more specific than that.

What he was addressing in that speech in the House of Commons in February 1922 was something that is once again a very live issue: the goddamned Irish border and its endless capacity to drive British governments to distraction. And so here we are again.

Churchill was speaking in a debate about the Anglo-Irish Treaty and the establishment of the Irish Free State. The context, therefore, was partition and the as-yet-unsettled question of where the border would be drawn. Churchill evoked the Great War in this context because he wished to recall a cabinet meeting in which he had participated just before that calamitous conflict broke out. The Home Rule crisis was still unfolding. The question being examined by the cabinet was whether parts of Ulster could be temporarily excluded from Home Rule and if so where the boundaries were to be drawn.

'I remember,' said Churchill, 'on the eve of the Great War we were gathered together at a Cabinet meeting in Downing Street, and for a long time, an hour or an hour and a half... we discussed the boundaries of Fermanagh and Tyrone. Both of the great political parties were at each other's throats. The air was full of talk of civil war. Every effort was made to settle the matter and bring them together. The differences had been narrowed down, not merely to the counties of Fermanagh and Tyrone, but to parishes and groups of parishes inside the areas of Fermanagh and Tyrone, and yet, even when the differences had been so narrowed down, the problem appeared to be as insuperable as ever, and neither side would agree to reach any conclusion.'

It is a poignant, almost tragic image: Europe is about to implode and the imperial cabinet in London is peering through a metaphorical microscope at the ragged boundaries of parishes in Fermanagh and Tyrone. I like to think of the grandees sitting around the table in Downing Street saying the strange Gaelic names to themselves in tones of pure bewilderment: Belcoo, Magheraveely, Rosslea, Aghalane, Derrygonnelly. But the first time is tragedy; the second time is farce.

Theresa May's cabinet is embroiled in a European war that is not so much a cataclysm, more a nervous breakdown. And beneath the noise and bluster, a low but persistent voice keeps whispering: Belcoo, Magheraveely, Rosslea, Aghalane, Derrygonnelly. The mock-heroic epic of Brexit is itself mocked by the contested contours of minute border parishes. Pathos has become bathos. But the same fundamental truth applies: the problem of the goddamned border is 'as insuperable as ever'. No one can, or will, 'reach any conclusion'.

23 September 2017

Theresa May delivers a big Brexit speech in Florence, formally asking for a transition period after March 2019. Her foreign secretary Boris Johnson goes on manoeuvres with a big essay of his own, staking out a hardline position.

Brexit is written in binary code. It is all zeros and ones – out of the European Union or in. In his long *Telegraph* essay last weekend, the British foreign secretary and totem of the Leave campaign Boris Johnson reiterated the iron imperatives of last year's referendum: 'The choice was binary. The result was decisive. There is simply no way – or no good way – of being 52 per cent out and 48 per cent in.'

This has an impeccable logic, in the way mad things often do. In her speech in Florence on Friday, Johnson's supposed boss Theresa May was trying, in her own weak way, to tweak that logic, to find some wriggle room in the relentless bind of the binary.

The concrete content of the speech may be less important than its signal of distress – though whether May is waving or drowning remains an open question. She is edging towards some way to be – however temporarily – at least a little bit in while moving out. This is what mathematicians call fuzzy logic, the logic of vagueness where there are infinite possible gradations between zero and one.

Her problem is that compared with the clean and clear choice that Johnson offers – in or out – the search for a transitional compromise deal is indeed fuzzy.

As she retreats from the confident, if rather ludicrous, tautology of 'Brexit means Brexit', she must wander into a no man's land of ambiguities and uncertainties. May's compromise offer is slight and tentative but the abandonment of the lofty rhetorical heights of last January is unmistakable.

Almost a year ago, the president of the European Council, Donald Tusk, prefigured Johnson when he suggested that 'the only real alternative to a hard Brexit is no Brexit'. From both sides of the English Channel, the binary view makes sense.

It is easier for the EU if the UK simply departs – a part in/part out arrangement, even for a few years, undermines the clarity of the rules of EU membership.

And, conceptually if not in practice, it is also easier for the Brexiteers. Since, as Johnson claimed, Britain outside the EU will be nothing less than 'the greatest country on Earth', why should it wait around in the anteroom of historic destiny?

In an essay that was much more interesting than its headline-grabbing mendacities and implied leadership ambitions suggested, Johnson was really delivering a classic breakup speech. And although he didn't actually use the old 'It's not you, it's me' line, he came pretty close.

Cleverly, instead of attacking the EU, he depicted Britain's membership of the union as just one of those relationships in which the lovers are bad for each other. They don't mean to be but they are. And he suggested that the Brits, unhappy and misplaced, had become impossible to live with: 'It is wrong for us to be there – always trying to make things different, always getting in the way, always moaning.'

Johnson's tale of the Brits as partners in a doomed marriage has a compelling moral: make a clean break. The couple who were never meant for one another will find a way to be perfectly civil, even friendly, in the future, but only if, to coin a phrase, they consciously uncouple first. No sentimental one-night stands, no teary evenings looking at the wedding photos, no possibility that they might, after all, give it another go sometime.

Theresa May, on the other hand, now finds herself edging towards the suggestion that the couple should share a house for a few years and not finalise the divorce until Britain is ready to occupy the apartment it has not yet begun to build.

The point is not that May is wrong – she isn't. It's that the binary logic is all on Johnson's side.

The strangeness of where the Brexit paroxysm has led us is that the hard Brexiteers once characterised by a close ally of David Cameron as 'swivel-eyed loons' are logical but not rational. The sensible compromisers are rational but not logical. The crux of the matter is this: compromise means mirroring the EU as closely as possible so you can still enjoy some of its benefits. 'Rule, Britannia' will segue into 'I Wanna Be Like You'.

And if you're going to be as like the EU as possible, why not stay in the EU? In Johnson's metaphor, if you're going to live in the same house, sleep together and with no one else, pay into a joint bank account and do your share of the domestic chores, why get divorced at all?

The answer, of course, is that you're trying to make the best of a very bad job. And that best is inevitably second best – Johnson was not entirely wrong to characterise the compromise position of staying in the single market and/or the customs union as one in which Britain is 'turned into a vassal state – taking direction from the EU, but with no power to influence the EU's decisions'.

If, as May signalled on Friday, the UK is moving away from the clean break she called for last January, the nation is indeed going to be, for some as yet undefined period, not the glorious British sun but a satellite locked into the EU's gravitational pull and palely reflecting its light. It is an oddly humiliating overture to what May still insists will be a heroic grand opera.

The underlying problem is with binary thinking itself. Where May and Johnson do not differ is in their insistence that people can belong to one thing or the other, but not to both. They can be British or European; they can be with us or against us. May, in the hubris before her general election humiliation, characterised pro-Europeans as 'citizens of nowhere'.

Johnson, in his essay, declared himself 'troubled with the

thought that people [in Britain] are beginning to have genuinely split allegiances' – with Brexit as the cure that will restore the binary choice between Britishness and Europeanness. Underlying the whole mad project is the idea of belonging and sovereignty as zero sum games – it is either/or, not both/and.

The British problem is that all the rationality is on the side of both/and, but all the emotional clarity is with either/or. If it is to avoid disaster, Britain needs to accept messy ambiguities. But it is still led by a party that allowed itself to be captured by the stirring simplicities of a stark choice between national failure and impending glory. The question after May's speech is the same as it was before she gave it: who has the authority to invest a painful climbdown with the emotional potency of a patriotic imperative?

26 September 2017

On the surface, all is well between Theresa May and her allies
in the DUP. But it is already clear that a rupture is inevitable.

I apologise to the Democratic Unionist Party. After it did a deal to keep Theresa May in power, I suggested it would eventually be stabbed in the back by its Tory friends. This has proved to be doubly wrong. It didn't happen eventually – it has happened already. And it has been stabbed, not in the back, but in the front. Sorry about that.

The DUP's enthusiastic support for Brexit is largely an exercise in identity politics, a way of expressing an emotional attachment to Britishness. But it has two political imperatives. The DUP's own voters do not want a hard border. And they do not want to lose the agricultural subsidies that account for 87 per cent of farm incomes in Northern Ireland.

They need their friends in London to swing these two big things for them. Otherwise Arlene Foster will look less like Moses leading her people to the Promised Land and more like a Scout leader who has lost the compass, forgotten the tents and dropped the sandwiches in the bog.

The DUP always acknowledged that a hard frontier is not just undesirable but impossible, a reality made starker by figures showing the border is crossed 110 million times a year. But it has been pushing a magical solution: technology. Some as-yet-undiscovered technology (vaguely imagined as having something to do with number plate recognition and data analytics) would allow the frictionless movements of goods and people.

There was something oddly touching in this act of faith, like one of those cargo cults that developed on remote South Sea islands when fridges and TVs washed ashore and were worshipped as mysterious messages from the gods. But, while the DUP was placing all its bets on this technological totem, its Tory friends dragged the poor beast out the back and shot it. At the end of July, Jeffrey Donaldson was still rhapsodising about the ingenious machines that were going to solve the border problem, sighing that 'Modern technology is a wonderful thing'. Two weeks later the Tory government published its long-awaited position paper on the Irish dimension of the Brexit negotiations.

It was a mercy killing without the mercy. The DUP's solution was dismissed in a single line, committing the UK to 'avoid any physical border infrastructure in either the United Kingdom or Ireland, for any purpose'. No physical border infrastructure means no magic machines. Unless it is going to suggest that border controls will be purely spiritual, it is hard to see where this leaves the DUP.

On agricultural subsidies, too, the DUP has been brushed aside by its Brexiteer mates. The party knows very well that agriculture matters much more to Northern Ireland than it does to England. And most of it is currently unthinkable without the cheque in the post from Brussels: Northern Ireland makes up 3 per cent of the UK population but gets almost 10 per cent of its European Union farm subsidies.

A beef farmer in Northern Ireland who followed the DUP's advice to vote for Brexit might typically have a commercial income of £14,745. The Brussels cheque is for almost twice that amount: £28,726. What's going to happen after Brexit? The DUP has a simple answer: London will send that farmer £28,726.

In the short term, this is probably true. The Brexiteers cannot afford an immediate food security crisis, so London will pony up for a few years. But in the medium term, frankly my dears, London doesn't give a damn. Remember the tragicomic episode in July when one of the arch-Brexiteers, Michael Gove, now the UK's food minister, visited a farm show in Antrim and was feted by the

DUP? He issued a statement praising the quality and worldwide renown of, um, Welsh lamb. Hard to blame him – all these rainy, hilly peripheries where people talk in funny accents do rather meld into one another.

What the Brexiteers really want is an ultra-free-market Britain, liberated from subsidies and regulations. George Eustice, the UK farming minister, has been clear about the implications: 'If subsidies equal direct payments, of course we want to move away from that.' The promise to protect farm subsidies is tied up with the idea that Britain will have a vast amount of money to spend because it will no longer be sending it to Brussels. Leaving aside the mendacity of the infamous £350 million a week that is supposed to be available, has the DUP noticed that this mythic sum has been promised yet again to the National Health Service, not to farmers? In the 4,326-word essay in which Boris Johnson revived these claims, he said nothing about giving a penny of the dividend to farmers.

The DUP needs to consult a self-help manual, *He's Just Not That Into You*, which is advertised as ideal for those 'who want to get past the crappy get-out lines fellas use'. The crappy get-out lines about the wonders of technology and the cheque in the post from London didn't disguise the truth that the Brexiteers are just not that into dealing with the complications of Ireland. Whether it likes it or not, the DUP has to join the rest of Ireland in trying to do so.

12 November 2017

The British ministers for defence and international affairs resign in separate scandals and the foreign secretary, Boris Johnson, is proving to be openly incompetent. A leaked EU position paper is scathing on the failure of the British side to come up with credible proposals on the Irish border.

In his magisterial history of the Hundred Years War, Jonathan Sumption recounts a complaint by the fourteenth-century French chronicler Jean Froissart about the difficulty of negotiating with the English: 'According to Froissart, it was a well-known trick of English diplomats to evade embarrassing questions by pretending not to understand them.'

It would be unfair to make the same charge against British diplomats now, but their political masters are clearly up to the old tricks. The most embarrassing question of all is: what now is Britain's place in the world? Instead of an answer, all the rest of the world gets to hear are self-evidently evasive pomposities about a gloriously global Britain. To which the world is increasingly inclined to reply: what globe exactly do you think you're on?

It does not seem entirely accidental that, in the past week, the three British ministers who deal most directly with the outside world have been such clownish embodiments of disarray. Defence, foreign affairs and international development are the ways in which a state formally conducts its relations with other countries.

The ministers in charge of two of them – Priti Patel and Michael Fallon – are gone from the cabinet. Whatever shred of credibility Boris Johnson had as foreign secretary has been stripped away. One of the most basic functions of any country's foreign office is to come to the aid of its citizens when they are in trouble abroad. That he, instead, placed Nazanin Zaghari-Ratcliffe at further risk of unjust punishment in Iran suggests a dysfunctionality. If the elementary tasks are being screwed up so badly, what chance is there of competent handling of the most complex talks in Britain's modern history?

The coming together of these three ministerial crises may owe much to coincidence, but apparently random events have a way of exposing deeper patterns. In this case, the pattern is hardly mysterious. Since the Brexit vote, there is a concerted pretence of incomprehension in the face of other people's alarm at what the long-time London correspondent of the *New York Times*, Steven Erlanger, recently called Britain's 'unmoored' position in the world.

We have been witnessing a very English farce, but one with a wholly new twist. In this version of *Fawlty Towers*, it is not Manuel the stereotypical foreigner who goes around saying: '*Qué?*' and: 'I know nawthing!' It is the all-too-English Basil, acting out a panto-mime of feigned perplexity.

In the immediate aftermath of the Second World War, Winston Churchill set out a vision of Britain's place in the world as a kind of square. He knew that the pre-eminent position that victory had given Britain could not be maintained in isolation. So, he articulated a complex sense of belonging. If Britain was one side of the square, the other three were: the United States, with which it would have its famously special relationship; the Commonwealth, which would look to the mother country for leadership; and, as Brexiteers like to forget, a united Europe, in which Britain would be a leading light and which, in Churchill's words, would banish 'tariff walls and passport networks'.

Brexit is a radical attempt to alter this geometry, to wrench Churchill's square into the shape of a golden triangle of Britain, the US and the Commonwealth (reimagined in the most feverish fantasies as Empire 2.0). However, everybody knows that this is not going to happen. The only triangle it actually resembles is the mythical one off Bermuda into which flights of fancy disappear.

In the aftermath of the Brexit referendum, the brilliant historian of post-war Britain, John Bew, suggested the only way forward was a 'reinvigorated special relationship' with the US that would, in turn, open the way for a deeper British engagement with Asia. In truth, this was always likely to be a problematic notion; after all, Tony Blair's special relationship with George W. Bush hardly did much for Britain's standing in the world. In any case, three months after Bew made this suggestion, Donald Trump was elected to the White House. The idea of Britain finding a secure place in the world as Trump's favourite caddy is about as appealing as it is plausible.

It is true that Trump won't always be around. However, if and when the Democrats return to power, there is no reason to think they will be any more inclined to sympathise with the Brexit project than the openly dismissive Barack Obama was before the referendum. Indeed, a fundamental problem for Britain's place in the world is precisely that Brexit is deeply linked in international discourse with the Trump phenomenon, as two manifestations of the same reactionary breakdown. A US that is recovering its senses is highly unlikely to want to cosy up to a Britain that has locked itself permanently in its own padded cell.

As far as the Commonwealth is concerned, it is striking that no one has yet been trampled in the rush to embrace the old mother country again. Most Commonwealth countries felt that they were pretty much ditched by Britain when it got into bed with Europe in 1973. Australia, for example, had to radically restructure its agricultural economy when it lost most of its access to the British market. It responded by remaking its own place in the world and becoming, in effect, a Pacific country. Maybe there is some Aussie soap opera in which the cruelly dumped lover drops everything and returns to the bastard who blew her off all those years ago, just because he clicks his fingers.

But real life is not going to be like this. All but the most deluded Brexiteers know all of this very well. They know what Churchill knew – that Britain's relationships with the rest of the world have to be anchored in its relationship with a gradually uniting Europe. They know that Brexit Britain doesn't even have a solid relationship with the rest of the archipelago it inhabits: last week's leaked European commission position paper raises, more starkly than ever, the impossibility of a clean Brexit that does not undermine the Northern Ireland peace settlement, prompting profound questions about the future of the UK itself.

They surely know that a country that is so deeply uncertain about where its own future borders will lie cannot deal confidently with the world beyond it. They must know, too, that reneging on the most important international commitments you have made in your modern history – the commitments of EU membership – is not a great advertisement for your potential as a future partner in international affairs. If it were a personal ad, it would read: 'Petulant bolter seeks stable, lifelong relationship.'

However, the Brexit project is a triumph of the unknown known. It is all about pretending not to understand its own obvious consequences. One of those consequences is that Britain will never be able to replace the prestige, influence and respect it has enjoyed as a leading but highly distinctive member of the EU. Bluster aside, all the Brexiteers have to say about that is: '*Qué?*'

14 November 2017

In 1962, the Ulster poet John Hewitt published a short poem called 'The Frontier'. It is ostensibly about crossing the Alps between France and Switzerland but, of course, not really. Hewitt's reflection on the absurdity of border-crossings is inevitably resonant of more insular experiences. The train he is on stops and 'small men in uniform drift down the corridor, thumb passports' and mark the travellers' bags with chalk as a sign that they have been duly inspected.

> We pass here into another allegiance,
> expect new postage stamps, new prices, manifestoes,
> and brace ourselves for the change. But the landscape does
>   not alter;
> we had already entered these mountains an hour ago.

Borders are often like this, arbitrary, accidental and at odds with a landscape that is sublimely indifferent to their merely human contingency.

They are an attempt to impose culture on nature, to privilege history over geography, to elevate the work of centuries or even decades over the work of eons, to insist that short human time triumphs over the long duration of geological time. The mountains don't give a toss about the small men in uniform. And, as Hewitt was slyly hinting, this is just as true whether the mountains are the soaring Alps or the sombre Mournes, majestic white peaks or low, wet drumlins.

I'm old enough to remember the men in uniform boarding the trains at Newry for what was, in the pre-Troubles time of my early childhood, a perfunctory ritual of inspection. I also remember the equally casual ticking of the bags with chalk by the bored Irish customs officials manning the barrier at Heuston station, like assembly line workers going through their repetitive motions.

Did they realise that the same kids who had gone up to Belfast that morning as skinny waifs were now sweating and obese because they were wearing three layers of cheap smuggled clothes? Sure they did – but so long as the bag was not bulging with obvious contraband, it received its quick benediction of chalk.

'Habit,' says Didi in Samuel Beckett's *Waiting for Godot*, 'is a great deadener.' We get used to pretty much anything. For people who actually lived and worked on the old Irish border of my childhood, it was always a daily irritant. And, of course, for militant Irish nationalists, it was an affront and a provocation. But most of the time, for most people, it was a habit, a dead ritual that must nonetheless be performed.

If the history were not so unsettled, and if had not become even more so, the reasons why this line was drawn here and not there, why to move from one field to the next was to 'pass… into another allegiance', would have been gradually forgotten. Habit would have deadened those questions; the border would be there because it was there.

But we broke the habit. These days, whenever I'm on the train from Dublin to Belfast, I know I've crossed the border only because my mobile phone burrs and my provider sends me a text message of unconscious but magnificent irony: 'You are now roaming in Europe.' There are still different postage stamps, different prices, different currencies and different allegiances. But we've been 'roaming in Europe' on our own island for almost twenty-five years now, ever since the single market came into force in 1993.

If this had never happened, if the men in uniform had sustained their officious ceremonies, the force of habit might have meant that, for all the minor irritations and all the atavistic animosities, the border would have retained its old power of deadening routine. Instead it's like smoking. If you smoke for decades, you don't notice how disgusting it is, don't smell the acrid tang from your clothes and furniture.

But if you've long since broken the habit, you can't bear the thought of going back to the raking cough and the clinging odour and the nicotine-stained fingers. Within a few years of giving up the smokes, you wonder how you ever started such an awful habit in the first place.

And after twenty-five years without the border-crossing rituals, they will, if they return, seem impossibly absurd.

Crossing the Irish border is ordinary: it is a thing that is done 110 million times a year. And in recent decades, it has been mostly a thing of geography, not of history.

Brexit threatens more and more to reverse this order, to turn this quotidian travel from a mere crossing of the indifferent landscape into a reminder of the capriciousness of history – 110 million annual lessons in the pettiness and folly of human efforts to impose our political meanings on the mountains and the rivers.

For what we know and have always known about the Irish border is that the rituals of inspection and the hurried chalk marks were just that, little ceremonies that did nothing to hold this imaginary line against the realities of a highly porous landscape. The strange thing about the present moment is that everybody knows we can't go back to those daft pretences – and yet back is the only current direction of travel. Unless we are roaming in Europe, we will be doomed to border on the absurd.

5 December 2017

*But nothing in this story is
ever straightforward.*

Just before lunchtime on Monday, European Council president Donald Tusk tweeted: 'Tell me why I like Mondays!' He had just got off the phone with the Irish prime minister, Leo Varadkar. Varadkar told Tusk that Ireland was happy with a formula of words the British government had already agreed to: that, after Brexit, there will be 'continued regulatory alignment' between both parts of Ireland. Behind this technocratic phrase, there was a great retreat by the British.

They had previously insisted that Northern Ireland is as British as Yorkshire and thus could have no special status after Brexit. The Irish government, with the full support of the European Union, had argued that this would mean the reimposition of a hard border on the island of Ireland and a real danger of undermining the Belfast Agreement of 1998 that ended the Troubles. This was always going to be the most difficult of all the problems posed by Brexit. While the British concession to the Irish position was no more than the beginning of a solution, it was 'sufficient progress' for the EU to conclude when its leaders meet on 14 and 15 December that they could at last open trade talks with the British.

Yet Tusk's tweet was inadvertently ominous. It was a play on 'I Don't Like Mondays', a hit song in 1979 by the Irish rock band the Boomtown Rats. The song in turn was inspired by a mass shooting in a US school playground. Asked why she did it, the shooter, a sixteen-year-old girl, replied, 'I don't like Mondays. This livens up the day.' The lyrics, written and sung by Bob Geldof, now a prominent campaigner against Brexit, had her adding that 'I wanna shoot that whole day down'.

Within hours of Tusk's playfully optimistic tweet, Monday's hopes would indeed be shot down. The shots came from Arlene Foster, the leader of the Democratic Unionist Party (DUP), a right-wing Evangelical party in Northern Ireland, whose ten members of the Westminster Parliament are keeping Theresa May's minority government in office.

For Prime Minister May, this was a double humiliation. First, she had conceded what she had promised never to concede – a special deal for Northern Ireland. This is itself hugely problematic for the whole Brexit project: as soon as word of the deal got out, the leaders of the devolved parliaments of Scotland and Wales and the mayor of London were asking why they couldn't have special deals, too. May's famous tautology – 'Brexit means Brexit' – falls apart if Brexit means many different things in different parts of the UK.

Yet she found herself entirely outmanoeuvred. The British had assumed that the Irish could be relied on to agree that 'sufficient progress' had been made even when there was nothing on the table but bland assurances of 'no return to the borders of the past'. This was a serious miscalculation, though an understandable one. Britain has always had the upper hand in its relations with Ireland. It was completely unprepared for the reality that Brexit is creating: a rapid waning of British diplomatic power. The Irish government knew that it had all of the other twenty-six EU member states, and the European Parliament, on its side. Since the negotiation process got under way in April, the Europeans have made it clear that their position is Ireland's position. Britain is isolated; Ireland has powerful allies.

The reasons for this European solidarity with Ireland are a mixture of idealism and realpolitik. On the one hand, the EU genuinely wants to protect the Belfast Agreement and the Irish peace process. For all its problems, that process is a great reminder of the EU's own primary purpose, which is to end the threat of war in Europe. On the other hand, siding so strongly with Ireland is a

115

very effective way of admonishing the British about what they are abandoning with Brexit – the protection and support of a large multinational institution. There is a simple message: Ireland is one of us and Britain is not. We look after our own.

Britain's agreement to accept Ireland's demands is an expression of its weakness: it can't even bully little Ireland any more. And this would have been bad enough for one day. But there was another humiliation in store. Having backed down, May was then peremptorily informed that she was not even allowed to back down. She left her lunch with the president of the European Commission, Jean-Claude Juncker, to take a phone call from the DUP's Arlene Foster, who told her that the deal she had just made was unacceptable. May then had to go back in and tell Juncker that she could not agree to what she had just agreed to. It is a scarcely credible position for a once great state to find itself in: its leader does not even have the power to conduct a dignified retreat.

In September, I suggested that the Irish question was like the Sphinx on the road to Thebes: its riddle must be solved before a final deal on Brexit can be approached. On Monday, the Sphinx seemed to be in a good mood, willing to allow the traveller to mutter an interim formula and pass at least a few more steps along the road. But she was only toying with the hapless May, like a cat letting a mouse go with one paw, only to grab it back with the other.

For what is clear is that the Irish question is more and more a British question: does any British government have the authority to make a deal on Brexit? The reckless decision to leave the European Union, and the fantasies that fuelled it, have destabilised the United Kingdom itself. There is a vacuum of authority, one that has been filled, most improbably, by the DUP, a party that received just 292,000 votes, or less than 1 per cent of the total cast, in the UK's general election in June. Before the Europeans can even think about a final deal with the British, they need to know whom exactly they are supposed to be dealing with. They can be forgiven for not understanding that it is the DUP.

There are forces outside the room, realities not represented at the negotiating table. Those are the unresolved realities of Britain's long and complex entanglement with Ireland. Until they are honestly addressed, the Brexit project will struggle to articulate itself in a way that the Europeans can respond to. The song he evoked in his moment of misplaced optimism must still be going round in Donald Tusk's head:

> *Now, it ain't so neat to admit defeat*
> *They can see no reasons*
> *'Cause there are no reasons*
> *What reason do you need, oh, whoah…*
> *[Tell me why]*
> *I don't like Mondays.*

8 December 2017

The question – are we going to see a border in the Irish Sea, with Northern Ireland remaining much more closely aligned to the EU than the rest of the UK? – turns out to be the critical one. Under pressure from the DUP, May agrees that Northern Ireland will remain aligned to both the UK and Ireland. Simple logic suggests that this means the UK remaining aligned to Ireland – and hence to the EU. The Irish question has, it seems, made a hard Brexit impossible.

Let's not understate the import of what Ireland has just achieved. It has not just secured an outcome that minimises the damage of Brexit on this island. It has radically altered the trajectory of Brexit itself, pushing that crazy careering vehicle away from its path towards the cliff edge. This saga has taken many strange turns, but this is the strangest of all: after one of the most fraught fortnights in the recent history of Anglo-Irish relations, Ireland has just done Britain a favour of historic dimensions. It has saved it from the madness of a hard Brexit.

There is a great irony here: the problem that the Brexiteers most relentlessly ignored has come to determine the entire shape of their project. By standing firm against their attempts to bully, cajole and blame it, Ireland has shifted Brexit towards a soft outcome. It is now far more likely that Britain will stay in the customs union and the single market. It is also more likely that Brexit will not in fact happen.

Essentially what this extraordinary deal does is to reverse engineer Brexit as a whole from one single component – the need to avoid a hard Irish border. It follows the Sherlock Holmes principle: eliminate the impossible and whatever remains, however improbable, must be the solution. The Irish government, by taking a firm stance and retaining the rock-solid support of the rest of the EU, made the hard border the defining impossibility. Working back from that, the Brexit project now has to embrace what seemed, even last Monday, highly improbable: the necessity, at a minimum, for the entire UK to mirror the rules of the customs union and the single market after it leaves the EU. And this in turn raises the biggest question of all: if the UK is going to mirror the customs union and the single market, why go to the considerable bother of leaving the EU in the first place?

The great surprise of the text of the joint report is that its language is actually much more favourable to Ireland than the text that was leaked on Monday as having been agreed. The language that caused the Democratic Unionist Party to threaten hellfire and damnation suggested that there would be continuing 'regulatory alignment' between the two parts of Ireland. What we've actually ended up with is much firmer and clearer – and it explicitly invokes the customs union and the single market as the source of these regulations: 'In the absence of agreed solutions, the United Kingdom will maintain full alignment with those rules of the internal market and the customs union which, now or in the future, support North–South co-operation, the all-island economy and the protection of the 1998 Agreement.'

The phrase 'in the future' is crucial – it means that every single change in the EU's rules will have to be mirrored north of the border. But this is now the wooden horse inside the walls of Troy because, to avoid the idea of Northern Ireland becoming a separate regulatory space, there will also have to be the same mirroring of the rules and regulations that continue to apply in Northern Ireland by the UK as a whole. The mathematics are simple: if A equals B and B equals C, then C equals A. A is Ireland's position in the single market and customs union, B is Northern Ireland's full alignment to that position and C is the UK's commitment not to differ from Northern Ireland. The commitment to have no barriers to east–west trade means that London is effectively a prisoner of Belfast.

I suggested earlier this week that we were seeing things being turned upside down: instead of, as DUP leader Arlene Foster insisted, Northern Ireland leaving the EU on the same terms as the UK, the UK will have to leave the EU on the same terms as Northern Ireland. This, in effect, is what is now agreed. We always knew the border is extremely porous, but what has now been smuggled across it is a minimum condition for the second phase of the Brexit talks: whatever trade arrangements eventually emerge, they cannot be ones in which Britain strays much beyond the existing customs and market arrangements. To adapt Henry Ford, Britain can have any Brexit it likes, so long as it is green.

Apart from all of its other consequences, this means the DUP's great bluff has been called. It was insisting on two contradictory things: no special status for Northern Ireland and completely leaving the customs union and single market. This contradiction has come back to haunt the whole Brexit project – the DUP has been forced to concede that if the first condition is to be satisfied, the second in effect cannot. The deal secured by Ireland does not necessarily force the UK to stay in the customs union and single market. It just forces it to act as if it has stayed in – a distinction without a difference. Call it what you like – if it acts like a customs union, moves like a customs union and is fully aligned like a customs union, it is a customs union.

But this, of course, is precisely why this deal is not just the beginning of the end of the Brexit talks. It is potentially the beginning of the end of Brexit itself. If the deal sticks, the dreams of a clean break, of throwing off the shackles of EU regulation and sailing off into the great blue yonder of Empire 2.0 are over – unless the 'swivel-eyed loons' can stage a coup, call off the talks process and crash out with no deal.

And as they themselves have always argued, if Britain is not making a clean break, what is the point of breaking up with the EU at all? Ireland has just pointed its neighbour towards one obvious answer to that question.

9 December 2017

It has never seemed more apt that perhaps the greatest work of English literature, William Shakespeare's *King Lear*, is about the consequences of a capricious loss of authority. Lear gives up his kingdom for no good reason and everything falls horribly apart. In his madness and despair he utters the most scathing lines ever written about political power: 'Thou hast seen a farmer's dog bark at a beggar?... There thou mightst behold the great image of authority.'

The great image of British authority this week was Theresa May travelling to Brussels on Monday essentially as a beggar, a suppliant desperately in need of the European declaration of 'sufficient progress' in the Brexit talks – and the bark of Arlene Foster peremptorily ordering the British prime minister to take back the promises she had made.

Theresa May was experiencing the double Irish, capitulating first to the Irish government and then uncapitulating on the orders of a very different Irish force, the Democratic Unionist Party. And then, in the early hours of Friday morning, there was a further twist – both May and the DUP essentially signing up to what had been agreed on Monday. It was a startling display of British powerlessness: there can hardly be a more unfortunate military manoeuvre than the retreat from a retreat.

But the image of cracked authority that will linger longest was Foster sweeping down the Stormont staircase on Monday afternoon, like the star of a Busby Berkeley musical flanked by her all-male chorus line, to deliver her royal command: Northern Ireland must leave the European Union on exactly the same terms as the rest of the United Kingdom.

It was an apparent moment of historic triumph: no Irish party leader had seemed to hold this much sway over a British prime minister since Charles Stewart Parnell and William Gladstone. But this historical parallel should have given the DUP pause. It is one thing for an Irish nationalist to lord it over the Brits, quite another for a unionist and 'British' party to do so.

For Foster's historic triumph was also a historic mistake. Each man, wrote Oscar Wilde, kills the thing he loves. The DUP on Monday helped to kill the thing it purports to love: the power and prestige of Britain.

It is easy to understand how exhilarating that moment must have been for the DUP in general and for Foster in particular. A year ago this month she was in very deep trouble over the 'cash for ash scandal', facing demands to stand aside. It seemed possible that her political career might come to an ignominious end. She cannot have dreamed then that she would find herself at the centre of European affairs, being able to call the British prime minister out of a meeting in which she was about to make a crucial deal and send her back in to say, in effect, 'Mrs Foster says I'm not allowed to play with you any more.'

The utterly unexpected result of the UK general election in June, in which the DUP soared and the Tories plummeted, was a vertiginous spin of the wheel of political fortune that had left her at an apparent summit of power.

It is also easy to understand why the DUP felt it had to issue its diktat on Monday. It was right to see May's agreement to guarantee 'full alignment' between the two parts of Ireland after Brexit as a defeat.

However technocratic the language, the agreement meant that Northern Ireland would, in practice, have to mirror both the customs union and the single market. That would mean that there were only two possible conclusions to the Brexit process, both of them unpalatable to the DUP. Either there would be a border in the Irish Sea or the UK as a whole would in effect stay in the customs union and the single market. The DUP's shock was almost certainly genuine.

Exhilaration and shock are powerful emotions, especially in combination. They provoked a response that was, for four thrilling days, highly satisfying for the DUP but, in the longer term, likely to prove disastrous.

The party is anchored in two, closely related things: the preservation of the union and a sense of 'Britishness' as a strong and stable identity. The union is the DUP's external orientation, Britishness its internal tribal marker.

If it were able to stand back and coolly appraise what it did on Monday, it would have to conclude that both of these things have been severely and perhaps permanently damaged. For both of them, like all political constructs, depend on an image of authority rather grander than the farmer's dog barking at the beggar.

The union is not a God-given reality: it is a recent political construct, and a fragile one. It has to be held together by the aura of power radiating from Downing Street. That goes doubly for Britishness, especially in the fraught context of Northern Ireland: it is a way of identifying not just with a country but with an idea of greatness.

In a famous passage of *The English Constitution* Walter Bagehot wrote of the need to preserve the illusion of the monarchy: 'We must not let in daylight upon magic.' The same is true of the British prime minister: at least in the conduct of vital international talks, she or he must exude authority.

And what the DUP did on Monday was to rip aside the curtains and let a cruel, harsh daylight in on poor Theresa May. As at the end of a cheap vampire movie, her authority crumbled to dust in front of the watching world. And with it went whatever magic still attaches to the image of post-imperial Britain.

By barking at May and having her cower in obedience, the DUP exposed the weakness of the very thing it purports to uphold. But the embarrassment was not just for May personally or even for her supporters. This was the mortification of Britain itself, the abject humbling of a once-feared power.

This is not a smart thing for the DUP to have done. It aligned the party more firmly than ever with the enemies of May's gradual shift towards pragmatism.

In doing so it has alienated a swathe of British opinion that would now prefer to see the DUP as a foreign body in its body politic. You don't save the union by making so many of its citizens revile you.

And for what? In the end, by making May and the British government seem ridiculous, all the DUP achieved was to make it more likely that they would have to capitulate on all the red lines of a hard Brexit. It accidentally confounded the desires of its own allies among the extreme Brexiteers by creating the circumstances in which Britain has effectively had to agree to be bound by the regulations of the single market and the customs union.

The sword it was waving at the Irish government turned out to be a pin that pricked both its own moment of power and the bubble of Brexit's grand self-delusions.

TIMELINE

18 January 2018:   The European Union (Withdrawal) Bill has its First Reading in the House of Lords.

14 February 2018:   Boris Johnson gives a major speech on Brexit.

28 February 2018:   The European Commission publishes the draft withdrawal agreement.

2 March 2018:   May gives a speech at the Mansion House in London on the UK's future economic partnership with the European Union.

14 March 2018:   The European Parliament endorses a resolution laying out a possible association agreement framework for future EU–UK relations after Brexit.

19 March 2018:   The amended draft withdrawal agreement is published.

26 June 2018:   The European Union (Withdrawal) Bill receives Royal Assent and becomes an Act of Parliament: the European Union (Withdrawal) Act.

13 February 2018

*Many Brexiteers assumed that there would be no Irish
border problem because Ireland would follow the UK out of
the EU. Nigel Farage visits Dublin to encourage what he and
a small bunch of Irish conservatives (including the Catholic
commentator John Waters) hope will be the beginning of Irexit.*

What Europhile quisling said this: 'Ireland belongs to Europe by history, tradition and sentiment no less than by geography. Our destiny is bound up with that of Europe... Our people have always tended to look to Europe for inspiration, guidance and encouragement'? That was Seán Lemass, who fought in the 1916 Rising as a boy, took the anti-Treaty side in the Civil War, built Fianna Fáil and could never be thought of as anything other than an Irish nationalist. He was speaking in Brussels in January 1962 on Ireland's hopes of joining what was then the European Economic Community. He stressed that he understood that Ireland was seeking to be part of a project that was about much more than economics and that he spoke 'in full awareness' of the EEC's underlying aim of 'ever-closer union'.

For all the fantasies of Nigel Farage and John Waters, Ireland will not follow the UK out of the European Union. It won't do it for reasons that Farage and his new-found Irish acolytes fail to fathom but that Lemass grasped very clearly. Brexit is an authentic English nationalist revolution, even if it depends on a ludicrous notion of the EU as England's imperial oppressor. Irexit would not be an Irish nationalist revolution. On the contrary, it would be the end of Irish nationalism. The logic of Irexit would be for Ireland to rejoin the UK – and that's why it hasn't a hope.

If we were to be brutal about it and strip away all the undoubted psychological satisfactions of nationhood, Irish independence was largely notional until we joined the EEC in 1973. In some ways, Ireland was rather like what Britain could yet become after Brexit – a satellite state. We were no longer represented at Westminster but we played largely by British rules. There were grand moments of national self-assertion (most obviously Irish neutrality during the Second World War) but day-to-day realities, as Lemass understood, were the realities of dependency. Our people continued to emigrate to British cities. Our economy was a British backwater.

In 1960, 75 per cent of Irish exports went to the UK. In 1972, the last year before we joined the EEC, the proportion was still 61 per cent. Now, just 18 per cent of Irish service exports and 14 per cent of Irish goods exports are to the UK. Conversely, Ireland's economic links to continental Europe were astonishingly weak. In 1971, our total exports to the EEC's six member states amounted to just £23 million. Just ten years later, Irish exports to EEC countries other than the UK stood at £968 million.

In one sense, of course, these figures mean nothing. They belong to a rational discourse of economic self-interest and Brexit has reminded us that self-interest may be neither here nor there in nationalist revolutions. The areas of England that will suffer the greatest economic hardship as a result of Brexit are also the areas most in favour of it. The pain of self-harm can be assuaged by the pleasures of self-righteousness. In principle at least the same could be true of Ireland – it is possible to imagine that we might get a masochistic thrill from shooting ourselves in one foot while trying to dance an authentically Irish jig with the other.

But there is an enormous difference in this regard between England and Ireland. England has thrown off an imaginary oppressor – we've had a real one. England has no idea what actual dependency feels like. It imagines that it is a vague feeling of irritation, a cranky seething at 'red tape' and 'interference'.

We know what dependency is really like. It's not Brussels sending you a big cheque and telling you not to spread slurry on your fields in return. It's not a nice man from Poland coming to install your bathroom or a Latvian woman who speaks five languages coming to work for an American multinational that wouldn't even be in your city if it couldn't recruit people like her. It's having to exist at the whim of foreign people, some of them jolly decent chaps and some of them cynical creeps like Farage.

Usefully, Brexit has reminded us of that stratum of English political life in which it is still perfectly okay – indeed compulsory – to treat Ireland with an arrogance undiminished by absolute ignorance. The rage at Irish impertinence in insisting on guarantees about the border and the Belfast Agreement was expressed by Tory MPs who talked airily about 'the Taoiseach of Northern Ireland Enda Kelly'.

The EU has deep problems but most Irish people will always prefer to take their chances with it rather than going back into the orbit of an England that does not even exert the gravitational pull of an imperial power. There is something irredeemably ridiculous about a notion of Irish independence that consists of mimicking the craziest contortions of Ireland's former masters. All our mammies had the answer to it years ago. 'Why did you do that?' 'Because my friend did it first.' 'And if your friend jumped off a cliff, would you do that too?' Even as a little kid, you'd have to be an awful eejit to say 'Yes, Mammy.'

20 February 2018

Did you ever see a cat stuck up a tree? It desperately wants to get down, but when a kindly human climbs up to rescue it, it hisses and claws. Even cats can't bear to lose face. Brexit is like this: England needs to climb down, but it can't bear to lose face. The only solution is to offer England enough ways to declare victory. In return for forgetting about Brexit, the European Union and member states will offer the following concessions.

1. Germany will agree that the penalty shoot-outs from the 1990 World Cup semi-finals and 1996 European Championship semi-finals will be restaged at Wembley. Chris Waddle, Stuart Pearce and Gareth Southgate will be allowed to take their penalties as many times as is necessary for them to score, ending decades of hurt. There will be mass chanting of 'two World Wars and *two* World Cups'.

2. Queen Elizabeth II will be permitted to add Queen of France to her titles for the remainder of her reign, in keeping with the claims of her predecessors. The title will have no extraterritorial significance, but the fleur-de-lis will be returned to the royal standard and will fly over all royal palaces.

3. The European Union will recognise British sovereignty over the northeast Atlantic islet of Rockall. Denmark, Iceland and Ireland will withdraw their rival claims and issue a joint statement recognising the inalienable Britishness of the rock. A helmeted Boris Johnson will be winched on to Rockall from a helicopter, waving a Union flag in each hand. He will be granted the title of sovereign lord of Rockall and will remain in residence for six months each year.

4. Beethoven's 'Ode to Joy' will be replaced as the official EU anthem with 'On Ilkla Moor Baht 'at'.

5. France will agree to import 1,000 tonnes of Cheddar each year until 2023. The Cordon Bleu institute of gastronomy in Paris will endorse an advertising campaign under the slogan 'Roquefort merde, Cheddar mmmm!'

6. Spain will agree to reissue all school atlases with Las Malvinas given their proper name, the Falkland Islands.

7. Spain will formally cede the Pie n Pint pub and Churchill's Sports Bar, in Santa Ponsa, and the EastEnders pub and Arfur's Cabaret Bar, in Magaluf, to Her Majesty's government, recognising them in perpetuity as British overseas possessions.

8. Marmite will be granted protected-designation-of-origin status by the European Union.

9. In recognition of distinctive English traditions and justified irritation at bloody Brussels interference, EU labour laws will contain a special derogation to allow for the employment in England of soot-faced child chimney sweeps singing 'Chim chiminey / Chim chiminey / Chim chim cher-ee!'

10. Jellied eels will be served at all formal EU dinners.

11. Ireland will agree that Oscar Wilde, Bernard Shaw, W. B. Yeats and James Joyce are Great British writers. (The status of Samuel Beckett will be referred to a special United Nations commission.)

12. Saoirse Ronan, Rory McIlroy, Graham Norton and Bono will agree that they are British when they win an Oscar / win the Masters / tell a good joke / make a good album but remain Irish when they make a dud movie / hit a round of eighty-two / tell a terrible joke / make a show of themselves. The Irish people will enter a solemn covenant not to whinge about this ever again.

13. Brussels sprouts will be renamed Little England cabbages.

14. English grocers will not be banned from selling only bendy bananas. English women will not have to turn in their old vibrators for recycling before buying new ones. English lorry

drivers will not be forced to give up rashers and eggs for muesli and croissants. (None of these things ever happened, but, largely thanks to Boris Johnson, people believe they did, so the 'concessions' will feel like a victory.)

15. The people of Paris will agree to stop being rude and pretending they don't speak English, especially when it is helpfully spoken at them slowly and very loudly.

These proposals have two great advantages. First, they are much more practical and achievable than the actual have-our-cake-and-eat-it demands of the British government in the Brexit negotiations. They involve some pain for the countries making the concessions, but they do not threaten vital national interests. Second, they are designed to send the *Daily Mail*, *Daily Telegraph* and *Sun* into paroxysms of patriotic ecstasy. A noisy orgy of triumphalism will fully cover the retreat from Brexit. A nation that is still celebrating the retreat from Dunkirk as a stunningly heroic deed will have enough fuel for self-love to last a century.

Above all, honour will be satisfied, face will be saved. The cat will be able to come down from the tree with a smile on its face and its tail in the air, knowing that it is its rescuer who has been humiliated. In years to come Brexit will be but dimly remembered and people will say what the grandfather says of the Battle of Blenheim in Robert Southey's poem: 'But what good came of it at last?' / Quoth little Peterkin. / 'Why that I cannot tell,' said he, / 'But 'twas a famous victory.'

25 February 2018

On 14 February, Boris Johnson, Theresa May's foreign secretary, gave a big speech in London on his 'vision for Brexit'. It assured Remainers that their feelings of 'grief and alienation' were unjustified and that Britons would 'continue ever more intensively to go on cheapo flights to stag parties in ancient cities, meet interesting people, fall in love' after Brexit. He did not suggest any such consolations for grief and alienation in Ireland. Meanwhile, the European Commission is about to publish its draft of a withdrawal agreement with provision for a 'backstop' clause to ensure that there will be no hard border in Ireland.

The culmination of the referendum campaign was the BBC's live Great Debate from Wembley on the evening of 21 June 2016. It lasted for two hours. After an hour and a half, someone finally raised the question of Britain's obligations under the Belfast Agreement of 1998 (often called the Good Friday Agreement) that brought an end to the longest and most vicious internal conflict in the history of the United Kingdom. Frances O'Grady, general secretary of the TUC, spoke passionately in a tone of pleading desperation: 'Many trade unionists in Britain and Ireland worked together for many years to support the peace process in Northern Ireland and it took a lot of hard work. And we've supported the Good Friday Agreement ever since... The Irish prime minister has said that if we come out of the EU, there will have to be border controls and, let me tell you, the way that is seen in Belfast and Derry, I worry for our future.'

It fell to Boris Johnson to reply to O'Grady on behalf of the

Leave campaign. 'I remember vividly,' he said, 'when the EU was given the task of trying to sort out the tragedy in the Balkans...' For those who had suspected that, for most of the Brexiteers, Ireland might as well be Montenegro, here was literal confirmation. Johnson spoke for two minutes. He did not address O'Grady's point at all. He did not manage even the most facile of clichés about the Belfast Agreement or the benefits of peace. He did, admittedly, raise the question of violence on the streets: 'I do worry about our security on the streets of this city.' This city was, of course, London. The UK cities that O'Grady had mentioned – Belfast and Derry – were neither here nor there.

Or perhaps it would be more accurate to say that they are very much 'there' – a foreign place barely glimpsed even in peripheral vision. Johnson has been utterly consistent in this. In his big Brexit speech on Valentine's Day, delivered as foreign secretary, he said about the Belfast Agreement exactly what he said in June 2016: not a word. There is some irony in the way he has implicitly adopted the great vernacular slogan of people in Northern Ireland during the Troubles: whatever you say, say nothing.

The consequences of Brexit for the Belfast Agreement have always been, for the most ardent Leavers, the thing that must not be seen or spoken. And in the way of such things, the whole Brexit process has been haunted by the return of the repressed. The EU has refused to pretend that there is no Irish problem. It has not gone along with the British government's airy assurances that 'there will be no return to the borders of the past' on the island of Ireland because everything is going to be frictionless, seamless and marvellous. The EU insisted, in the first phase of negotiations, on turning these airy assurances into solid commitments.

This week, Brussels will publish its draft withdrawal agreement, a legally binding text under which the UK will, in effect, commit itself to keeping Northern Ireland in the single market and customs union, unless a future free trade deal or a magical technological solution manages somehow to avoid a hard border. It will also bind both parties to recognising in all negotiations the 'paramount importance', as Theresa May wrote in her Article 50 letter, of the Belfast Agreement.

This has enormous repercussions. The sleeping beauties on the Tory right, for whom ignorance of Ireland was Brexit bliss, are finally waking up to these implications. A fog of denial and self-delusion is beginning to clear and they can at last see what should have been obvious all along: you can have a hard Brexit or you can have the Belfast Agreement but you can't have both. And it is increasingly clear which choice they want Britain to make: throw the dead weight of the peace process overboard so that the Brexit balloon may soar into the blue skies of its triumphant future.

The Tory right has never been fond of the Belfast Agreement, even though it was John Major who (with considerable courage) prepared the way for it by explicitly removing any British claim over Northern Ireland other than the democratic wishes of its people. In *The Price of Peace*, Michael Gove's pamphlet for the right-wing Centre for Policy Studies, published in 2000, he characterised the entire peace process as nothing more than a capitulation to the IRA which he likened to the appeasement of the Nazis in the 1930s. But this hostility lapsed over time into mere indifference – until, very late in the day, Brexit's true believers began to understand that they have an Irish problem.

Hence, as the EU prepares to publish its draft legal text, what seems like a concerted campaign to clear the greatest moral and political obstacle from the path to Brexit glory. The Belfast Agreement must be made not to matter. The failure of attempts to re-establish a power-sharing Executive in Belfast opens up the opportunity to say that the whole 1998 deal is no longer worth bothering about.

And so the former Northern Ireland secretary Owen Paterson tweeted that 'The collapse of power-sharing in Northern Ireland shows the Good Friday Agreement has outlived its use'. Labour's staunchest Brexiteer, Kate Hoey, follows up by declaring the agreement 'unsustainable'. The leading Tory intellectual Daniel Hannan in his *Daily Telegraph* column, dismisses the agreement as nothing more than 'a bribe to two sets of hardliners' in Northern Ireland. He claims, rather astonishingly, that it did not bring peace because Northern Ireland was already at peace: 'The Belfast Agreement was a consequence, not a cause, of the end of terrorism.' And to crown the campaign, Jacob Rees-Mogg, also writing in the *Telegraph*, announces that this whole Irish business does not really exist – it is an 'imaginary problem' caused by the Irish government.

The Belfast Agreement is not holy writ and the collapse of the power-sharing talks between Sinn Féin and the Democratic Unionist Party does, indeed, point to the problematic nature of one part of it – the internal arrangements for the governance of Northern Ireland. If the context were less febrile, the twentieth anniversary in April of the agreement would be an apt opportunity for a thoughtful review of those structures.

But let's not kid ourselves. These attacks on the agreement are not coming from a sudden interest in the minutiae of devolved government in Montenegro – sorry, Northern Ireland. They are all about Brexit. The real subject here is not a deal made in Belfast in 1998. It is the deal Theresa May signed in December to conclude the first phase of the divorce negotiations. Bizarre as it may seem, many of the leading Brexiteers seem not to have understood that deal or the radical implications of the commitments May made in it, commitments that, she concurred, 'must be upheld in all circumstances, irrespective of the nature of any future agreement between the European Union and United Kingdom'.

It is worth recalling that when May did this deal in December, the first instinct of the Brexiteers was to characterise all the language in it about Ireland as just more meaningless verbiage to stop the Irish from whining on. The Brexit secretary David Davis told Andrew Marr: 'This was a statement of intent more than anything else. Much more... than it was a legally enforceable thing.' This was entirely untrue – as we will see this week, the deal will be turned into a legally binding text – and Davis quickly reversed himself and claimed to have been misunderstood. But his claim revealed a deeper mindset: an inability to grasp the underlying reality that the Belfast Agreement sets very tight limits on the UK's final arrangements with the EU.

The problem for the Brexiteers is that, in December, May signed up to two different things, apparently without grasping the connection between them. The first of these is that the Belfast Agreement effectively demands that there be no hard border between Northern Ireland and the Republic. Thus, whatever else happens – even if there is an ultra-hard, no-deal Brexit – the British will 'maintain full alignment with those rules of the internal market and the customs union which, now or in the future, support North–South co-operation, the all-island economy and the protection of the 1998 Agreement'.

This is a big commitment in itself, but it could be implemented in a way that had relatively little impact on post-Brexit Britain by, for example, creating customs borders between the two islands of Britain and Ireland rather than within Ireland. Except that this kind of arrangement is anathema to the DUP, on whom May depends for her Commons majority. So, in desperate need of a deal, she also gave the DUP what it wanted: an equal commitment that there will be 'no new regulatory barriers' between Northern Ireland and Britain. The mathematics of this are quite simple. Northern Ireland has to remain fully aligned with the Republic, which is to say with the customs union and single market. Britain has to remain aligned to Northern Ireland. So Britain has to remain aligned to the customs union and single market. Exit hard Brexit pursued by the Belfast Agreement.

One way to deal with this is heroic denial. The Brexit minister Robin Walker told MPs on Thursday that the text agreed in December 'is not talking about full alignment' – even though 'full alignment' is exactly what it says. The other is to dig out the root of the whole problem, the Belfast Agreement itself. In a sense, this is the more honest approach, not least because it implicitly acknowledges that the driving force in Brexit is a specifically English nationalism for which the rest of the UK is ultimately dispensable.

But even then there is a problem for the zealots. Their whole vision of a glorious post-Brexit future is based on Britain's ability to do great trade deals and be a trusted partner on the world stage. Yet to get there they now have to start by tearing up two of the most important international deals Britain has signed in its recent history, both of them legally binding. They have to renege on the pact May signed in December, that placed the Belfast Agreement at the centre of the Brexit process. And they have to pull out of the agreement – which, contrary to what they seem to believe, is not an internal British deal but a binding international treaty between two sovereign governments registered with the United Nations and effectively underpinned by both the United States and the EU.

They would have Britain stand before the world, knee-deep in shredded treaties, and say, 'Sign here, trust us!' One can but wish them the best of British luck with that one.

27 February 2018

Marxism is alive and well in British politics. The irony, though, is that its strongest influence is not in Jeremy Corbyn's Labour Party. It is on the Tory right. Perhaps the oddest thing about the Brexit zealots – though there is a great deal of competition for this title – is that they cling to a particularly crude form of Marxist economic determinism.

Their whole project is predicated on the belief that a cabal of capitalist bosses can issue orders that the entire European Union would rush to obey. The all-powerful clique in question is made up of the principal shareholders of Volkswagen, BMW, Audi, Opel, Porsche and Mercedes. It would be hard to overstate just how large these German industrialists have loomed in the consciousness of the Brexiteers and their media cheerleaders. They were to be Britain's saviours. It was they who would ensure that the EU would be forced to give Britain all the benefits of the single market and the customs union even after it departed from both. It was they who would provide the lubrication for the zipless, frictionless Brexit of the Leavers' dreams.

Boris Johnson encapsulated the proposition in the BBC's big set-piece final debate before the referendum in June 2016. 'Everyone knows this country receives about one-fifth of Germany's entire car manufacturing output,' he said. 'Do you seriously propose that they are going to be so insane as to allow tariffs to be imposed?'

The key word here is 'allow'. How telling it is. It reveals an entire view of how the world really works. Even while Brexit was posing as an exercise in returning control to the populace, Johnson was letting slip his understanding of where control really lay.

The chain of reasoning began with a factual proposition: the

Germans sell a hell of a lot of cars to the UK. The next link in the chain is rational: therefore, the German car manufacturers would not want any tariff barriers to be created after Brexit. And then, in the way of magical thinking, there is the great leap.

Seeing their interests threatened, Frau Mercedes and Herr Audi would lift the phone to Angela Merkel. 'Merkel!' they would bark. 'There must be no tariff barriers. We will not allow it!' The chancellor in turn would call Jean-Claude Juncker and Donald Tusk: 'The British must have their cake and eat it. Understood?' 'Yes, Ma'am!' Hence, BMW stands for Brexit Made Wonderful.

This fantasy really was at the heart of the Brexit strategy. David Davis, now the Brexit secretary, said during the referendum campaign that 'the first calling point of the UK's negotiator in the time immediately after Brexit will not be Brussels, it will be Berlin to strike the deal. Absolute access for German cars and industrial goods in exchange for a sensible deal on everything else.' A year after the referendum, when Davis was in fact the UK's chief negotiator, Andrew Marr put it to him: 'You basically argued that the German car industry, and German industry generally, would put pressure on the German chancellor who would put pressure on the EU to ensure that we got a good deal. Is that still your view?' 'Oh,' replied Davis, 'that's where it will end up, yeah.'

Even as the Brexit project retreats ever further into chaos and absurdity, this fantasy survives. Pro-Brexit papers continue to run headlines like the *Daily Express*'s 'Merkel's Brexit NIGHTMARE: 18,000 German car firm jobs at risk.' The *Sun* reports on the 'pleas from German car manufacturers, led by BMW, builders of Britain's electric Mini, for Brussels to stop punishing Britain'. This in spite of the explicit statements from those same German car bosses that the integrity of the single market matters much more to them than the disruption of their trade with Britain.

There are many ironies in all of this, not least the reliance on Germans to save an English nationalist project and the fact that most Marxists (including Marx) have long since abandoned this very crude idea of how economic interests translate into political actions. But the greatest irony of all is that Brexit itself is a particularly powerful example of how political sentiment can outweigh economic self-interest.

If people acted solely on the basis of what is good for their own pockets, Brexit would not be happening. Many of the parts of the UK that voted most enthusiastically for Leave (the northeast of England, for example) are also those which will be hardest hit by it. Indeed, if there is anything noble about the whole project, it is in this willingness to accept economic pain in pursuit of an ideal, however misplaced that idealism may be.

This is one of the great contradictions that have made Brexit so incoherent as to be impossible. You can't both 'take back control' and place your fate in the hands of imaginary omnipotent German moguls. There is no fleet of blacked-out Mercedes filled with Teutonic tycoons coming to rescue Theresa May and bring the EU to heel. There is only a broken-down old banger, driven into a dead end. Wouldn't it be funny if it is the actual Marxists in Labour who get to reverse it on to more solid ground?

3 March 2018

*With the publication of the EU's draft legal text, the
implications begin to sink in. But the British government
and the unionists of the DUP continue to cling to the hope
that some as yet uninvented technologies can keep the border
invisible even while the UK leaves the customs union and
single market. Boris Johnson explains that it can all be
done as simply as the congestion charge in London.*

Many unionist politicians are people of deep faith. After this week's momentous European Union proposal for a legal text on Britain's withdrawal from the EU, they had better pray for a miracle. A miracle, that is, of technology.

Last July, the DUP MP Jeffrey Donaldson spoke in tones of pure rapture about the fabulous scientific solutions that would make the problem of the Irish border after Brexit disappear: 'Technology is a wonderful thing.' It had better be – for if it is not, the DUP's support for Brexit will have done more to undermine unionism than Irish nationalism has managed in almost a century.

Reacting last Wednesday to the special protocol on Ireland in the EU's draft text, Theresa May said it would 'threaten the constitutional integrity of the UK'.

She is, in this at least, entirely right. She should not have been surprised, however – it was obvious all along that Brexit would undermine the constitutional integrity of the UK.

May also said that 'No UK prime minister could ever agree to it'. In this she was entirely wrong – a British prime minister already did. Her name is Theresa May and she signed up to it last December. But as with the broader undermining of the integrity of the UK, she and her allies in the DUP can be surprised only if they never knew what they were doing in the first place. They have gambled the future of unionism on the sudden emergence of a technology that has yet to be invented.

If you're a unionist, Wednesday's text is disastrous. It is like one of those forensic anthropology documentaries in which experts put a face and muscles and hair on the bones of an exhumed ancient skeleton so we can see in retrospect what the person might have looked like.

The bare bones are what May signed up to on 8 December, in particular Article 49 with its agreement that, in the absence of other solutions, Northern Ireland will retain 'full alignment' with the rules of the customs union and the single market, in order to preserve the Belfast Agreement and the all-Ireland economy.

But when you put the legal flesh on this skeleton, it looks, from a unionist perspective, like a monster. It means that Northern Ireland, after Brexit, becomes a radically different political and economic space from the rest of the UK.

It remains, in effect, part of the EU customs union. Its citizens remain, if they so choose, full EU citizens. EU customs officials will work alongside their UK counterparts at Northern Irish ports and airports. EU rules on state aids to industry will continue to apply in part to Northern Ireland even when they disappear in Britain. That great bugbear of the Brexiteers, the European Court of Justice, will retain significant jurisdiction in the North.

If this text becomes law – and it seems extremely unlikely that the EU will agree to weaken it – Margaret Thatcher's famous declaration that Northern Ireland is as British as Finchley will have a historic rejoinder: Northern Ireland will be almost as European as the Republic of Ireland.

If you're a unionist, there are in theory two ways to prevent this monstrous chimera – a Northern Ireland that is neither inside nor outside the EU and therefore neither inside nor outside the UK – from being born. But, in reality, there is only one.

The first possibility is an impossibility: the frictionless free trade between the UK and the EU in which everything pretty much carries on as it is now and the border doesn't matter. This is simply not going to happen – even the British government is looking instead for 'managed divergence'.

Which leaves us with the single possibility: the technological miracle.

Unionism – both British and Northern Irish – has written itself into a 1950s science fiction B-movie called 'The Thing from Brussels'. Its world is threatened by an alien being: a half-European Ulster. And it is desperately hoping for a heroic rescuer in the form of a scientist in white coat with geeky glasses. He (it would definitely be a he) has been working away in a basement on a magical formula for creating frictionless borders. His colleagues have been sneering at him. But now his hour has come. He will save unionism.

And this is about as plausible as most 1950s sci-fi movies. To understand this, consider Boris Johnson's claims on BBC Radio 4 last Tuesday that the Irish border could be just like the border between Camden and Westminster. As motorists cross that line, incurring a congestion charge, they are monitored by technology 'anaesthetically and invisibly [taking] hundreds of millions of pounds from the accounts of people travelling between those two boroughs without any need for border checks whatever'.

Leaving aside the obvious problem that an external EU border is not exactly like a London borough division, there is still an enormous difficulty here. For Johnson seems to have read neither his own government's position paper on Ireland and Brexit, published last summer, or the agreement that Theresa May signed in December. Both of these documents commit the British, not just to having no personal border checks in Ireland but, in the British government's own words, to 'avoid any physical border infrastructure in either the United Kingdom or Ireland, for any purpose'.

London's congestion charge works because it has a very large physical infrastructure: 646 cameras mounted on big gantries at 203 different sites. Even if number plate recognition were the solution for Ireland (which it is not), there would have to be many more cameras to cover the 110 million annual trips across 300 different border crossings. And the erection of those big gantries is exactly what the British government, entirely of its own volition, has pledged not to do. So Johnson's comparison is either astonishingly ignorant or wildly disingenuous.

But perhaps there is a crack team of boffins working away on some other technological solution that requires no physical infrastructure? Actually, two of the very few questions we can answer with certainty about the Brexit process are: who is working on this and what have they come up with? The answers are: nobody and nothing. Hard as it may be to fathom, given that the future of unionism depends on it, the British have done damn all to create their technological solution. The people whose job it is to come up with the technological solutions not only have no plans – they have no plans to make plans. If the integrity of the UK depends on this approach, it doesn't have a prayer.

6 March 2018

Theresa May gives a big speech on Brexit at the Mansion House in London. It returned, yet again, to the promise of technological solutions to the border question.

History is a funny business. When most of us think about a united Ireland (which is not very often), we imagine it as a grandiose final scene from an epic movie. But history now turns on small and dull matters. Just now, if you want to think about the future of Ireland as a whole and of its relationship with Britain, you have to think about boring stuff – stuff like the functionality of UK border controls. It is as if the GPO in 1916 had really been all about the British postal system.

In 2016, more than 310 million people and nearly 500 million tonnes of freight crossed the UK's borders. If this continues to happen in a 'frictionless' way after Brexit, the disturbances to the status quo in Ireland will be limited. If it doesn't, hang on to your hats. Frictionless trade is the only condition under which Brexit can happen without inflicting a hard border on Ireland. It is almost certainly a political impossibility if the UK leaves the customs union. But even if it could somehow be agreed in principle, there is another enormous obstacle: the actual capacity of the British to handle it.

On Friday, after Theresa May's big set-piece speech on Brexit, the DUP leader Arlene Foster issued a glowing endorsement. She referred back to a paper issued by the UK government last August: 'Those proposals can ensure there is no hard border between Northern Ireland and the Republic of Ireland after we exit the EU.' Foster recognises how much unionism is staking on that document and on the ability of the UK's bureaucracies to deploy technology to take the sting out of the potentially toxic irritant of the Irish border.

This forces us to consider something that would previously have been of little interest to Irish people: the recent and dismal history of the UK's adventures in using digital technology to control its borders. In 2003, the British established a spanking new 'e-borders system' which was meant to collect and analyse advance passenger information for people travelling into the UK. It had a generous timescale – the full programme was meant to be in place by 2011. In 2010, the Home Office admitted that it was so useless it had to be abandoned. By then, it had spent £340 million (€380 million) on the programme.

The cancellation of the contract led to a legal settlement for another £150 million (€168 million). The Home Office then spent another £303 million (€340 million) on a new programme, bringing expenditure to £830 million (€940 million). In 2015, the National Audit Office reported that all of this expenditure 'has failed, so far, to deliver the full vision' of what was supposed to be achieved. The current date for completion of the programme is 2019. The whole thing will have taken a mere sixteen years. On the same timescale, the new post-Brexit systems on which the future of Ireland may hinge would be delivered in 2035.

In 2015, fifty-five million UK customs declarations were made by 141,000 traders. Once Brexit happens, that will increase fivefold to 255 million. Leaving aside all the issues of political principle, this is the vast logistical challenge that will have to be dealt with if May and Foster are to get the Brexit they want. This brings us back to the paper on customs the British produced back in August and that Foster hailed last Friday as 'innovative'. Actually, the words that paper used about its own proposals are 'an innovative and untested approach that would take time to develop and implement', which is management speak for 'nobody has done this stuff ever before, we have no evidence that it would work and we have only the vaguest outline ideas about it'. In relation to the idea of a 'customs partnership' (as opposed to a customs union) with the European Union, which May embraced on Friday, the August paper says: 'This is of course unprecedented as an approach and could be challenging to implement.'

The one big idea on which the DUP places much of its hopes is the 'trusted trader' scheme – companies whom the customs authorities get to know and trust to fill out all their own declarations honestly. There is nothing, of course, to stop the UK from using this system right now for trade outside the EU. So I wondered how many 'trusted traders' the UK has designated so far. Of the 141,000 companies using its systems, a grand total of 604 are trusted traders. That's 0.43 per cent. Which prompts an obvious question – if this is such a great solution, why are more than 99 per cent of UK companies not using it? Why are UK authorities not currently taking any steps to promote it?

The cross-party public accounts committee of the House of Commons put it succinctly in a report in November: 'Government departments' poor track record of delivering critical border programmes, such as e-borders, leaves us sceptical that they are up to the challenges of planning for the border post-Brexit.' If the UK's own parliament doesn't believe in the frictionless future, for the rest of us to take it on trust would be bordering on gullibility.

28 April 2018

In spite of all the evidence to the contrary, the Brexiteers cling to the belief that Ireland can be bullied into dropping its pesky objections to a hard border.

The performance artist who created and sustains the absurd persona called Jacob Rees-Mogg is one of the great satirists of our times. He carries off with great conviction a unique blend of English comic prototypes: Warren Mitchell's Alf Garnett and Al Murray's Pub Landlord seamlessly combined with P. G. Wodehouse's Gussie Fink-Nottle and *Monty Python*'s Upper Class Twits. His latest burlesque, delivered this week with his usual deadpan aplomb, was on the subject of how Britain should show Brussels who's boss in the Brexit negotiations by threatening, of all things, Irish beef.

'If,' he warned, Britain 'were to apply the common external tariff on Irish beef, the Irish agricultural industry is in serious trouble. You've got to ask the EU: does it want to sacrifice the economy of Ireland on the altar of EU ideology? My guess is that the answer is no, and therefore we are in a very strong negotiating position.'

What makes Rees-Mogg so clever, of course, is that his most ardent admirers take him for a real person and his pronouncements for real strategies. This idea that Ireland and the European Union can be brought to heel by making war on our sirloins and Sunday roasts will lift the hearts and stiffen the backs of the Brexit ultras who believe that Europe secretly knows that it will be destroyed if it does not give Britain everything it wants. It is therefore worth examining.

To think about the implications of Brexit for the food industries on these islands we have to grasp a concept that many Brexiteers seem to find extremely difficult: Northern Ireland is part of the United Kingdom. You would not have known this, admittedly, during the Brexit referendum debates, and it does not seem to have become any more obvious to the true believers in the period since their great victory. But it is a fact.

And it forces us to ask a supplementary question to the one posed by Rees-Mogg – not whether the EU wants to 'sacrifice the economy of Ireland on the altar of EU ideology' but whether the Brexiteers want to sacrifice the economy of that part of the UK known as Northern Ireland on the altar of their own ideology.

When Ireland was partitioned, almost a century ago, it made some rough sense to think of the North as primarily industrial and the South as primarily agricultural. The image of the North was a great Harland & Wolff ocean-going liner, of the South the cattle boat across the Irish Sea.

To many Brexiteers this division seems to be alive and well, hence Rees-Mogg's notion that hurting the beef trade would be a death blow to the Irish economy and the implication that 'industrial' Northern Ireland would somehow escape this fate.

But this stuff just isn't true any more. Food production is very important to the Republic's economy – but it is even more important to Northern Ireland's.

Food and drink is the North's biggest manufacturing industry. One in every ten jobs in Northern Ireland is in food production. And a lot of these jobs rely on food exports to the European Union: Northern Ireland exports £1.1 billion, or about €1.25 billion, worth of food to the EU every year, making the EU its largest export market for food.

Crucially, more than 70 per cent of this food is exported either to or through the Republic. It has to cross the border – a simple thing now but a nightmare if Northern Ireland is dragged out of the customs union and the single market.

Yet the actual complications would be even worse than this. More than a quarter of all the milk produced by farmers in

Northern Ireland is processed south of the border. Forty-two per cent of all the sheep and lambs raised in the North are slaughtered and processed in the South. Restaurants and hotels on either side purchase and serve fresh food sourced across the border. In one recent study food-related businesses in Armagh and Down reported sustained growth in their trade with the Republic, which now accounts for 30 per cent of their sales. In fact Northern producers are much better at selling to the South than vice versa.

In the Rees-Moggian world view (apparently shared by some in the Democratic Unionist Party) none of this greatly matters, because a glorious future of trade with the world beyond the EU will open up after Brexit. For Northern Ireland this would require a miraculous transformation. Currently, for example, Northern Ireland sells £221 million, or €253 million, a year of beef and lamb to the Republic and the rest of the EU. It sells £19.5 million (€22.3 million) to the rest of the world. In other words the imagined post-Brexit future global trade will start out as much less than a tenth of the business being done within the EU.

This, moreover, is just one side of the story, the part that will be disrupted if there is a hard border on the island. If Britain leaves the customs union the only alternative to this internal Irish border is, in effect, a border in the Irish Sea – trade barriers between Northern Ireland and the rest of the UK.

This, too, would be a nightmare for the flow of food. As a recent report by the Food Research Collaboration, in London, has pointed out, 680,000 tonnes of food leaves Northern Ireland every year for Britain – and 680,000 tonnes goes in the opposite direction. Seventy per cent of the food bought in Northern Ireland comes from one of the three big British supermarket chains, all of which depend on fast, frictionless just-in-time movement of food within the EU. Such is the integrated nature of food production and consumption that a lamb dish being eaten in Magherafelt probably began with an animal being taken across the border to a processing plant, exported from the Republic to France, reimported to Britain and then re-exported to Northern Ireland.

This is why the threat to slap tariffs on Irish-produced food to make the Europeans submit to Britannia's rules is so fatuous. A hard Brexit would certainly do immense damage to Ireland's food trade, but it would be just as terrible for Northern Ireland.

As the Food Research Collaboration report puts it, 'It would raise important challenges for food safety, put jobs at risk, potentially constrain Northern Ireland's access to health-supporting foods such as fruit and vegetables, and create opportunities for food fraud and crime.'

Unless, of course, Northern Ireland simply doesn't matter. Rees-Mogg, as he so often does, has exposed the contradiction at the heart of the Brexiteers' rage that the Irish border has become such an infuriating obstacle to their project.

On the one hand they are professed unionists who see Northern Ireland as an integral part of their homeland. On the other hand they see the border issue as a foreign irritant, as if the border had only one side – the Republic – and its fate were therefore not a vital UK interest too.

Notions like attacking Irish agriculture as a way of chastening the dastardly Europeans can occur only to those for whom Northern Ireland is an irrelevance. People who knew anything about the realities of Irish food would think twice before opening their mouths.

26 May 2018

The border question raises again the prospect of a
united Ireland, which seems to offer an easy way out
of the great Brexit dilemma. But it is not so simple.

I t was easy to forget that this week saw the twentieth anniversary
of a momentous Irish referendum. Oddly enough, it is all the
easier to forget because this one was almost eerily consensual.
It was supported by 1.4 million people – just 86,000 voted No.
There was no rural/urban divide, no tribal warfare, no setting of
young against old. The result was almost the same everywhere in
Ireland. In every single constituency, more than 92 per cent voted
yes, almost mirroring the national result of 94 per cent in favour.

What proposition could possibly be so bland and uncontentious
that Irish people couldn't be bothered to have a decent row about
it? Nothing less than the bloodiest, bitterest and most fiercely
contested issue of all, one that made the abortion wars seem like
a lovers' tiff. One for which a real civil war had been fought. What
was at stake in the vote on the 19th Amendment to the constitution
was nothing less than the definition of Irish nationalism. On 22 May
1998, voters in the Republic went to the polls on the same day that
those in Northern Ireland were voting on the Belfast Agreement.

They had two proposals to vote on. One was to approve the
relatively minor Amsterdam Treaty of the European Union. The
other was a huge change to the very definition of the state itself.
Voters were asked to remove the keystones of Éamon de Valera's
1937 constitution, articles 2 and 3, and replace them with radically
new versions. They did so with overwhelming enthusiasm.

But as Brexit brings the existential questions of Irish nationhood back into play, we might look back and wonder. It may be an impertinent question to pose in a democracy, but it has to be asked: did we really think about what we were voting for? Do we really understand just what a revolutionary change Irish nationalism was making in its official self-definition?

Loose talk about the imminence of a united Ireland suggests that the enthusiasm of 1998 had more to do with the idea that we were voting for peace than with the radicalism of the 19th Amendment. What happened through that referendum was not just a new definition of Irish nationalism. It was arguably a new way of thinking about nationalism itself. It didn't just shift the ground – it shifted away from the ground. It stopped thinking about nationalism as being a claim to land, a title to territory, and started thinking about it as a process of reconciliation.

It is a rather startling thing to have done and perhaps if people had understood just how radical it is, it would not have received such a virtually uncontested endorsement. The old articles 2 and 3 were classic territorial claims. They said, respectively, that 'The national territory consists of the whole island of Ireland, its islands and the territorial seas' and that the laws made in Dublin would have effect south of the border 'Pending the re-integration of the national territory, and without prejudice to the right of the parliament and government established by this constitution to exercise jurisdiction over the whole territory'. In the seventy-one words of the two articles, the word 'territory' or its derivatives appeared five times. This was about land.

What voters did so overwhelmingly twenty years ago was to replace these words with profoundly different statements. These new statements are not primarily about land. They are about people.

The new article 2 says: 'It is the entitlement and birthright of every person born in the island of Ireland, which includes its islands and seas, to be part of the Irish nation. That is also the entitlement of all persons otherwise qualified in accordance with law to be citizens of Ireland. Furthermore, the Irish nation cherishes its special affinity with people of Irish ancestry living abroad who share its cultural identity and heritage.'

And instead of the claims in article 3 about 'jurisdiction over the whole territory', the new version expresses 'the firm will of the Irish nation, in harmony and friendship, to unite all the people who share the territory of the island of Ireland, in all the diversity of their identities and traditions, recognising that a united Ireland shall be brought about only by peaceful means with the consent of a majority of the people, democratically expressed, in both jurisdictions in the island'.

The five uses of 'territory' are reduced to one, and even that is utterly transformed, from a contested land to a shared space. It is the people who share it who are what matters.

And in the most radical move of all, we set in constitutional stone an acceptance that 'all the people' is not the same thing as 'the people', for that 'all' is echoed in the key phrase about 'all the diversity of their identities and traditions'.

In the long tradition of nationalism since the eighteenth century, 'the people' is a single thing that must not be subdivided. Irish nationalism, on that day twenty years ago, broke with this tradition and officially reimagined the people as a plural entity.

And yet it sometimes seems as if this seismic shift had never happened. Do we collectively grasp the idea that Irish nationalism no longer claims to integrate a territory but, rather, desires to unite a diverse people in harmony and friendship?

Do we really understand that Irish unity can no longer be imagined as the creation of a monolithic identity but must instead be understood as the reconciliation of multiple identities?

In fairness, it is not entirely the fault of Irish nationalism that there is a tendency to slip back into old habits of mind. The violence that Brexit does to the island of Ireland is precisely that it re-territorialises the Irish question. It throws us back on to the ground by forcing us to ask how that ground is divided, bordered, controlled, policed.

We can see already Brexit is forcing Catholics in Northern

Ireland to think about a united Ireland – even when they don't want to. One of the most interesting details in the fascinating study of attitudes published this week by researchers at Queen's University Belfast is just how big a difference Brexit makes. Only 28 per cent of Catholics in the North would vote for a united Ireland if the UK changed its mind and remained a full member of the EU. However, 53 per cent of Catholics would vote for a united Ireland if there was a hard Brexit in which all of the UK left the customs union and single market.

But we can't let the follies of Brexit railroad us into a return to a pre-1998 Irish nationalism. The radical changes of twenty years ago came at the cost of more than 3,500 lives in the Troubles. It was necessary to think differently in order to escape from a hellish trap. And it is still necessary to think differently in order to avoid the danger of returning to one. Brexit itself is fuelled by an English nationalism as crude and self-deluded as Irish nationalism used to be. The best response is not to match it like for like. It is to remember that we chose to move beyond dividing up territory and accepted instead the larger task of uniting people.

29 May 2018

*On 25 May, Ireland had a referendum on the previously
divisive issue of abortion. The constitutional protection
for 'life from the moment of conception', inserted in 1983,
is overturned by a majority of two to one. The whole
process contrasts starkly with the way the Brexit
referendum had been conducted and points to how
any second referendum might be handled.*

In all the excitement of what happened in Ireland's referendum
on abortion, we should not lose sight of what did not happen. A
vote on an emotive subject was not subverted. The tactics that
have been so successful for the right and the far right in the UK, the
US, Hungary and elsewhere did not work. A democracy navigated
its way through some very rough terrain and came home not just
alive but more alive than it was before. In the world we inhabit,
these things are worth celebrating but also worth learning from.
Political circumstances are never quite the same twice, but some
of what happened and did not happen in Ireland surely contains
more general lessons.

If the right failed spectacularly in Ireland, it was not for want
of trying. Save the 8th, one of the two main groups campaigning
against the removal of the anti-abortion clause from the Irish
constitution, hired Vote Leave's technical director, the Cambridge
Analytica alumnus Thomas Borwick. Save the 8th and the other
anti-repeal campaign, Love Both, used apps developed by a US-
based company, Political Social Media (PSM), which worked on
both the Brexit and Trump campaigns. The small print told those
using the apps that their data could be shared with other PSM

clients, including the Trump campaign, the Republican National Committee and Vote Leave.

Irish voters were subjected to the same polarising tactics that have worked so well elsewhere: shamelessly fake 'facts' (the claim, for example, that abortion was to be legalised up to six months into pregnancy); the contemptuous dismissal of expertise (the leading obstetrician Peter Boylan was told in a TV debate to 'go back to school'); deliberately shocking visual imagery (posters of aborted foetuses outside maternity hospitals); and a discourse of liberal elites versus the real people. But Irish democracy had an immune system that proved highly effective in resisting this virus. Its success suggests a democratic playbook with at least four good rules.

First, trust the people. A crucial part of what happened in Ireland was an experiment in deliberative democracy. The question of how to deal with the constitutional prohibition on abortion – a question that has bedevilled the political and judicial systems for thirty-five years – was put to a Citizens' Assembly, made up of ninety-nine randomly chosen (but demographically representative) voters. These so-called ordinary people – truck drivers, homemakers, students, farmers – gave up their weekends to listen to forty experts in medicine, law and ethics, to women affected by Ireland's extremely restrictive laws and to seventeen different lobby groups. They came up with recommendations that confounded most political and media insiders, by being much more open than expected – and much more open than the political system would have produced on its own.

It was these citizens who suggested entirely unrestricted access to abortion up to twelve weeks. Conservatives dismissed this process, in Trump style, as rigged (it wasn't). They would have been much better off if they had actually listened to what these citizens were saying, and tried to understand what had persuaded them to take such a liberal position. The Irish parliament did listen – an all-party parliamentary committee essentially adopted the proposals of the Citizens' Assembly. So did the government. And it turned out that a sample of 'the people' actually knew pretty well what 'the people' were thinking. If the Brexit referendum had been preceded by such a respectful, dignified and humble exercise in listening and thinking, it would surely have been a radically different experience.

Second, be honest. The yes side in the Irish debate handed its opponents a major tactical advantage but gained a huge strategic victory. It ceded an advantage in playing with all its cards turned up on the table. Technically, the vote was merely to repeal a clause in the constitution. There was no need to say what legislation the government hoped to enact afterwards. But the government chose to be completely clear about its intentions. It published a draft bill. This allowed opponents of reform to pick at, and often distort, points of detail. But it also completely undercut the reactionary politics of paranoia, the spectre of secret conspiracies. Honesty proved to be very good policy.

Third, talk to everybody and make assumptions about nobody. The reactionary movements have been thriving on tribalism. They divide voters into Us and Them – and all the better if they call us 'deplorables'. The yes campaigners in Ireland – many of them young people, who are so often caricatured as the inhabitants of virtual echo chambers – refused to be tribal. They stayed calm and dignified. And when they were jeered at, they did not jeer back. They got out and talked (and listened) without prejudice. They did not assume that an elderly lady going to mass in a rural village was a lost cause. They risked (and sometimes got) abuse by recognising no comfort zones and engaging everyone they could reach. It turned out that a lot of people were sick of being typecast as conservatives. It turned out that a lot of people like to be treated as complex, intelligent and compassionate individuals. A majority of farmers and more than 40 per cent of the over sixty-fives voted yes.

Finally, the old feminist slogan that the personal is political holds true, but it also works the other way around. The political has to be personalised. The greatest human immune system against the viruses of hysteria, hatred and lies is storytelling. Even when we don't trust politicians or experts, we trust people telling their own tales. We trust ourselves to judge whether they are lying or being truthful. Irish women had to go out and tell their own stories, to make the painful and intimate into public property.

This is very hard to do, and it should not be necessary. But it is unstoppably powerful. The process mattered, political leadership mattered, campaigning mattered. But it was stories that won. Exit polls showed that by far the biggest factors in determining how people voted were 'people's personal stories that were told to the media', followed by 'the experience of someone who they know'.

Women, in the intimate circles of family and friends or in the harsh light of TV studios, said: 'This is who I am. I am one of you.' And voters responded: 'Yes, you are.' If democracy can create the context for that humane exchange to happen over and over again, it can withstand everything its enemies throw at it.

12 June 2018

Buzzfeed releases a secret recording of Boris Johnson
addressing a private dinner for Brexit supports in
London. As well as suggesting that Donald Trump
would be the man to negotiate Brexit with the EU,
he reveals his rage at the awkward bloody Irish.

What's the best cinematic version of Brexit? I've previously suggested the final sequence of *The Italian Job*, where the truck is suspended halfway over a ravine and the crew can't get at their great pile of gold bars without tipping themselves into the abyss. But from an Irish point of view, we probably need a double bill in which it is shown alongside another British classic from the same era, *The Wicker Man*. Some horror fans have already noted the prescience of Summerisle, where most of the film is set. It is an Atlantic island that has cut itself off from the mainland and adopted a crazy cult. The cult is led by Lord Summerisle, a man with a self-consciously orotund vocabulary, mad hair and a great line in sacrificing the young generation for his bonkers beliefs – Christopher Lee as Boris Johnson, in other words.

But the most interesting parallel is the arrival on Summerisle of Edward Woodward's Sergeant Neil Howie, innocently intent on doing his duty of investigating a suspected murder. He thinks of himself as embodying the majesty of the British state. He is upright. He is judgemental. He is righteous. And he is very devoutly Presbyterian, possibly even of the Wee Free variety. He is, of course, the DUP. Howie becomes increasingly aware that he has no idea where he really is, that he has taken a one-way trip to a place with its own fatal laws. Lord Summerisle eventually summons him

161

to his horrible death: 'We confer upon you a rare gift, these days –
a martyr's death. You will not only have life eternal, but you will
sit with the saints among the elect. Come!'

Lord Boris did not say these words in that private dinner with
Tory diehards last week. But what he says on the recording leaked
to Buzzfeed places Irish unionism right inside the giant Wicker Man
with the torches just about to touch the kindling. It is not so much
the idiocy of Johnson's repeated belief that an international border
is just like moving around London, though having previously
compared the Irish frontier to passing from one London borough
to another, he now compared it to travelling on the Tube: 'You
know, when I was mayor of London... I could tell where you all
were just when you swiped your Oyster card over a Tube terminal,
a Tube gizmo. The idea that we can't track movement of goods,
it's just nonsense.'

Fatuous as these comparisons are (a 500-kilometre-long border
barrier with turnstiles that open when we brush our passports
against the 'gizmo'?), the real point is what came next, the hissy
fit about this whole bloody Irish border business: 'It's so small and
there are so few firms that actually use that border regularly, it's
just beyond belief that we're allowing the tail to wag the dog in
this way. We're allowing the whole of our agenda to be dictated by
this folly.' Infantile as this is, it expresses a kind of truth – one that
is not yet spoken in public but soon will be. The truth is that the
Brexiteers don't give a flying fig for Ireland North or South – and
that includes Irish unionism and the DUP.

Johnson and his chums ignored Northern Ireland in their
Brexit campaign. That seemed to be the ultimate height of irres-
ponsibility, but they have now gone further – they are exploiting
it. Their current strategy is to use the EU's offer of a special deal
for Northern Ireland, preserving many of the advantages of the
single market even while leaving it, as an opening through which
they can force the EU to concede the same have cake/eat cake
privileges to Britain. They are trying to turn the sympathy that
comes from a horrible conflict, in which nearly 2 per cent of the

population was killed or injured, into a way of getting one over on Michel Barnier. This is political depravity.

But it won't work and when it doesn't, the rage that Johnson uttered in private will become more open and explicit. The Brexit balloon is supposed to soar into the skies when it cuts the ropes that bind it to Brussels. But its occupants are realising that there is another rope that keeps them earthbound – the one that ties them to Newry and Strabane.

To salvage their fantasies, they will cut that rope, too. Brexit is an English nationalist project – it cannot allow the English bulldog to be wagged by an Irish tail. If the tail has to be cut off – sorry but pass the shears, old man. The DUP thinks it's the dog, of course, but it's not. To the Brexit believers, we are all part of the same Irish 'folly'. The DUP has gone one further than poor Sergeant Howie and helped to construct the wicker cage in which unionism will be torched to appease the gods of Brexit. It could still save itself by voting with the opposition when the EU Withdrawal Bill returns to the House of Commons today. Or it can murmur ecstatically Kipling's 'Ulster 1912': 'We are the sacrifice'.

TIMELINE

26 June 2018:   The European Union (Withdrawal) Bill receives Royal Assent and becomes an Act of Parliament.

6 July 2018:   The cabinet meets at Chequers to agree a collective position for the future Brexit negotiations with the EU.

9 July 2018:   David Davis resigns as secretary of state for exiting the European Union and is replaced by Dominic Raab. Boris Johnson resigns as foreign secretary and is replaced by Jeremy Hunt.

24 July 2018:   UK government publishes white paper on future UK–EU relations.

23 August 2018:   UK government publishes the first collection of technical notices providing guidance on how to prepare for a no-deal Brexit.

10 July 2018

On 7 July Theresa May holds a cabinet meeting at Chequers and pushes through an agreement that the UK will seek to remain closely aligned to the customs union and single market after Brexit. David Davis resigns as Brexit secretary, followed by Boris Johnson as foreign secretary.

The best headline about British prime minister Theresa May's short-lived triumph over the hard Brexiteers last Friday was undoubtedly the one on Pádraig Collins's report in the *Guardian*: 'Possum rescued after getting head stuck in Nutella jar'.

Admittedly, Collins was actually reporting, not from Chequers, but from Brisbane, Australia. Yet the accompanying photograph was the perfect image of what May is trying to do. It showed the furry creature all curled up and immobilised with its head completely encased in a glass jar streaked with visible residues of sticky brown stuff. As a spokesman for the Australian RSPCA explained, the dumb animal 'managed to get his head in the jar, but obviously couldn't get it out'. The rescuer put 'towels around the possum so she could get him out of the jar without getting scratched by his claws'.

The story saves me the trouble of thinking up a metaphor. The Brexiteers have their heads stuck in a jar of sticky brown stuff that seemed so sweet and enticing. May's compromise deal and the white paper she is still expected to publish this week are the towels wrapped round the Brexiteers' claws so that their heads can be pulled out of the jar without her premiership getting scratched to death.

The only problem is that David Davis and Boris Johnson, having been successfully extracted, decided to bare their claws again. As any possum or two-year-old child will tell you, sticking your head inside a glass jar is quite a thrill. You get to see the world through a distorting lens that creates a comforting distance between you and reality. You can't hear unwanted voices raising awkward questions. Brexit has so far been conducted through a glass darkly. It has been seen through glorious fantasies of imperial revival and layers of self-pity about imaginary oppression. What May has been attempting, very late in the day, is to force her more deluded colleagues to get their heads out of the jar and look directly at Brexit.

She has shown them the best-case scenario, the most desirable possible outcome. And though in colour it may look like Nutella, it is actually a different kind of sticky brown stuff. 'Human kind,' said T. S. Eliot, 'cannot bear very much reality', and the same is surely true of Davis, Johnson and their fellow diehards. May has finally managed to disenchant the Brexit project, to strip away its heroic veneer. And instead of a date with destiny, it looks awfully like a loveless marriage, entered into with a heavy heart because the only alternative is unbearable loneliness.

The Brexit the British are now officially seeking is indeed miserable. Instead of the *Star Trek* vision of boldly going where no imperial-nostalgic society had gone before, it would not have enough thrust to get the UK out of the gravitational pull of the European Union. And instead of freeing British businesses from Brussels red tape, it proposes to wrap them up like mummies in layers of staggeringly complex bureaucracy, with two completely different tariff regimes operating side by side. And this, remember, is what the UK is asking for, not what it will get.

In real negotiations, as Davis knows from experience, things can only get worse: the role of the hated European Court of Justice will loom much larger and the opt-outs for future UK parliaments will disappear. If a deal is to be done at all, the last vestiges of fantasy Brexit will have to be stripped away and what will be left is a state that has negotiated its way from full partnership to the status of a rule-taking satellite of the EU.

When you take away all the heroic elements of Brexit, all the epic thrills of throwing off the oppressor and beginning a new history, what you are left with is just this – a country that has gone to enormous trouble to humiliate itself. Brexit has reached the point where the best possible outcome is the worst of both worlds, a state that is neither in nor out, neither on its own nor part of something larger.

This is what all the patriotic bombast has brought Britain to: a humble request that the EU play nice and grant it a subordinate status. Imagine that at some point in the past, the EU had actually offered this to the British. How dare they!

Can there be the slightest doubt that the British would have been up in arms, demanding nothing less than full EU membership? Has any country ever gone into international treaty negotiations hoping to emerge with a status greatly inferior to the one it already enjoys? What do we want? National humiliation. When do we want it? Now.

Davis and Johnson know this is the reality they helped to create. They hadn't the stomach either to face it or to publish a credible alternative. That is because the only alternatives to a mortifying Brexit are stark. One is to be honest and admit that the whole project has already failed and must be stopped before it is too late. The other is to stick your head back in the Nutella jar. If May goes, there may be no one left to pull the poor possums out.

14 July 2018

The British government's white paper, formalising the Chequers proposals, makes it clear that Britain would be swapping a first-class for a second-class membership of the EU. This is not what anyone said Brexit would be like.

The one thing standing between the British people and a way out of the shambles in which they find themselves is a misunderstanding of democracy. The exit from Brexit is by way of a second popular vote – anything less would pollute British politics for at least a generation with the toxic taint of betrayal. But there is a reluctance to go back on the moment when the 'people's will' was expressed, the decisive day of 23 June 2016. It is, on the surface, a decent kind of hesitancy: the Brexit vote was an impressive exercise in mass democracy. Civilised politics depend crucially on the willingness of the beaten side to accept the results of a vote they have lost.

But there is an enormous difference between a general election and a referendum or plebiscite. An election result is for the immediate future – it creates a mandate for a few years, one that will later be either renewed or annulled. It is by definition reversible.

It is also limited – the essence of democracy is not just that the majority forms a government but that it is still tightly constrained by courts, constitutions and the rights of minorities. Brexit, on the other hand, is not for the immediate future. It is for good. It is an entirely different kind of democratic gesture, one that purports to bind not just a short span of national history but many generations to come.

The Brexiteers' motto might be taken from Bob Dylan: 'Don't think twice, it's alright.' But it is patently not alright and thinking twice is the essence of real democracy. Democracy is innately humble. It is a system of trial and error. Its method is experimental. As voters, we try this lot and see how they get on, knowing that if we have made a mistake, it can be corrected. We can try the other lot and see how they in turn get on. Democracy rests on the wisdom of the people – but equally on the ability of the people to regret and correct their own follies.

The Brexit vote, too, was an experiment – and the early results are coming in. Even for the true believers, they are obviously not what they were supposed to be. Almost nothing that was promised is proving to be possible. Conversely, nobody at all suggested in the referendum campaign that what Britain should seek is what it has now been reduced to pleading for: a subordinate status as a satellite of the EU, half in and half out, neither a full partner nor a free-standing state. If anyone had proposed in the run-up to June 2016 what Theresa May's white paper has proposed this week, there would have been howls of derision from all sides.

If Brexit had been a general election, the winning 'party' would now be facing certain defeat. It made wild promises and has kept almost none of them. We can be pretty sure what 'the people' would do – kick out that lot and put the other lot in. So why is this way of thinking, so deeply ingrained in British electoral democracy, anathema when it comes to the Brexit vote? How come a perfectly normal democratic impulse has suddenly become an outrageous assault on democracy?

The essential problem is that the notion of the Brexit vote as a point of no return appeals, for different reasons, to people on both the left and the right. There are reasons why Jeremy Corbyn is just as adamant in his opposition to a second referendum as Theresa May or Boris Johnson are. For both the left and the right are drawn to the notion of Year Zero, a single point in time when history starts again from scratch. Corbyn and some of those around him have their emotional roots in revolutionary communism, in the idea of the single longed-for moment at which everything changes.

Brexit – which is essentially an ultra-Thatcherite project of deregulation – has completely the wrong content for this fantasy but it has the right form. In its own bizarre way, it is a kind of English revolutionary storming of the Bastille or the Winter Palace.

On the right, this idea of the single historic moment from which there is no going back has an even greater – and more contemporary – appeal. Autocrats have been drawn to the 'democratic' plebiscite ever since 1802 when French voters were asked to answer yes or no to the question *'Napoléon Bonaparte sera-t-il Consul à vie?'* – 'Should Napoleon Bonaparte be consul for life?' Adolf Hitler, Benito Mussolini and Augusto Pinochet used such votes to try to legitimise their rule.

But in our time, the 'illiberal democracy' pioneered by Vladimir Putin has refined the idea. Once the strong man (Putin, Viktor Orbán, Recep Tayyip Erdogan) has taken power, he embodies the will of the people and is therefore entitled to control the media and the judiciary and crush dissent.

It should not be forgotten that Theresa May tried a milder version of this last year. With the Brexit press howling classic revolutionary slogans – 'Enemies of the people!', 'Saboteurs!' – at judges and dissenting parliamentarians, she called an election, not because she lacked a majority but because she wanted a supermajority, one in which there would be no more than token resistance to 'the people's will' for a hard Brexit. She failed – the British people still have more sense than to fall for this authoritarian rhetoric. But the consequences of that failure have still not sunk in for the Brexiteers. They still hanker after that once-and-for-all gesture, the notion that everything was transformed on 23 June 2016.

But this is bad law, bad history and bad politics. It is bad law because the Brexit vote was not properly speaking a referendum at all – it was a mere plebiscite. The UK does not have a written constitution that can be changed by referendum, so in that sense the vote itself changed nothing. It is bad history because these fantasies of a single irreversible moment of truth when all is changed, changed utterly, are always disastrous, whether they come from the left or the right.

The historical irony is that nothing is less durable than 'eternal' moments of transformation – what always follows such moments is a profound instability. This eternity almost never lasts more than a few decades at most. And it is bad politics because fetishising the 'will of the people' as a one-time-only offer undermines the right of the people to change its mind.

None of this is to dismiss the Brexit vote of 2016. It is simply to say that it has to be honoured by accepting that it can be undone only by an equivalent vote – this time on a much more concrete proposition.

The undeniable fact is that the proposition put to the UK electorate in 2016 is no longer valid. There is no quick-and-easy uncoupling with no divorce settlement to be paid. There is no ability to simply ignore the Belfast Agreement of 1998. There is no end to immigration. There is no queue of former British colonies dying to return to the embrace of the mother country with fabulously advantageous trade deals. There is no £350 million a week bonanza for the National Health Service.

There is only the horribly complicated, utterly compromised and ultimately humiliating Brexit offered in this week's white paper. Would the British people ever have voted for that? There is only one way to find out – ask them.

28 July 2018

I have to open the Yeats Summer School in Sligo. It should be a welcome relief to think about poetry. But Yeats has long since been drawn into this nightmare.

There are many ways to measure the state of the world and economists, ecologists and anthropologists labour mightily over them. Opening the Yeats International Summer School in Sligo last week, I suggested another one: the Yeats Test. The proposition is simple: the more quotable Yeats seems to commentators and politicians, the worse things are. As a counter-example we might try the Heaney Test: if hope and history rhyme, let the good times roll. But these days, it is the older Irish poet who prevails in political discourse – and that is not good news.

After the election of Donald Trump, there was a massive surge in online searches for – and presumably readings of – Yeats's magnificently doom-laden 'The Second Coming'. Frank McNally has reported in the *Irish Times*, based on analysis from the media database Factiva, that the poem, written largely in response to the Bolshevik Revolution of 1917, was more quoted in newspapers the first seven months of 2016 than in any other year of the past three decades. Its popularity seems not to have abated much since: there is even an entire Twitter account called Widening Gyre that does nothing except send lines from the poem out into cyberspace without further comment.

'The centre cannot hold' was tweeted or retweeted 499 times on 24 June 2016, the morning after the Brexit vote. Thereafter it continued to appear thirty-eight times a day. It also appeared 249 times in newspapers in the first seven months of 2016. In a quick Twitter search of very recent usage, the phrase is quoted by everyone from the veteran US conservative Bill Kristol to the business editor of BBC Africa, Larry Madawo, from the poet laureate of Indiana Adrian Matejka to the comedian Avery Edison, and from an apocalyptic Zimbabwean preacher to an Indian nationalist campaign. (I am particularly glad to see that one of the many Africans who have tweeted it lately uses the Twitter handle Optimistic Guy.)

Three other phrases from 'The Second Coming' – 'mere anarchy is loosed upon the world'; 'The ceremony of innocence is drowned'; and 'The best lack all conviction, while the worst / Are full of passionate intensity' – turn up all the time. And, of course, 'Things fall apart' over and over. Other phrases from 'The Second Coming', like the 'rough beast' (slouching towards the White House) have been called into service. The most frequent triggers for these quotes in 2016 were the Paris and Brussels terror attacks, the rise of Trump and the Brexit vote. But continuing global instability and the sense of foreboding it induces have made Yeats's apocalyptic vision as quotable as a chart-topping song.

Some of this appeal is simply a tribute to the way great phrase-making acquires a timeless quality. But Yeats made lots of great non-doomy phrases, too. The grim ones ring especially true right now because he lived through such turbulent times, his poetic antennae picking up the distress signals of Ireland's civil wars, the Great War, the Russian Revolution and the rise of fascism in Europe. His brilliance lay in his ability to turn these immediate anxieties into words that seem capable of articulating every kind of epic political disturbance. As Ed Ballard noted in a *Wall Street Journal* article of the resurgence of Yeats quotations, he created 'a sequence of images dark enough to conjure a sense of doom and vague enough to be invoked by anybody looking for a more highbrow way of saying "the world is going to hell in a handbasket"'.

This is demonstrably true. Yeats's lines can be claimed by right, left and centre. The guru of the new right, Jordan Peterson, tweeted six lines from 'The Second Coming' to his fan base in August 2017.

The post-Marxist philosopher Slavoj Zizek, in response to the Paris attacks, said the poem 'seems perfectly to render our present predicament: "The best lack all conviction, while the worst are full of passionate intensity".' And here's our own minister for finance Paschal Donohoe in his 2016 budget speech: 'I alluded to "The Second Coming" by W. B. Yeats when I said that it was the job of those in the middle ground of Irish politics to show that things won't just fall apart and the centre can hold – and stay firm.'

It is, of course, this very adaptability that makes Yeats's images so useful to those of us who are in the business of reacting to the latest atrocities of word or deed. He had a genius for reflecting specific historic events in his own lifetime without allowing his language to be confined to or defined by them. 'Great hatred, little room' was hard to avoid during Northern Ireland's Troubles. (Tony Blair's key adviser, Jonathan Powell, used it for the title of his book on the peace process.) 'We are closed in, and the key is turned / On our uncertainty' from 'The Stare's Nest by My Window' works equally well for that conflict and for the present state of Brexit Britain. 'We had fed the heart on fantasies, / The heart's grown brutal from the fare' from the same poem seems to speak to almost every historic moment when the rhetoric of zealots is in the ascendant – and to the contemporary world of 'alternative facts' and ecstatic slogans.

In one way, the reference back to Yeats in contemporary political discourse is quite helpful. It reminds us that we've been here before, that the current sense of profound unsettlement is not unique in modern history. Perhaps especially on social media, where everything exists in a continuous, frantic present tense, the insertion of Yeats might do something to provoke a wider reflection on the big things that are happening around us and where they might lead.

The problem, though, may be that with so much bad news, the Yeats images are becoming so overused that they are in danger of sinking into the linguistic mire of cliché – a fate no great poet deserves. Given that the gloom is unlikely to lift anytime soon, will we get to the point where 'Things fall apart' replaces 'There are no strangers here; only friends you haven't yet met' (which Yeats did not write but which bears his name on a million tea towels, T-shirts and pub signs) on kitschy consumer products?

We need to renew the store of Yeats images that seem to comment on our times. Here is one, from 'Nineteen Hundred and Nineteen', that says it all about fake news and the pre-fascist culture of hatred:

> We, who seven years ago
> Talked of honour and of truth,
> Shriek with pleasure if we show
> The weasel's twist, the weasel's tooth.

The sense of foreboding in 'The Second Coming' is equally well captured in 'Coole Park and Ballylee':

> All is changed, that high horse riderless...
> Where the swan drifts upon a darkening flood.

What better descriptions can there be of a Donald Trump speech than 'an old bellows full of angry wind' ('A Prayer for My Daughter') and 'the barbarous clangour of a gong'('Nineteen Hundred and Nineteen')? Yeats even anticipated the trend for stupid hair among right-wing male politicians (Trump, Boris Johnson, Geert Wilders) in 'The Tower':

> There lurches past, his great eyes without thought
> Under the shadow of stupid straw-pale locks
> That insolent fiend...

We really should quote him on that.

31 July 2018

The British government has drawn up plans for a possible no-deal Brexit, hoping to bring the Irish and the Europeans to their senses. But they are too scary to publish.

Given the trouble British industry is facing, I am happy to offer a sure-fire winner to its entrepreneurs. There is bound to be a huge market in T-shirts, posters, mugs, pillowcases, postcards, and perhaps even tattoos imprinted with a Tudor crown and the words in white capitals on a red background: KEEP HYSTERICAL AND CARRY ON. The original poster, designed in 1939 by the Ministry of Information as part of its preparations for an impending world war, was revived ironically in recent decades, and perhaps its appeal as an affectionate parody of the traditional English virtues of composure and resilience should have been a warning. The only stiff upper lips on display in England now belong to the victims of botched Botox jobs.

Admittedly, my idea has been slightly pre-empted by the Royal Mail. In one of those coincidences that you couldn't make up, it issued in June a set of stamps to mark the fiftieth anniversary of the first screening of the long-running wartime sitcom *Dad's Army*. One of them has the catchphrase 'Don't Panic! Don't Panic!' printed on a still from the series of Clive Dunn's elderly Home Guard soldier, Lance Corporal Jones, mouth agape, glasses askew and, of course, in an awful funk. Here in a single mass-produced image is a masterly summary of Britain's current Plan B for Brexit.

Theresa May's government drew up contingency plans for a no-deal Brexit to put the fear of God into the damned Europeans. They would show the Brussels bullies just who they were dealing with – a people famed for their infinite stoicism who will eat rats in dark cold cellars before they agree to be enslaved like, um, Norway.

And when the British government looked at these contingency plans, they scared themselves so badly that they decided they must not be published after all. As Oscar Wilde said of the death of Little Nell in Charles Dickens's *The Old Curiosity Shop*, you'd have to have a heart of stone not to laugh. The effigy created to frighten the notoriously lily-livered continentals into acknowledging the God-given British right to eat cake and have cake has turned back on its makers and made them cringe in terror.

One minister explained the core of the plan to the *Sunday Times*: 'You would have to use all your services to provide essential supplies to people. The elderly and vulnerable would be in a difficult position. It would be the end of March (when Brexit happens) but it might still be cold. You've got to think about the energy supply and keeping the lights on.' Another source explained indelicately why the actual contingency plan cannot be shown to the British people after all: 'People will s**t themselves and think they want a new referendum or an election or think the Tory party shouldn't govern again.' Or: here is a special broadcast by the minister for contingency planning, Lance Corporal Jones – 'Stockpile Spam! Armed forces surround Tesco! Stockpile candles! Stockpile paraffin! Cut down those cherry trees for firewood! Arrest saboteurs! Don't panic! Don't panic!'

In this national nervous breakdown, a peacetime country is dreaming itself back into its finest hour. A major academic report published last week, *Feeding Britain: Food Security after Brexit*, deals with what it would take for the UK to export food to the United States as an alternative to its current trade with the EU: it 'would require a vast food flotilla and logistics operation exceeding that of the 1940–45 Atlantic convoys.' Never mind the practicalities of this – how on earth did the Second World War Atlantic convoys become part not of the British past but of a feverish vision of its possible future?

The British, in their own heads, long ago replayed the Second

World War's tragedy as farce – what other culture could have not only produced *Dad's Army* but lapped up the jaw-dropping French Resistance saucy sitcom *'Allo, 'Allo!* that ran for eighty-five episodes in the 1980s and 1990s. But if you've already turned tragedy into farce, what do you turn the farce into? As it happens, you turn it into public policy. In Plan B Brexit, nostalgia for wartime morphs into a weird mash-up of *Dad's Army* and *Mad Max*. 'Who do you think you are kidding Monsieur Barnier / We're preparing to kill each other for a can of Spam'.

It's all at once deadly serious and gloriously camp in that self-dramatising, stroppy manner that kids can adopt when they're not getting their way, making a big performance out of starving themselves because you won't let them eat ice cream before their dinner. I'll die of hunger and then you'll be sorry, but it will be too late and I'll look down at you crying at my funeral and I'll laugh at you. As a negotiating strategy, this seldom works for kids. It is probably not a great move in international talks either, especially when everyone can hear the rising notes in the voice behind it: Don't panic! Don't panic!

TIMELINE

5–6 September 2018:   Further UK–EU Article 50 negotiations.

13 September 2018:   The government publishes an additional twenty-eight technical notices, providing guidance on how to prepare for a no-deal Brexit.

19–20 September 2018:   EU leaders hold an informal summit in Salzburg. On the evening of the first day, Theresa May gives a ten-minute Brexit speech over dinner. There is deep dismay that she does little more than read woodenly an op-ed article already published in *Die Zeit*.

15 September 2018

Boris Johnson is manoeuvring ever more
openly against Theresa May.

As Winston Churchill did not say, never in the field of human conflict has so much harm been done to so many by a mere chancer. Never has a great democracy's fate hung on so fatuous a figure. Boris Johnson is not fundamentally malign. And he is certainly no mastermind, evil or otherwise. He is just deeply unserious, a man-child whose public life has been no more continent than his private life. He acts on impulse, pursuing his own pleasures and ambitions. He understands the world as a kid understands a sweetshop – a store of possibilities for immediate self-gratification.

And yet, future historians may have to deal with this man of no consequence as the most consequential figure in early twenty-first-century British politics.

The next few weeks, leading up to the Tory party conference at the end of September, may well decide Johnson's place in history. If Theresa May does not find the courage to denounce him for what he is – a narcissist loyal only to his own immediate desires – he could destroy not only her premiership but the British state as we know it.

When he came out in favour of Leave, Johnson assured the then prime minister David Cameron that 'he doesn't expect to win, believing Brexit will be "crushed"'. This is a fundamental truth about Brexit but one that is so absurd that the brain refuses to hold on to it as fact and lets it seep down into the cognitive sludge of half-remembered dreams and half-forgotten fantasies;

for a critical section of its supporters, and in particular for the effective leader of the Leave campaign, Brexit was always meant to be a Lost Cause.

For Johnson, the whole thing was supposed to be a heroic failure, a grand gesture. The ideal outcome would have been 55 per cent Remain, 45 per cent Leave – with a majority of Tory voters backing Brexit. It would have been a fine showing, a splendid performance against insuperable odds. It would have the romance of, say, the Confederacy in the Southern states of the US; a thoroughly bad cause given a veneer of nobility by honourable defeat. It was not meant to be a victory.

Johnson's face on the morning after the referendum told a remarkable story – written on those oversized features were shock, bewilderment and the panic induced by the realisation that consequence-free rhetoric had to be somehow transformed into a viable reality.

Of course Johnson couldn't do that. The logic of Brexit was undoubtedly that he, as the leader of the revolution, should take power. But he wasn't up to it. And when Theresa May made him foreign secretary, he wasn't up to that either. To exercise power, you have to be able to take some responsibility. That is precisely what Johnson is incapable of doing.

When the imperative is to actually devise workable plans and make difficult decisions, he is gone like a shot off a shovel – 'shot' arguably containing the wrong vowel. And so what we are now seeing is Johnson desperately trying to turn Brexit back into what it was supposed to be. He is trying to snatch glorious defeat from the jaws of his accidental victory, to recreate Brexit as a Lost Cause – lost, of course, not by the fecklessness and incompetence of Johnson and his fellow Brexiteers but by the treachery of Remoaners, judges, citizens of nowhere and the bloody Irish.

But the voters did back Brexit and the EU, for some strange reason, does not see the virtue of giving a non-member state a place in its decision-making processes. And there are real-life consequences. The farce on stage may well become a tragedy on the streets and in the factories. What would any patriot – any decent human being – do when he's made such terrible mistakes? Own up and try to limit the damage. This is not just a political obligation – it's a moral imperative.

But Johnson is doubly evasive. He leaves other people (principally the hapless May) to mop up his mess and then takes a vast amount of money for criticising them in his newspaper column for not doing it properly. This is the ultimate in what one of Johnson's favourite authors, Rudyard Kipling, called the prerogative of the harlot throughout the ages: power without responsibility.

Theresa May could do a great deal to rescue her lost credibility if she were to say this in public and at great length. Her biggest mistake has been to indulge the most self-indulgent creature in contemporary British politics, to give him the free pass of 'Boris being Boris'. Boris being Boris is Britain being destroyed. His bad jokes are all on the country he purports to love. May needs to explain, with cold fury, why they are not funny any more.

22 September 2018

As the Brexit negotiations enter what seems to be the crucial stage, the British side is trying to use the concessions the EU has made to allow Northern Ireland to remain effectively in the customs union and single market to argue that Britain should also be given full access to EU markets even when it leaves both.

According to the well-known model created by Elisabeth Kübler-Ross, the first three stages of grief are denial, anger and bargaining. In their approach to Northern Ireland and the Irish border, the Brexiteers have broadly followed this pattern.

First, clothing their naked indifference in wilful ignorance, they denied that the problem existed at all. Next, they resorted to anger at the bloody Irish, the perpetual disturbers of the British peace without whom Brexit would have been, as promised, the easiest deal in the history of the world. And now we are at the bargaining stage.

But there is a dramatic twist: the bargaining is not so much *about* Northern Ireland. It is bargaining *with* Northern Ireland. The sheer cynicism of what is going on is so breathtaking that it is hard to credit and thus easy to miss.

The British approach to Brexit has been so chaotic that it has seemed silly to look for method in the madness. In relation to the Irish dimension of Brexit, we've become inured to magical thinking (the wonderful efficacy of not-yet-invented technological solutions), blithe misapprehension and sheer fatuousness (Boris Johnson's insistence that the border is just like that between two London boroughs).

This has been oddly comforting. Since this stuff is so evidently childish, we can wait for the adults to enter the room.

But the comfort is false. The adults did enter the room. The Brexit negotiations are now in the hands of serious, skilful, professional mandarins. And they've done something remarkable with the Irish question. Remarkable in that it takes some nerve even to contemplate it. For what it comes down to is a strategy of using the human suffering of the Troubles to try to extract a favourable post-Brexit trade deal from the EU. You have to be very clever to think of trying this – and utterly shameless.

Essentially what has been taking shape in British strategy is a reversal of the old Irish nationalist adage: England's difficulty is Ireland's opportunity. Ireland's tragedies are being deployed as England's last opportunity to achieve what the Brexiteers promised: the advantages of EU membership without the obligations. If we leave aside its amorality, there is an element of brilliance here. The strategy takes the biggest weakness of the British position and seeks to transform it into the greatest strength.

To understand how this strategy has evolved, we need to go back to last December. On Monday 4 December, Theresa May and Michel Barnier agreed a text on the so-called backstop, the default commitment to avoiding a hard border after Brexit.

It essentially conceded to the position of the EU and the Irish government: that no hard border means keeping the North effectively inside the customs union and large parts of the single market. But May was summoned from that meeting to take a call from DUP leader Arlene Foster effectively vetoing the deal.

So May returned to London, negotiated with the DUP and went back to Brussels on Friday 8 December. There she agreed to the same backstop proposal but added a politically crucial rider: just as there would be 'full regulatory alignment' between Northern Ireland and the Republic, the same would apply between Northern Ireland and Britain. So no hard land border on the island and, in the rather hyped-up term, 'no border in the Irish Sea'.

Logically this double backstop can have only one outcome.

If the North is aligned to the Republic (and hence to the EU), and Britain is aligned to the North, then it follows that Britain remains aligned to the Republic – and hence to the EU.

In simple terms, Britain remains in effect within the customs union and the single market. So Theresa May had essentially signed up to the softest of soft Brexits and had done so because there is no other way both to honour her commitment to avoiding a hard Irish border and to keep the DUP happy.

Except that she had no political cover for this dramatic manoeuvre. It is not an outcome she had ever promised, articulated or prepared for. Hence the stalemate in the talks on the withdrawal agreement: May has been unwilling and unable to say what it is she signed up to in December. It is an agreement that dare not speak its name.

This is where the brilliance and the cynicism come in. What if the metaphors were to change? For the Brexiteers, Ireland is the poison that has seeped into their great project, sapping all its vitality. But, as the mandarins took full charge this spring, they realised that Ireland might be thought of rather as the magical elixir that could bring a dead project back to life.

The thinking is in itself simple enough. The EU has accepted from the outset of the negotiations that Northern Ireland is special. It is special because it has suffered – the bodies of the dead and maimed are the eloquent argument for a recognition that this place needs to be treated tenderly.

What that tenderness translates into is have cake/eat cake. Northern Ireland can be allowed to be what the Brexiteers have always fantasised about: it can formally leave the EU while retaining the benefits of membership. The whole point about this is that a massive, rule-based organisation such as the EU can do it only in a very special case. For the North it is doable because (a) the place is very small and (b) the suffering has been so great.

But what the British have done is to seize on this tenderness as a weakness in the EU's position. The North is to be the aperture through which the hopeless fantasy of have cake/eat cake can be reborn. The EU has conceded that this fantasy double existence is possible for this one part of the UK. And the December agreement says that Northern Ireland must remain aligned with the rest of the UK.

So the EU must concede that the UK as a whole can have all the special benefits that it has offered to the North. *Voilà!* Northern Ireland is not the tail wagging the British dog, it is a different kind of beast altogether – the Trojan horse within which all of Brexit is smuggled into the promised land of frictionless access to EU markets without the political obligations of membership.

Clever as this is, it won't work because, were the EU to concede to it, it would be signing its own death warrant. And even if it is cunning, it is a very low cunning indeed. Britain is not solely responsible for the Troubles, but it bears a huge responsibility for creating the conditions in which they happened and in prolonging them through ineptness and misgovernment. It faced those responsibilities in the peace process and, it seemed, thought well of itself for doing so.

It is really quite something to seek now, in the midst of a self-inflicted crisis of authority in Britain, to turn the North's suffering and the EU's care for it to advantage. The dead are surely not to be bargained with.

The next stage in the grieving process after bargaining is depression. Perhaps we are moving into it now, for it is deeply depressing to find what is still in many ways a great country giving way to such cynicism. It is a reminder that the damage from Brexit is not just economic or political. It is also moral.

29 September 2018

*Oddly enough, there is already a part of British territory
that is outside the EU's customs union but has a land border
with an EU country: Gibraltar. While the future Irish border
is subjected to all sorts of abstract speculation, I wondered
what this real-world example might have to tell us.*

Some of the titles still on the shelves of the old Garrison Library in Gibraltar: Charles Mayer's *Jungle Beasts I Have Captured*; G. P. Sanderson's *Thirteen Years Among the Wild Beasts of India*; the Maharajah of Cooch Behar's *Shooting in Cooch Behar: A Record of Thirty-Seven Years of Sport* and my favourite, Major A. E. Wardrop's *Modern Pig-Sticking*.

The library was founded in 1793 and remained as a refined retreat for the officers of the British military garrison until 2011. Inside the elegant Georgian building, there is a stellar gathering of historians at a conference called *Bordering on Brexit*, itself part of a wider project called 'Embers of Empire'. Outside, looming above the lush back garden, is the massive Jurassic bulk of the Rock of Gibraltar surmounted by a huge Union Jack on which, I can report, the sun does actually set. Few places on earth are at once so real and so symbolic.

Gibraltar is, in a sense, all border. Its historic importance is that it marks and controls the border between the Atlantic and Mediterranean. And its contemporary importance is that, along with the Irish border, it will be, after Brexit, the other land frontier between the European Union and British territory.

In that regard, it has some things to tell us about both the physical realities of Brexit and the complexities of the post-imperial

Britishness that surround it. For just as 'no hard border' has entered our political phrasebook, the Gibraltarian government says of Brexit that its priority 'will be to give people certainty on the fluidity of the frontier' with Spain.

In a sense, the Gibraltar border is a massively simplified version of our own. From the top of the Rock, you can look down and see it all laid out: the Spanish town of La Linea, the narrow isthmus, the border fence and the runway of the Gibraltar airport that almost immediately abuts it.

Politically, it is a frontier almost as fraught as our own: Spain does not accept long-term British sovereignty over the Rock and also disputes the area on which the airport was built. But geographically, it could not be more straightforward. It is 1.2 kilometres long compared to Ireland's 500 kilometres. It has a single, controlled crossing point, compared to 208 official crossings on our island and an infinite number of unofficial ones. If ours is the *Finnegans Wake* of frontiers, this is *Borders for Dummies*.

But, even so, the first thing you see when you come out of Gibraltar airport is the very thing we never want to see again in Ireland: physical border infrastructure. It is relatively small and it is pleasantly topped on the southern side by the flags of the UK, Gibraltar and the EU but it is exactly what you would expect to see if you were crossing, for example, from the United States to Canada or from France to Switzerland: buildings, barriers, police, border guards.

This is striking because, for now, both sides of this border are in the EU. How can this be? The reason is highly significant from an Irish point of view: Gibraltar, when it joined the Common Market along with Britain and Ireland, stayed out of the customs union.

So what you're seeing when you look at the Gibraltar border is exactly what the line between a member of the customs union (Spain) and a non-member looks like. You are not just looking at the present, you are looking at what, without a satisfactory deal on the UK's withdrawal from the EU, is Ireland's future.

It is true, of course, that Gibraltar is not in the Schengen travel area while Spain is, so there are passport checks. Assuming, as everyone does, that the Common Travel Area between Britain and Ireland remains intact after Brexit, this will not be our problem.

But even if Gibraltar and Spain were not in different travel areas, they would still have to have the same infrastructure because of customs checks. Since the British government insists that Northern Ireland must leave the customs union, the situation will in this regard be the same.

And this raises a very stark question: if the British know of some magical technological way to have a customs frontier with no physical infrastructure, why have they not already applied it in Gibraltar?

The other obvious thing about the Gibraltar border is that it is inescapably political. In one sense, what has happened here in recent decades is very similar to what has happened on our island. This frontier was so bitterly contested that Spain, under General Franco, closed it entirely between 1969 and 1985, ironically solidifying the British identity of the enclave's indigenous people.

It has since been, to use another current term, 'de-dramatised', just as ours was in the 1990s. Thousands of people move back and forth daily for work and pleasure. But what has been de-dramatised can always be re-dramatised at a moment's notice.

When I drove out of Gibraltar last Sunday afternoon, passport at the ready, there were actually no checks at all. But the driver, Chris, an English expat who lives on the Costa del Sol and ferries passengers to and from the enclave all the time, said that there have been times when he has been delayed for five and a half hours at the border and the queues of cars and trucks have snaked all the way around the Rock.

As recently as 2013, there was a serous diplomatic incident when the British government accused Spain of conducting 'excessive' searches of vehicles at the Gibraltar border and 'torturing' travellers. Contested borders will never be entirely 'frictionless'. They will always be political pressure points.

The other way in which Gibraltar resonates with Northern Ireland is, of course, in its Britishness and more specifically in what it says about the relationship between Britishness and Brexitness. The DUP and many of its supporters would undoubtedly see the Gibraltarians as political kith and kin: doughty defenders of a British identity under siege.

But while the DUP not only campaigned for Brexit but has aligned itself with the Rees-Moggian ultras, the Gibraltarians take a radically different view of their interests. A Soviet-style 96 per cent of them voted against Brexit in the 2016 referendum. And the tone you hear from Gibraltar's government and officials is calm, pragmatic, carefully focused on limiting the damage and getting the best possible outcome.

Joe Bossano, aka Sir Joseph Bossano KCMG, is probably one of the best negotiators alive. He has been a huge figure in the life of Gibraltar for the last fifty years, first as a ferocious labour organiser, agitator and founder of the Socialist Labour Party, and later as chief minister of the territory.

He led dockworkers and seamen to victory in a four-year-long campaign of strikes and blockades to win pay parity with their British counterparts. He has dealt with successive British governments, with Spanish antagonism, and with the EU. He is a dedicated Marxist who negotiated with international capitalists to turn Gibraltar into a haven for their money and used the proceeds to subsidise public housing and free university education. At seventy-nine, he is still minister for economic development and when I had dinner with him last Saturday night he said he plans to stand for re-election next year.

Given all of this, I asked him what he thought about the Brexit negotiations. His answer is the best short summary I've yet heard: 'There were only three possibilities. One was the status quo, which the British have decided they don't want.

'The second is something better than the status quo, which the EU can't possibly give them. And the third is something worse than the status quo, but since the status quo was not acceptable to you, something worse than the status quo couldn't be acceptable either. It is quite simple: if you enter into a negotiation in which all of your options are impossible, you can't win.'

If you leave aside his Marxism and his atheism – admittedly rather a lot for the DUP to leave aside – Bossano has much in common with the DUP. Gibraltar is an iconic outpost of Britishness, and he is one of the people who have fought to keep it that way. Like the DUP, he has often been more British than British governments, driving them crazy with his hardline resistance to any compromise with Spain on the issue of sovereignty. Like the DUP, he has also insisted on local self-government.

When you see the steps of the main passageway up the Rock from the old town of Gibraltar painted in the colours and form of the Union Jack, like kerbstones in loyalist estates, you don't have to stretch too far for the connections. And, astonishingly, Joe Bossano tells me that he spent his early childhood in, of all places, the Paisleyite heartland of Ballymena. During the Second World War, the British rather ruthlessly evacuated the civilian population of Gibraltar to Britain. Joe's family ended up living in a Nissen hut in what was effectively a refugee camp in Co. Antrim. Back in Gibraltar, he was briefly educated by the Irish Christian Brothers before, as he puts it, 'we parted by mutual agreement'.

He became a deckhand in the merchant navy, moved to West Ham in London's East End and joined the Seamans' Union. He learned his negotiating skills the hard way, dealing with shipowners in a very rough industry.

Which brings us back to Brexit. 'When you are going in to a negotiation,' he says, 'the most important thing you need to know is: what happens if I fail? You must have a way out – you try to get what you want but if that's not possible, you have to be able to retreat and fight another day.'

In a week when the Irish border continued to bedevil Brexit and British politics was resounding with the drama of 'humiliation' and demands for 'respect', it was all the more poignant, watching the sun go down over the Rock, to be reminded of such solid advice from a veteran fighter for Britishness: don't go into talks when there is no good outcome and always leave yourself a way out.

In this outpost of empire, the natives knew something the mother country had forgotten.

6 October 2018

At the Conservative Party conference, Theresa May pledges herself to protect above all the 'precious precious union'.

Arlene Foster spoke this week about the DUP's 'blood red line' of avoiding any post-Brexit differences between Northern Ireland and Britain. The image was not in good taste, but it was revealing. When politicians resort to such overheated rhetoric, it is usually because they know deep down that they are protesting too much.

To really understand the hysteria about 'the territorial integrity of the union', we have to understand that it is not about what it seems to be about. Beneath the surface of anxiety about the EU's Brexit proposals is a deep pool of panic about the union itself. For even the DUP must know that the blood red line of Britishness is now a thin red line. It has been worn away, not by the EU, but by the English. The union is being undermined, not by Michel Barnier, but by John Bull.

In his 2002 survey of modern British identity, *Patriots*, the historian Richard Weight noted of the English: 'They have woken up en masse to the fact that their blithe unionism is no longer reciprocated and that their seamless Anglo-British identity is effectively redundant.' Since then, three very strange things happened.

The first of them is nothing. Almost the entire British political class pretended that nothing was happening in England and therefore did nothing about it.

The second was what usually happens when something very big is building up and everyone is trying to keep the lid on it: an explosion. The Brexit referendum vote on 23 June 2016 was about many things, but one of the main ones was the non-metropolitan English blowing the lid off.

And the third thing that happened is the most astonishing of all: after the explosion, the political class, as we saw again at the Tory conference this week, went back to pretending that it didn't happen. The thing to be defended at all costs in the Brexit negotiations is the very thing the English were so deeply unhappy about – the union.

In the past few weeks, it has become clear that if there is to be the disaster of a no-deal Brexit it will be because, as Theresa May re-emphasised in her conference speech, the Tory party, egged on by the DUP, has made 'the integrity of the union' into the reddest of red lines. Customs checks on goods moving between Britain and Northern Ireland, even very low-key ones in warehouses or onboard ships, would be an outrageous affront to the union. Hence, there can be no compromise on the Irish border question; hence there may well be no deal.

This is all very well – unionism is a perfectly legitimate political principle on both sides of the Irish Sea. Except that to fetishise it at this moment is to miss the point spectacularly. The point is not just that the Brexit referendum showed how disunited the union is: Scotland and Northern Ireland voted one way, England and Wales another. It is that the great force that lay behind it is the emergence of English nationalism. The English blew the union up into the air. It is Brexit itself that raises fundamental questions about the 'integrity of the union'. The great show of rallying round the Union flag and dying in the last ditch of unionism is nothing more than the usual last resort of panicky governments: denial and distraction.

Before Brexit there was a reasonable excuse for paying no attention to what is in fact the most remarkable political phenomenon on these islands in the twenty-first century: the astonishingly rapid emergence of a specifically English political identity. The excuse is habit. In the (relatively short) history of the union since 1707, it was generally a fair assumption that trouble would come, if it came, from the smaller 'partners': the Irish of every stripe, of course; the Scots; possibly the Welsh.

The idea that Englishness would be the problem was absurd – England was so unaware of itself as a separate political community that its politicians and journalists could use 'England' when they meant 'Britain' and vice versa. The English had folded their national identity into two larger constructs – the empire and the union – and it would surely never be unfolded again.

But the empire evaporated, and the union's long-term future began to look more and more uncertain. Two big things happen in the 1990s. The Belfast Agreement of 1998 made Northern Ireland's place in the union an explicitly open question: Britain accepted that it could leave whenever a majority of its population wished this to happen. And the following year, the Scottish parliament was established. Over the next decade its existence would gradually establish the idea that Scotland's place in the union is also contingent: the British government agreed in 2014 that the result of the referendum on Scottish independence would be binding – the Scots were shown the door even if they decided not to go through it.

Yet it seemed to occur to very few people in the political mainstream that the English might react to any of this. Their 'blithe unionism' would be unaffected. In fact, it was very profoundly affected. This was obvious in the 2011 census: fully 60 per cent of the people of England identified themselves as solely English. Remarkably, given that people could choose 'English' and 'British' if they wanted to, only 29 per cent of the English identified themselves as feeling any sense of British national identity at all.

Even more starkly, the important Future of England surveys in 2012 and 2013 showed that this re-emerging English identity was highly political. The English were saying very clearly that they did not see Westminster and Whitehall, the institutional pillars of the union, as being capable of representing their collective national interests.

The pace of this withdrawal of support from the institutional status quo is dizzying: in 1999, when the Scottish parliament was just established, 62 per cent of English respondents agreed that 'England should be governed as it is now with laws made by the UK parliament'. By 2008, this had fallen to a bare majority, 51 per cent. But by 2012 it was down to 21 per cent.

This mass disaffection fed Brexit: there was a direct correlation between those who expressed a strong English identity and those who voted for Brexit. What happened in 2016 was essentially that the English outside the big multicultural cities staged a peaceful national revolution. And yet for the very people who claim to be on their side, it seems they need not have bothered. It is one of the weirdest facets of the current crisis that the DUP, which clings to a fantasy of an eternal union, has a much louder voice in Theresa May's Brexit strategy than the English people, who have shown that they do not.

England's roar has been muted; the stirring music of loyalty to an unchanging union turned up to eleven. But what if the defence of the union ends up doing terrible harm to the English? What, in the end, will there be for Northern Ireland to be united with?

16 October 2018

Hello, Mrs Mouth, may I introduce you to Mr Money? When we cut to the chase, Arlene Foster's bluster comes down to a brutal and basic question: will the Little Englanders put their money where the DUP's mouth is? And there is a brutal and basic answer: not bloody likely.

We are, finally, at the point when Arlene Foster's 'blood red line' must be crossed if a Brexit deal is to be done. The DUP has gambled the union on the belief that the Brexiteers are above all unionists and will never concede to any post-Brexit arrangements that differentiate between Northern Ireland and Britain. In this they are deluded to the point of insanity. To understand why, forget the mouthy platitudes and just listen to Mr Money. What Mr Money is saying very clearly to the DUP is: sayonara.

Northern Ireland's place in the United Kingdom has a price. It costs English taxpayers roughly £10 billion (€11.38 billion) a year. An average of £14,020 (€15,955) per head was spent on public services in Northern Ireland in 2016, compared, for example, with £10,580 (€11,446) in the southeast of England. This (rather than the DUP's flagship Renewable Heat Incentive) is what keeps the home fires of Ulster burning.

It is also what makes a united Ireland currently impossible: the taxpayers of Ballydehob are not going to subsidise better public services in Ballymena than they get themselves. Northern Ireland's place in the union depends entirely on the willingness of English taxpayers to pony up.

And, after Brexit, to pony up even more: it is they who must, for example, replace the 60 per cent of farm incomes in the North that comes in subsidies from Brussels.

So, if we strip away all rhetorical decor, this is what the union means: the voter in Gloucestershire loves the union enough to share her money with Arlene and Michelle. And here is the really big news: if she's a Brexiteer, she damn well doesn't. In the latest Future of England survey, there is a buried landmine.

It has received some attention for the breathtaking revelation that fully 83 per cent of Leave voters and 73 per cent of Conservative voters agree that 'the unravelling of the peace process in Northern Ireland' is a 'price worth paying' for a Brexit that allows them to 'take back control'.

But there is actually an even more explosive finding, less immediately lurid but of far greater consequence for the DUP. The proposition put to these English voters is this: 'Revenue raised from taxpayers in England should also be distributed to Northern Ireland to help Northern Irish public services.' Just 25 per cent of Leave voters, and 29 per cent of people who said they voted Conservative in 2017, agree.

What is even more striking is that antipathy to sharing English tax revenues actually rises if Northern Ireland is explicitly included in the question. In the abstract, 38 per cent of Leave voters agree that revenue raised from taxpayers in England should be spread across the whole of the UK. That falls to 25 per cent when Northern Ireland is explicitly mentioned.

Tories and Brexiteers in England are literally not buying the union any more. On the only real test that matters – the willingness to share their money with their kith and kin in Ulster – three-quarters of English Leave voters have their hands firmly in their pockets. The message could not be clearer: Kith? My arse!

And here's the true idiocy of the DUP's alliance with the Brexit ultras: the only people in England who are still willing to subsidise Northern Ireland are Remainers. The DUP has taken sides with the enemies of the union against its friends. While just 25 per cent of Leave voters are okay with it, 52 per cent of Remain voters in England agree that their taxes should pay for Northern Ireland's public services.

On every similar question, it is Remainers who still believe in UK solidarity and British identity – the Leavers have tilted decisively towards an English version of Ourselves Alone. The DUP may not be able to stay in bed with Sinn Féin in Belfast, but it has entangled its destiny with that of the English Shinners.

While any unionist with a stim of wit would understand that Northern Ireland's future in the union depends on the Remainers, the DUP is aggressively biting the only hands still willing to feed it: screw you and your money!

The DUP's delusion is that it can emotionally blackmail the English by screaming 'don't leave me now with the precious union in my arms!' To which the mass of Brexit supporters in England will say: 'Right you are then. Ta-rah!'

TIMELINE

29 October 2018: In what is supposed to be the last budget before the UK leaves the EU, Chancellor Philip Hammond announces just £500 million for no-deal Brexit preparations.

14 November 2018: The UK and the EU negotiating teams reach an agreement in principle on the withdrawal agreement. This establishes the terms of the UK's departure on 29 March 2019.

15 November 2018: Brexit secretary Dominic Raab resigns from the cabinet, citing his opposition to the prime minister's draft withdrawal agreement. Several other ministers resign, including Suella Braverman (junior Brexit minister) and Esther McVey (works and pensions secretary).

25 November 2018: At a special European Council meeting, EU27 leaders endorse the Brexit withdrawal agreement and approve the political declaration on future EU–UK relations.

5 December 2018: Theresa May suffers three Brexit defeats in the Commons and the government is also found to be in contempt of parliament.

10 December 2018: The prime minister gives a statement to the House of Commons on Exiting the European Union and announces a delay to the meaningful vote, originally planned for the following day.

| 12 December 2018: | Sir Graham Brady, chair of the 1922 Committee, announces that enough Tory MPs have a requested a vote of confidence in Theresa May as Conservative leader. In the ballot later in the evening, Theresa May wins the vote of confidence by 200 to 117. |
| 13 December 2018: | The European Council (meeting as EU27) adopts conclusions on Brexit, including further assurances on the Northern Ireland backstop. |

6 November 2018

I t is probably not a good sign that the best role model for Theresa May as she approaches Brexit's make-or-break moment is Caligula. The most notorious of Roman emperors needed a military triumph to bolster his faltering authority. He gathered legions and supplies, the historian Suetonius tells us, 'on an unprecedented scale' and led them towards the French coast facing the English Channel.

He wrote despatches berating the people of Rome for enjoying themselves while he was facing all the hazards and hardships of war. He staged a few harmless skirmishes in Gaul, after which he awarded himself and his sidekicks victory crowns decorated with the sun, moon and stars. Finally, he got to the Channel, ready, it seemed, to embark on an invasion of Britain.

Suetonius tells us that Caligula then drew up his army and his great siege machines in battle array on the shoreline. 'No one had the least notion what was on his mind when, suddenly, he gave the order 'gather seashells!' He referred to the shells as 'plunder from the ocean… and made the troops fill their helmets and tunic-laps with them'.

He then wrote to Rome with orders to 'prepare a triumph more lavish than any hitherto known'. This incident is generally taken as evidence of Caligula's 'brainsickness' and perhaps it is. But the world would be a better place if all glory-hunting megalomaniacs instructed their soldiers, instead of carrying out futile massacres, to collect shells on the beach.

And I can't help thinking that this story is quite instructive in relation to Brexit. Brexit is also a strange kind of mock fight, intended to make a point about British greatness rather than to achieve some real benefit. We have had the phoney, melodramatic skirmishes, and the whole Brexit army is now lined up in battle array on the shoreline with nowhere left to go. It is time for Theresa May to take the Caligula option: gather whatever seashells can be rescued from the debacle, claim them as tribute from Michel Barnier, award all the leading Brexiteers victory crowns decorated with the sun, moon and stars, and declare a triumph more lavish than any hitherto known.

We must never forget how important it is for Britain to save face. National honour is no less potent for being idiotic. For example: what would have happened if the EU had said to the UK in 2015 when David Cameron was demanding concessions – Out! You're expelled! We're sick of all your moaning – just go!? Oh yeah, you and whose army? How very dare you talk to us like that? Staying in just to spite the damn Europeans would have become a great patriotic cause.

That didn't happen, of course, and we are left with the need for May to perform that trickiest of manoeuvres: saving face while climbing down.

Since there is no possible outcome better than the status quo, Brexit was always going to go one of two ways. One was the insane self-sabotage of no deal. The other was a messy and profoundly unsatisfactory compromise. It was a choice between irreparable damage or reluctant damage limitation. The sane choice is still pretty grim, and it has taken almost a year for May to face up to its inevitability.

Since last December we have had what might be called the with-drawal agreement for slow learners. It was completely obvious to anyone who read the agreement without red-white-and-blue-tinted spectacles what it meant: in order to avoid both a hard border in Ireland and a 'border in the Irish Sea' the UK as a whole will have to stay in the customs union. That's what May signed up to – and so did her government, including Boris Johnson and David Davis.

And it is a miserably anti-climactic ending to what was supposed to be an epic of national liberation: the UK will remain tied to the EU for a 'temporary' period that will end on the Twelfth of Never. Caligula himself would have known the line from Horace: *Parturient montes, nascetur ridiculus mus*. The mountains labour and give birth to a ridiculous mouse. The people who were promised a glorious Brexit are entitled to ask: Is that it?

And yet it is in everyone's interest to declare the mouse a lion, and to hail May as a negotiating genius who has forced the EU – and the uppity Irish – into submission. Ireland is going to get what it wants and needs: no hard border and, in effect, the softest available Brexit. The British will get, in return, a declaration that if it can solve the Irish problem it can have its Canada-style trade deal – which is like saying that May can win *Strictly* as soon as she learns to dance.

But we must button our lips and look glum. The British are still going on about Dunkirk – a retreat reimagined as a glorious victory. It is crucially important that May is allowed her Dunkirk moment.

And to do that she must be allowed to talk up her success in getting all the great things that will follow if the Irish problem is ever solved. Don't say: good luck with that. Do say: oh, what lovely seashells!

13 November 2018

When future historians try to understand how Britain ended up with a choice between chaos and becoming a satellite of the European Union, one question will stump them. Were these people telling deliberate lies or were they merely staggeringly ignorant? Where does mendacity stop and idiocy begin? Historians generally have to assume that people in power have a basic grasp of what they are doing, that their actions are intentional. They may use deception as a tactic and they may be deluded in what they think they can achieve. But they must, at least at the beginning, have some grasp on reality – otherwise they would not have achieved power. Yet, for the poor historians trying to make sense of Brexit, this assumption will be mistaken.

There is, of course, plenty of straightforward mendacity for them to identify. Boris Johnson's whole journalistic and political career has been driven by his talent for taking minor regulations and distorting them into wildly exaggerated claims of oppression by the Eurocrats. This can't be done by mistake. For example, you cannot by accident take, as Johnson did, a Council of Europe (not EU) convention on the repatriation of corpses and turn it into a repeated claim that 'There really is European legislation on the weight, dimensions and composition of a coffin'. There isn't. This is not ignorance – it is a knowing falsification of the truth. So let's leave that aside. Historians will know it when they see it.

Their problem will be, rather, with the shades of obliviousness. Here our future scholars will have to try to distinguish between three kinds of ignorance: deliberate unknowing, crass self-delusion and what we can only call pig ignorance. So, for their benefit, here is a brief spotter's guide.

Deliberate unknowing is when you are fully aware of something but then choose to suppress that consciousness. A good example is Theresa May speaking about the Irish border on 21 June 2016, just two days before the referendum: 'Just think about it. If we are out of the European Union with tariffs on exporting goods into the EU, there'd have to be something to recognise that, between Northern Ireland and the Republic of Ireland. And if you pulled out of the EU and came out of free movement, then how could you have a situation where there was an open border with a country that was in the EU and has access to free movement?' So she knew full well that a Brexit that involved leaving the customs union would create a hard border. And then, as prime minister, she insisted on the opposite: that a hard Brexit was perfectly compatible with no return of a hard border. She unknew what she had known.

Crass self-delusion is when you start with an ideological premise that you believe to be true even though it isn't and then draw apparently reasonable conclusions from it.

Thus, for example, David Davis sincerely believed the EU is just a front for German domination of Europe. Hence he also believed quite genuinely that the Brexit negotiations would be conducted not with Brussels but over a convivial Weissbräu and Schnitzel in Berlin and that frictionless trade would be decreed immediately because the German car manufacturers wished it so: sincerely fatuous self-delusion.

And then there's pig ignorance – the genuine hallmarked, unadulterated, slack-jawed, open-mouthed, village idiot variety in which the people who are in charge of the British state don't know stuff that anyone off *Gogglebox* could tell them. The Brexiteer MP Nadine Dorries admitted in effect that she didn't know what a customs union is. Her comrade Andrew Bridgen said last month: 'As an English person, I do have the right to go over to Ireland and I believe that I can ask for a passport. Can't I?'

Karen Bradley, the actual secretary of state for Northern Ireland, said: 'I freely admit that when I started this job, I didn't understand some of the deep-seated and deep-rooted issues that there are in

Northern Ireland. I didn't understand things like when elections are fought, for example, in Northern Ireland – people who are nationalists don't vote for unionist parties and vice versa.'

And last week the actual Brexit secretary, Dominic Raab: 'I hadn't quite understood the full extent of this, but if you look at the UK and look at how we trade in goods, we are particularly reliant on the Dover–Calais crossing.'

What's charming about this is that Bradley and Raab's ignorance is publicly self-proclaimed. It's not just that they didn't know basic stuff, it's that they didn't think there was anything shameful in not knowing. This is the purest form of ignorance: it's not just that you don't know, but that you don't even know that you're meant to know.

Historians will in time get to the bottom of the deliberate unknowing and the crass self-delusion. They can be charted. But this pure ignorance, innocent and unalloyed, is unfathomable. It will be impossible not to conclude that it was all part of some great strategic plan, that, if only we could plumb its depths, we could reveal the hidden truth of Brexit. How will they ever believe that the hidden truth is so asinine?

17 November 2018

The draft withdrawal agreement finally emerges: in the (highly likely)
event that the EU and the UK cannot agree a final trade deal that is
so frictionless that there is no need for a hard border in Ireland,
all of the UK will stay in something very like the customs union.
Northern Ireland would, in effect, remain in the single market, too.
It raises the fundamental question: why bother leaving at all?

In Ambrose Bierce's *The Devil's Dictionary*, published in 1911, we find the following definition: 'Road, n. A strip of land along which one may pass from where it is too tiresome to be to where it is futile to go.' A pithy summary of the draft UK withdrawal deal from the EU, which was finally published this week, might be: 'Brexit, n. A meandering road from where the British found it too tiresome for them to be to where it is futile for them to go.' The deal spells out what Brexit actually looks like: second-class membership of the European Union.

Faced at last with this reality, Britain has three options. It can retrace its steps and return to the ordinary tedium of EU membership and with it to its true status as a prosperous but unexceptional European country.

It can carry on towards the futility of a new arrangement patently worse than what it already has. Or it can wander off the road altogether, into the unmapped and treacherous mire of a no-deal Brexit.

Or, perhaps, there is a fourth option: it can stand in the middle of the road and, like the lisping Violet Elizabeth Bott in Richmal Crompton's great (and terribly English) *Just William* stories, declare 'I'll thcream and thcream 'till I'm thick'.

All hell broke loose on Thursday morning as it became ever clearer that Brexit has created a vacuum of political authority in the UK. Theresa May, in her stoical and stolid way, has tried to fill it by leading her country towards a realisation that there is no happy ending to this story, just a painful resignation to the least worst outcome.

But it looks like she will be drowned out by the Violet Elizabeths who believe that, if they scream and scream until they are sick, they will get their way in the end.

The strange thing about this moment is that it has been coming for almost a year. On the morning of Friday 7 December 2017, when the agreed draft of the withdrawal agreement was released after late-night talks in Brussels, I wrote about what it meant. It was not full of dazzling insight, merely a statement of the obvious logic of what had been agreed: 'After one of the most fraught fortnights in the recent history of Anglo-Irish relations, Ireland has just done Britain a favour of historic dimensions. It has saved it from the madness of a hard Brexit. There is a great irony here: the problem that the Brexiteers most relentlessly ignored has come to determine the entire shape of their project. By standing firm against their attempts to bully, cajole and blame it, Ireland has shifted Brexit towards a soft outcome. It is now far more likely that Britain will stay in the customs union and the single market. It is also more likely that Brexit will not in fact happen.'

The reasoning here was pretty basic. Theresa May had agreed that, in order to avoid a hard border, 'in the absence of agreed solutions, the United Kingdom will maintain full alignment with those rules of the Internal Market and the Customs Union which, now or in the future, support North–South co-operation, the all-island economy and the protection of the 1998 Agreement'.

These are the very same words, albeit in a slightly different order, that appeared in the final draft agreement released on Wednesday night. They are the kernel of the whole deal, and they were there in black and white almost a year ago.

Their meaning was not obscure: barring the magical solutions that the Brexiteers kept promising, the same rules of the single market and the customs union would continue to operate on both sides of the Irish border.

But May had also agreed, to appease the DUP, that 'the United Kingdom will ensure that no new regulatory barriers develop between Northern Ireland and the rest of the United Kingdom'.

You didn't need to be very good at mathematics to see what this meant: the Brexiteers could posture all they liked about 'global Britain' and the fabulous trade deals with the rest of the world that awaited them after the great leap out of the EU. But unless and until they could make these airy fantasies real, what Brexit actually means is a rather dismal and decidedly humdrum half-in/half-out existence to be maintained for an indefinite period and exited only if and when the EU agrees.

This in turn raised two big questions.

First, could the Brexiteers in fact come up with some other solution?

After all, two of their leaders, Boris Johnson and David Davis, were then senior members of Theresa May's cabinet (though you would not know it, from his subsequent complaints, Davis was actually in charge of the Brexit negotiations).

Since they had signed up to this deal in December, it seemed safe to assume that they knew what it meant and that they had a plan to avoid this backstop ever being used. The backstop is just an insurance policy – just because you have fire insurance you don't let your house burn down. The key words then were 'in the absence of agreed solutions' – or, as this week's final draft has it, 'unless and until an alternative arrangement implementing another scenario is agreed'.

This was a straightforward challenge to the Brexiteers: come up with some other way of achieving the same aims and they could render the backstop entirely irrelevant.

The second big question was: is it worth it?

If they could not come up with some other way of dealing with the Irish border question, the British were placing themselves in a position that is, from any point of view, frankly weird. They must bind themselves to the EU's rules, not just as they exist at the time of Brexit in March 2019 but on a 'dynamic' basis, meaning they would have to adopt all the new ones as they came in.

But they would have no say in the making of those rules. The glorious dream of a Great Escape from Brussels regulation would be over but the UK would not even enjoy its current status as a full and equal member of the EU. Words like 'vassalage', 'slave state' and 'colony' – all thrown out by Brexiteers (and indeed by Remainers) this week – are as ridiculous over the top as all of the Brexit's rhetoric has been. But there is no doubt that the whole exercise would amount to swapping first-class membership for the second-class status of a satellite locked into the orbit of Planet Europe.

Hence, it seemed obvious last December that it had become 'more likely that Brexit will not in fact happen'. No one with his or her country's interests at heart would wish it to go on the futile journey towards such a mediocre destiny.

To understand how we got to where we are this week, we have to grasp what happened to these two big questions over the last year: bugger all.

First, it became clear that Johnson, Davis and their allies simply didn't understand what they had signed up to, either in its form as a solemn international agreement that could not simply be torn up, or in its content and implications.

But even as the light of reality slowly pierced their mental fogs, they did nothing except complain about it. As the negotiations wound on and on, apparently going nowhere fast, it became clear that they had much more time to think and act than anyone had imagined this time last year. All they did with that time was to waste it – and indeed by making it more and more difficult for May to negotiate with a clear mandate, to waste everybody else's time, too.

On the first question – the alternative solution that would render the backstop irrelevant – we know what the hard Brexiteers have repeatedly said they want: a glorious Canada-style free trade deal between the EU and the UK that would deliver frictionless trade all round, including, of course, on the island of Ireland.

But there was and is an obvious problem with this: a Canada-style deal would not in fact get rid of the need for a hard Irish border. Very substantial regulatory checks would still be needed. The UK would be outside the customs union and the single market, and the Republic would be inside.

You can't move between different customs and market regimes without checks. And the only theoretical solution therefore would be to make those checks digital rather than physical. So the hard Brexiteers, to save their dream, had the best part of a year to come up with a serious proposal for what this technological solution would be and how it would work.

Here, then, is the House of Commons select committee on Northern Ireland, after extensive hearings on the issue, reporting in March this year: 'We have had no visibility of any technical solutions, anywhere in the world, beyond the aspirational, that would remove the need for physical infrastructure at the border. We recommend the Government bring forward detailed proposals, without further delay, that set out how it will maintain an open and invisible border. These proposals should provide detail about how customs compliance will be enforced if there is regulatory and tariff divergence between the UK and Ireland.'

At that time, Davis and Johnson were still members of the government to whom this recommendation was addressed by their own parliament. They were being asked to tell the House of Commons and the world precisely how their preferred technological solutions would move 'beyond the aspirational'. The best that Johnson ever came up with was his fatuous suggestion that the Irish border could be managed like the congestion charge in London.

So, there are really only two possibilities. Either there are no magical technological solutions and they were just fig leaves for a naked disregard of the implications of Brexit for Northern Ireland.

Or there are such solutions but the Brexiteers are too lazy to come up with them – even when their epic dreams of freedom from the EU are at stake.

As for the wider question – is it worth it? – things have taken an even more extraordinary turn. In his resignation letter in July, Boris Johnson wrote to May that 'we appear to be heading for a semi-Brexit, with large parts of the economy still locked in the EU system, but with no UK control over that system'. This was for once, entirely accurate. His further claim that 'we are truly headed for the status of colony – and many will struggle to see the economic or political advantages of that particular arrangement' was typically inflated, but let's assume, since he has repeated it this week, that he meant it.

What Johnson was saying was that his country was heading towards an arrangement that, as he explicitly put it more recently, is 'substantially worse than staying in the EU'. What would any patriot do in these circumstances? Johnson's younger brother Jo drew the obvious conclusion: go back to the people and ask them if this is what they really want.

But neither Boris Johnson nor any of the leading Brexit ultras has had the guts to follow this inexorable logic. They know they have led the UK towards a position that is 'substantially worse' than its current status. But they will neither accept responsibility for this nor support the only thing that could prevent it: a second referendum.

It is easier to keep pretending that, if only May had stuck it to the Europeans in the negotiations, the perfect have-cake/eat-cake Brexit would have been delivered. The critique of May by the Brexiteers is based on the old British rule for how to behave with the continentals: if they don't understand your language, shout louder: 'GIVE . . . US . . . CAKE!' It is easier to scream and scream until everybody is sick than to reflect on how and why the British public was sold a fantasy Brexit that had no possibility of ever becoming real.

Let them scream. And let responsible and patriotic politicians repeat over and over the five words that lie beneath each one of the 500-plus pages of the draft withdrawal deal: it is not worth it. The destination is not what it looked like in the travel agents' glossy brochures, all sunlit uplands and lush green pastures. It is grey and grim and horribly provincial.

Why not, before the flight takes off, turn around and go home?

19 November 2018

Brexit has been derailed, as it was always going to be, by the Irish question. And, amid the chaos, there is something oddly comfortable about this. Isn't that what the bloody Irish always do – disrupt an otherwise placid British polity with their hopelessly convoluted and unresolvable feuds? In 1922, reflecting on the way Ireland had dominated imperial politics even on the eve of the great catastrophe of the First World War, a rueful Winston Churchill told the House of Commons: 'It says a great deal for the power which Ireland has, both nationalist and orange, to lay their hands upon the vital strings of British life and politics, and to hold, dominate, and convulse, year after year, generation after generation, the politics of this powerful country.'

In this very familiarity lies the lure of self-delusion: Brexit would have been gloriously harmonious if only the orange and green disruptors hadn't laid their hands upon its vital strings and played on them their own eternally discordant tune. Already, among the Brexiteers, there is this self-exculpatory narrative: it wasn't us, m'lud, who brought our country to this disgraceful state. It was the usual suspects across the Irish Sea.

But beneath this tatty comfort blanket there are two starkly naked truths. They are not at all familiar – indeed they are startlingly new. They are so novel that the British system has been completely unable to fully recognise or process them. And it is this inability that has made the Brexit negotiations so tortuous and their outcome so miserable.

One of them has to do with a breathtaking shift in the balance of power. The other concerns the inability of the existing political culture to deal with the rise of English nationalism and its vast implications for the existence of the United Kingdom. To resort to the old familiar blame game is to miss what is really going on.

First, negotiations will always be determined by the balance of power. The very poor outcome of the Brexit negotiations for Britain reflects the realpolitik: there was a relatively small and isolated country up against a huge multinational bloc. This is the accustomed way of such things. But this time there has been a staggering variation: the places have changed. Britain, not Ireland, is the relatively small and isolated country. Ireland, not the British empire, has on its side the power of a huge multinational bloc.

This in itself is deeply disorienting. It is a new thing: the first time in 800 years of Anglo-Irish relations that Ireland has had more clout. No wonder the Brexiteers and the British government found it impossible for so long even to recognise this new reality. They operated – and some of them continue to operate – under the old rules, in which the game would be settled between the big powers, and the interests of a small country such as Ireland could be easily shoved aside. The Irish would get a few platitudes about peace but the real deal would be done between London and Berlin.

Yet it has not been like that. In part, this is because of simple arithmetic: Ireland is not isolated, it is part of a bloc of twenty-seven states. There is a basic lesson here for the Brexiteers: even a very small country inside the EU has more influence than a much larger country on the outside. In part, too, it is because of basic statecraft. The Irish government and diplomatic service, backed by a near-unanimous consensus in the Dublin parliament, had a very clear sense of where Ireland's vital national interest lay, and hence of what they needed to achieve.

There was one big thing Ireland could not get: Ireland cannot, much as it would love to, force the UK to stay in the EU. Given this reality, Ireland had three priorities. One was to avoid the reimposition of a hard border between Northern Ireland and the Republic. The second, to protect the 1998 Good Friday Agreement and the rights of everyone in Northern Ireland to continuing Irish – and therefore EU – citizenship. The third, to preserve the close personal and economic relationships on these islands by preserving the common travel area and keeping the UK as closely intertwined with the customs union and single market as possible.

Ireland got exactly what it wanted in the draft withdrawal agreement. This undoubtedly shaped the entire deal; but instead of whining about this, the Brexiteers might reflect that if they had been as clear about their aims and as skilful in achieving them, we might not all be in the current mess.

The other big new thing is that the force that has shaped one side of Anglo-Irish relations for centuries – British unionism – is visibly faltering. Visibly, that is, everywhere except in Westminster. There is a weird disjunction between what is actually happening in Brexit and the official narrative that has framed it. In part because of the quirk of fate that gave the balance of power at Westminster to a minority Northern Irish party, the DUP, Brexit has been shaped around a sentimental story of rallying behind what Theresa May calls the 'precious, precious union'.

But this is fundamentally phoney. There is overwhelming evidence that the English people who voted for Brexit do not, on the whole, care about the United Kingdom and in particular do not care about that part of it called Northern Ireland. Just last week, in a major Channel 4 survey, asked how they would feel if 'Brexit leads to Northern Ireland leaving the UK and joining the Republic of Ireland', 61 per cent of Leave voters said they would be 'not very concerned' or 'not at all concerned'.

These are two seismic shifts. Neither of them is caused by anyone in Ireland. They are products of the rise of English nationalism and of the great Brexit upheaval that has left Britain so deeply uncertain about its identity and its place in the world. To throw up one's hands in exasperation at the old familiar eruption of the Irish question is to miss the whole point of this moment – which is, of course, the English question.

20 November 2018

On Friday morning, trying to get away from Brexit, I got on an exercise machine to mortify the flesh. Fleeing the radio, I turned my iPod on to Shuffle.

Up popped a random song that I must have heard before but didn't remember: Nic Jones singing a ballad about the disillusioning aftermath of a nineteenth-century gold rush:

> Farewell to the gold that never I found
> Goodbye to the nuggets that somewhere abound
> For it's only when dreaming that I see you gleaming
> Down in the dark, deep underground.

So much for escaping Brexit. Only when dreaming could they see it gleaming. Brexit has always existed in the deep dark underground of the English reactionary imagination. And this is what gives it such a strange, hallucinatory quality.

It is hard sometimes to remind yourself that it is really happening, that we won't awake soon and turn to our partners and say, with Bottom in *A Midsummer Night's Dream*: 'I have had a dream – past the wit of man to say what dream it was. Man is but an ass if he go about to expound this dream.' But if you write about Brexit, this is what you become: an ass who goes about expounding someone else's dream.

At 5.30 on the morning of Friday 7 December 2017, I was sleeping soundly in Laurel Villa, a lovely guest house in Magherafelt, Co. Derry. In my dream, my mobile phone was buzzing angrily on a bedside table and some mad person with an English accent was saying things about Theresa May and Michel Barnier and Brussels and the withdrawal agreement.

I distinctly remember thinking that it was not a good thing that this stuff was invading my dreams, that, if my sleeping brain was conjuring these invasive images, I really needed to get a life. And then it struck me that I was in fact awake, that I had actually answered the phone and that someone in London really was asking me to go on the radio and comment on the deal that was emerging after all-night talks. I had experienced one of those eerie moments of befuddlement, probably no more than a second or two, where you hang between two states, one that is imaginary but seems real and one that is all too real but seems like it ought to be imaginary.

I've never quite been able to shake off the feeling that this is oddly apt: Brexit does have that weird logic of dreams, where things seem to flow from one another in some rational sequence but also leap from impossibilities to absurdities.

In July, when Boris Johnson with his usual propensity for walking away from the trouble he has created, resigned from Theresa May's cabinet, he lamented in his letter to her that: 'The dream is dying, suffocated by needless self-doubt.'

The metaphor is awkwardly mixed – how do you suffocate a dream? – but this dream language was striking nonetheless. It was echoed in a mournful editorial in the *Daily Telegraph* (where Johnson soon found a luxury lifeboat from which to whine about everybody else's failure to do what he had so ignominiously failed to accomplish himself), lamenting May's Chequers plan for Brexit: 'This was the weekend that the Brexit dream died… the dream has been dashed.'

I started to think about this dreaming: what is it that gleams in the deep dark underground of England's dreams? That great Anglo-Irish thinker Johnny Rotten told us, of course, that there is no future in England's dreaming. But what past is there then? It has to be a kind of counter-factual past, a landscape of dark myths. For how else can we explain the force that underlies Brexit: imaginary oppression?

At some level, in order to get to Brexit, a society has to dream itself into a condition that it never experienced. Indeed, it has to dream itself into exactly the opposite condition to the one it actually did experience.

A great colonial power has to imagine itself as having been colonised by the EU. A country still obsessed by the war it won – the Second World War – has to imagine itself as having been defeated (this time sneakily and stealthily) by the Germans. These are very, very strange things for a country to do to itself and they require some explanation. So after Boris Johnson's claim that 'the dream is dying' I decided to write a short book exploring what I call English Dreamtime, that mental landscape of heroic failure in which loss and grief are somehow more solid than success and contentment.

It became, I'm afraid, a little treatise on self-pity as a pleasurable indulgence, even as it leads to self-harm. In another kind of history this would seem neither here nor there, too far out to have any immediate connection to unfolding political and economic realities. In another, more rational time, dark fantasies of imaginary oppression would be confined to the pages of dystopian counter-factual thrillers. But right here and now, who can deny that English Dreamtime is a nightmare from which we are all struggling to awake?

24 November 2018

In February 2016, just as the Brexit referendum debate was getting going, the *Evening Standard* columnist Anthony Hilton wrote, 'I once asked Rupert Murdoch why he was so opposed to the European Union.

'That's easy,' he replied. 'When I go into Downing Street they do what I say; when I go to Brussels they take no notice.'

At the time Murdoch did not deny this but later that year, when his bid to take over all of Sky made his political power a sensitive subject, he insisted that: 'I have never uttered those words. I have made it a principle all my life never to ask for anything from any prime minister.'

Hilton, in turn, stood by his story and said the remarks were made in the early 1980s, when Hilton was city editor of Murdoch's *Times*.

Proof will never be available either way. But what is undoubtedly true is that, for the billionaire press barons used to wielding such immense influence in London, Brussels is infuriatingly impervious. The EU is largely indifferent to them.

That is one of the reasons they have promoted a relentless campaign of lies about it. The other reason is simpler: Brussels is boring. Most of what it does is pretty tedious – if you want to sell papers, making up luridly entertaining stories is much more effective than reporting the truth.

What we have to remember, though, is the astonishing reality that this lying is the bedrock of Brexit. Britain could not have been brought to its current state had a majority of its citizens not been convinced of one 'truth': that the EU has been interfering non-stop in every part of their daily lives, from the way they have sex to what they eat and drink, from what they wear to what happens to them when they die.

If the consequences were not so serious, there would be a pure fascination to this long-term propaganda campaign. It is made up, not of one big lie, but of an endless succession of little lies, each in itself so absurd as to seem harmless, yet cumulatively amounting to a profound distortion of public reality.

What was distorted was the English perception of influence. When Scots and Welsh people were asked in 2012 to identify which layer of government had most influence over their lives, just 8 per cent and 7 per cent respectively cited the EU. This was very much typical of responses in regions throughout Europe from Bavaria to Brittany.

The great exception was England, where 31 per cent of people cited the EU as the most influential layer of government. Why? Because the English have been lied to by most of their press and made to believe that 'Brussels' is a factory for mad schemes to meddle with their lives in ever more ludicrous ways.

What has made this lying so effective, though, is that, viewed piece by piece, it is comic, absurd and amusing, a saucy sitcom in which the implied soundtrack is a camp 'ooh-er, Missus!' and a mockney 'would you Adam-and-Eve it?'.

It is competitively inventive: the journalists get great fun out of thinking up the next outrage. And, at its most vivid, it conjures visual images that lodge in the brain.

For example, there is the *Sun* headline of 19 October 1994: 'EU to push for standard condom size'; 'Brussels is set to produce a standard Euro condom, whilst refusing to implement the subsidiarity principle so that Member States can take into account the different national characteristics of the male organ. The resultant compromise is simply not large enough to house British assets.'

There's the punning on 'member states', a boring Europhrase turned into a reference to the erect penis and an assertion that our blokes have bigger mickeys than the Europeans. But there's also an invitation to form in the mind a ridiculous image of the well-endowed Anglo-Saxon trying to fit himself into a tiny continental-size condom.

Or: 'Circus performer must walk tightrope in hard hat, says Brussels' (*The Times*, 23 July 2003): 'A tightrope-walker says that his career has been placed in jeopardy by legislation originating in Brussels which dictates that he must wear a hard hat to perform.'

Or: 'EU's plan to liquify corpses and pour them down the drain' (*Daily Express*, 8 July 2010).

Or: 'Shake 'n back – EU tells women to hand in worn-out sex toys' (*Sun*, 4 February 2004): 'Red-faced women will have to hand in their clapped-out sex toys under a new EU law. They must take back old vibrators for recycling before they can buy a new one.'

Or 'Get netted: we won't play Ena Sharples, fishermen storm at Europrats' (*Daily Star*, October 1992), the claim being that the EU was forcing fishermen while working at sea to wear hairnets like that sported by the *Coronation Street* character.

Or: 'Shellfish (especially mussels and oysters) must be given rest breaks and stress-relieving showers during journeys of over 50km' (*The Times*, 29 January 1996).

This is a distinctive genre of English fiction – one of the tragedies of Brexit is that it will become redundant. It covers a range of comic forms from seaside postcards (the condoms and sex toys) to *Python*esque gender confusions (the butch fishermen in their hairnets might as well be singing 'I'm a lumberjack and I'm okay') to the deliciously grotesque (those liquefied corpses) to Dadaist surrealism (oysters being given rest breaks).

But each of these vignettes – and hundreds more over the years – has a common quality: memorability. It creates a visual image that lodges in the brain. And it is the accumulation of these images that expresses itself in every vox pop on Brexit from an English market town. These repeated pantomimes have congealed into a history play.

When English people say they are sick of Brussels' interference, it is these crazy little yarns that are weighing on their minds. It is hard to think of anything quite like this in history, where perniciously effective propaganda has come in the form of such extravagant daftness.

It used to be claimed that Britain's destiny was shaped on the playing fields of Eton, but here we have a country in thrall to a different kind of sport, a game of knowingly outrageous mendacity, a decades-long spoofing contest in which journalists – to serve the interests of an elite of super-rich media owners – dared each other to come up with the most outlandishly ingenious fabrication.

And this is also why Brexit has proved so hard to give a rational shape to. If you turn political reality into a *Monty Python* sketch, it is very hard to take it seriously again, even when you really, really need to.

27 November 2018

The EU council approves the withdrawal deal. All May has to do now is get it through the House of Commons.

One thing you can say for the whole Brexit story is that it is not like buying a piece of furniture in IKEA. You don't have to construct the sardonic commentary yourself.

It comes with all the satirical metaphors fully assembled and ready for use.

You don't even have to say, 'Alexa, order me a mordantly derisive Brexit image.' It literally comes through your letterbox: here's Michael Palin's new book, *Erebus: The Story of a Ship*. It is about one of two vessels that featured in the most tragicomic episode of heroic failure in British history before Brexit, John Franklin's doomed expedition to find the Northwest Passage in 1848.

Franklin was, as Stephanie Barczewski puts it in her superbly illuminating history, *Heroic Failure and the British*, 'a failure on a monumental scale, but he nonetheless became one of the greatest Victorian heroes'. The horribly farcical outcome of Franklin's blithely optimistic voyage was not just that he and his men were lost but that enormous amounts of effort and money were expended trying to find them. By 1854 the Admiralty had spent £600,000 (hundreds of millions in today's values) looking for Franklin. 'Some of the rescue expeditions,' as Barczewski wryly notes, 'themselves had to be rescued.'

As a metaphor for Brexit, Franklin's voyage offered itself on a plate in September 2016 when, shortly after the referendum, his flagship, HMS *Terror*, suddenly emerged out of the Arctic wastes. But now Palin's book on Franklin's other ship, the *Erebus*, offers an even more apt image. Writing of the ship's approach to Antarctica on its previous voyages under James Ross, Palin is struck by 'how many of the names given to physical features mirrored the mental states of those who named them. 'Apart from Danger Islets, there is Cape Longing, Cape Disappointment, Delusion Point and Exasperation Bay...' Yet again, the metaphor arrives as part of Brexit's self-satirising service. No need for fiddly Allen keys.

Now that the deal is done (though very much undusted), HMS *Brexit* has drifted past Cape Longing. The pure yearning for an escape from the ordinary and unheroic present tense of British history has evaporated. There is no way back to that state of uncomplicated desire. But the expedition has now arrived simultaneously at Cape Disappointment, Delusion Point and Exasperation Bay – respectively Theresa May's deal, no deal and the demand for a second referendum.

Cape Disappointment is the deal that May concluded with the European Union on Sunday. It is not the worst place to land – the ground is solid and the place is perfectly habitable.

But as a destination it is deeply disappointing: a rather grey suburb of the downtown EU, too close to be its own location, too distant to be at the heart of things. The problem with it is not that it is particularly horrible but that it just doesn't seem worth the voyage. Why bother going all that way to end up in a worse spot than you were in already?

Delusion Point is where the hard Brexiteers – the DUP, Boris Johnson, Jacob Rees-Mogg, David Davis, Dominic Raab, and the rest of the motley crew – have stranded themselves.

It is, at this point, a wilful self-delusion. They stand on their bleak headland and, peering through the icy fog, insist that they can see the blessed isles of a sun-drenched Global Britain just over the horizon. If everybody will just go back and start again at Cape Longing, if they will all just believe hard enough in the destiny that awaits them, the Northwest Passage to freedom and prosperity will open up like the Red Sea did for Moses.

And everybody else has sailed into Exasperation Bay. There is an increasing sense of furious disbelief: how the hell did we end up here, stuck between the disappointed and the deluded?

How did we end up with a choice between May's second-class EU membership and the chaos of a no-deal Brexit? And: when will this all end? Are we really going to set our course for another decade of tedious negotiations and destabilising uncertainties? Can we not rethink this whole voyage before we reach the point of no return?

With an expedition as crazy as this one, it remains impossible to say where it will all finish. But a tentative guess is that the zealots will remain marooned on Delusion Point and become increasingly irrelevant. They have proved themselves to be cowardly and incompetent – they had power but lacked the guts and skill to use it. So the real struggle will be between the disappointed and the exasperated.

The disappointed have history on their side: the British entered the EU in 1973 with an air of gloomy resignation, so perhaps they will leave in the same mood, settling on Cape Disappointment because they have nowhere else to go. But there is still time for exasperation to be a force powerful enough to fill the sails and point the way back to sanity. What's needed is a properly led mutiny.

11 December 2018

Liechtenstein! As in the mountaintop microstate of 37,877 people. To appreciate the state that the whole Brexit project is likely to arrive at in the next few days, consider this: many of the sensible, decent people in British politics may by the end of this week be hoping to save their country by engineering an alliance with Liechtenstein. And not just an alliance either – what they're hoping for is an arrangement in which Liechtenstein will be an equal partner and will have a significant say in what Britain does in the future. And, to make all of this even more surreal, a say on what happens with the Irish border.

Nobody talks much about the Liechtenstein option of course. They talk instead of Norway, and indeed of Norway Plus. Norway is a serious kind of country – Vikings, trolls, Ibsen, resistance to the Nazis, oil money, Ada Hegerberg coolly brushing off the idiot who asked her about twerking. But Norway Plus is also Liechtenstein Plus. A rose by any other name may smell as sweet, but I'm not sure a Brexit Plan B by any other name would smell less like old cod.

There is, as we are about to see, no majority in the House of Commons for Theresa May's Brexit deal. And, as will also become apparent, there is no majority for exiting the EU with no deal either. Hence we will be left with two possibilities: a people's vote with the option of staying in, or Liechtenstein Plus. This second option is favoured by many thoughtful people who just want to get their country out of this mess with the least amount of damage. But I'm not quite sure they understand how bizarre it is and how much humiliation it involves.

Liechtenstein comes into it because Plan B involves the UK leaving the EU but joining (in fact rejoining) the European Free

Trade Association and, through EFTA, the European Economic Area (EEA). The EEA is a kind of adjunct to the EU single market – its members are in the single market but not part of the EU's political structures. And the EEA has three members: Norway, Iceland and Liechtenstein. They are equal partners – Liechtenstein has the same weight in these arrangements as Norway does. It has a veto over what happens in the EEA.

So first of all, Britain would have to get Liechtenstein's permission to join the EEA. And second, even if it did get into the EEA, it would need Liechtenstein's approval every time it wanted to do something important like having a new EU regulation transposed into EEA market rules. This is of particular interest to us because if we are to maintain an open border, this procedure would have to be done on a regular basis to ensure that market regulations in the North maintained their alignment with the South. A Liechtenstein veto could cause us big problems.

Now, let us push this just a little bit further. My vast knowledge of the Liechtenstein constitution tells me that it grants a veto over all laws to His Serene Highness Hans-Adam II, Prince of Liechtenstein, Duke of Troppau and Jägerndorf, Count of Rietberg, sovereign of the House of Liechtenstein and Knight of the Order of the Golden Fleece. So here we are: having found it utterly intolerable to be 'interfered with' by the EU and its Court of Justice, the British are wishing themselves into a situation in which their laws and regulations would be subject to the agreement of the hereditary owner of an Alp. Brexit finally becomes what J. G. Ballard, in refusing a CBE, called 'a Ruritanian charade'.

But the real humiliation here is not that this is likely to happen. It is that it won't happen because even Liechtenstein won't agree to it. Nobody – not Norway, not Iceland, not His Serene Highness Hans-Adam II – wants to be stuck with the Brexit mess. It has reached the point where in order to stay alive it has to swallow more and more absurdities. And it has led to the very thing it was supposed to overcome. It was fuelled by imaginary humiliation and it is creating the real thing. It was bad enough in the 1960s when Britain's desire to join Europe was rebuffed by General de Gaulle. Now it is getting the bird from Norway, Iceland – and Liechtenstein.

The truth, which will surely begin to dawn in the next few days, is that there is no way forward with the present deal, no chance of renegotiating it substantially even if Theresa May were replaced by Jeremy Corbyn, no real political support for a suicidal no-deal exit and not even a viable Liechtenstein option. A general election in which Corbyn's 'alternative' to May's deal is just another fantasy of leaving the EU while retaining all the benefits of membership cannot resolve anything because it cannot present a genuine choice. There is only one way out and that is to go back to the people. Those people know that every time they buy a train ticket they have to accept the terms and conditions. The terms and conditions of Brexit now seem to have been written by the Marx Brothers.

15 December 2018

Theresa May loses three Brexit-related votes in the Commons and survives a motion of no confidence from her own MPs. She is neither expelled from power nor capable of exercising it.

The political chaos in London has now created a zombie prime minister to go along with a zombie Brexit, a dead project that carries on in its own brainlessly destructive way. At this low point for British politics, it is almost impossible to remember a startling fact: this is the easy bit. The cacophonous discord created by the withdrawal agreement is just the overture to the mad opera of Brexit. Unless the UK gets itself out of this mess now, it will be set for at least a decade of conflict, uncertainty and instability.

Even if Theresa May somehow manages to force her deal through by delaying it until the only other option is a catastrophic no-deal departure on 29 March 2019, the tribulations will not be over. That highly unlikely achievement would not be the beginning of the end. It would be merely the end of the beginning. What would follow would be a world of trouble.

This has been the easy bit because the withdrawal agreement had to deal with just three things, helpfully summarised by Michel Barnier at the start of the process: people, money, Ireland. People means the mutual rights of EU and UK citizens currently living in each other's territories. There was always going to be a deal precisely because the needs are mutual. Money meant the divorce bill that the UK would have to pay to meet the commitments it has made to the EU budget. It is an emotive question and there was some ridiculous shape-throwing from the likes of Boris ('go whistle') Johnson. But, in the end, it's just money – a figure was not that difficult to agree.

And that left, of course, the dreary steeples of Fermanagh and Tyrone. In effect, the British had, in this phase of Brexit, one job to do: come up with a way to live up to its own guarantees that, whatever happens, there will be no reimposition of a physical infrastructure on the Border. It is important to bear in mind that these guarantees were not – as is now being widely suggested – forced on the British as part of an evil Irish plot to trap them in bondage to the EU.

Theresa May's own words, in her speech in Florence in September 2017, were: 'We will not accept any physical infrastructure at the border.' It was Britain, not just Ireland and not just the EU, that insisted a way had to be found to avoid in all circumstances this unacceptable outcome. It failed to do this, even after it agreed to the now-notorious backstop in December 2017. The all-party House of Commons committee on Brexit summed things up in its latest report, issued last weekend: 'In December 2017, we said that we did not see how it would be possible to reconcile maintaining an open Border on the island of Ireland with leaving the single market and customs union, which would inevitably make the Northern Irish Border the UK's customs and regulatory border with the European Union. Since then, we have seen no realistic, long-term proposals from the Government that would address this.'

May's government had one job to do and it didn't do it. That failure meant that the withdrawal agreement had to create a default in which the UK remains in a customs union with the EU and Northern Ireland remains effectively tied to the single market, too. Hence, as we've seen, all the Mayhem. The border question is admittedly a damnably difficult one, but the fact is that this one thing alone has led to the open collapse of political authority in the UK. So how, then, will Britain deal with the huge array of difficult questions that will arise if the Brexit show somehow stays on the road? For there can be no illusion that if only May can pull off the near-impossible trick of getting a withdrawal deal through parliament in January, all the rest of the way will be clear.

Consider the issue that, for May herself, is the single defining purpose of Brexit: control of immigration. She believes – and Jeremy Corbyn is in uncomfortable agreement with her on this – that ending freedom of movement is what Leave voters most desire and that if it is delivered, all the pain of Brexit will be justified. So where is the British government's post-Brexit immigration policy? On 17 October 2017, the then home secretary, Amber Rudd, told the home affairs committee at Westminster: 'We have our White Paper coming out on immigration by the end of the year [i.e. 2017].' On 28 March 2018, Rudd told the same committee: 'We have decided to wait until the migration advisory committee reports in its entirety in September this year to go forward with the policy and the White Paper after that.' On 10 July 2018, the current home secretary, Sajid Javid, told the committee: 'The timeframe that we set out... is a White Paper in the autumn followed by an immigration Bill early next year.' On 2 December 2018, Javid told the BBC, 'it's very unlikely to be published before the vote' on the withdrawal treaty.

Could it be that the white paper on immigration has not been published because the simplistic promises that were made as part of the pitch for Brexit cannot be fulfilled? It is extremely difficult to reconcile the needs of businesses and the NHS, the desire of non-European ethnic communities for more immigration from their countries of origin and the expectation of many Leave voters that immigration would simply cease after Brexit. As rhetoric meets reality, tensions will surely rise.

But the biggest problems will come if and when the British and the EU start to negotiate their future relationship. They have a political declaration but it is much thinner than anyone expected it to be even a year ago. Once those negotiations start, the British may become nostalgic for the good old days when there was only the Irish backstop to give them migraines. Instead of one big issue, they will have to deal with trade in goods and services; foreign policy, security and policing co-ordination; participation in EU agencies; agriculture; fisheries; data protection; labour mobility and the mutual recognition of professional qualifications; broadcasting; intellectual property; public procurement; consumer safety and standards; aviation; freight; energy; medicines; and scientific co-operation. And instead of dealing with the EU27 as a bloc, they will have to face twenty-seven countries, each with a veto and each with its own particular interests to defend. All of this – bear in mind – while also trying to construct a trade deal with, for example, Donald Trump.

And by July 2020, Britain will have to decide whether it wishes to ask for an extension of the transition period or accept the implementation of the backstop. The first will involve more payments to the EU and a longer period of rule-taking – cue explosions of outrage. The second is already imprinted in political consciousness as a disaster. So more political chaos. And in principle this could be repeated annually as the same choice returns until a final settlement is reached.

This, remember, is the benign scenario, in which the withdrawal agreement somehow passes through Westminster. The alternative – no deal – is much, much worse. Brexit is not leading Britain through the current political desert to a land of milk and honey, but through one desert into another. The only rational course of action is to stop the caravan while there is still time.

16 December 2018

*Looking in at Britain from a country that has a
very recent experience of the potential cost of
a political breakdown, it is hard to fathom the
wilful descent into institutional chaos.*

Vincent Gookin, the seventeenth-century English colonist in
Ireland, wrote ruefully that 'the unsettling of a nation is an
easy work; the settling of a nation is not'. One way to understand why the Irish question has been so fatal for the Brexit project
is to think about two islands and their degrees of unsettlement.

For Britain, the Brexiteers have done the easy work of unsettling
a nation. Both parts of Ireland, meanwhile, have been involved in
the much harder business of settling a nation long torn apart by
deep divisions of allegiance and aspiration. The great paradox of
this moment is that the imperative of not endangering the fragile
settlement on one island is profoundly unsettling for the other.

What is so striking about the political chaos at Westminster is
the sheer wilfulness of it all. It is not a response to a plague or a
famine, a war or an invasion. Britain's crisis has deep causes, of
course, though most of them (the effects of austerity, the loosening
of the union) are self-generated. But at the political level most of
it seems to be happening purely for its own sake. It is all gestures
and poses.

The whole Brexit project has been, in Gookin's terms, easy work.
Make up lies about the European Union, throw patriotic shapes, get
a smugly overconfident prime minister to call a referendum whose
dynamics he does not understand, tell more lies, make promises
you don't believe in yourself, use stolen Facebook data to target

voters with xenophobic images, tell everybody that they will have all the benefits of membership with none of the costs. Easy work, all of it: no plans, no complexities, no responsibilities.

On the morning of the referendum result in June 2016, the image that came into my head was that amazing trick that some people can do of whipping a tablecloth away while leaving all of the dishes and cutlery in place. Except the trick was being tried by a drunk. The idea was that a whole layer of politics that had been there for forty-five years – the EU – could be whipped away and yet all the others – government, parliament, the law, the union itself – would not be upset. It was never going to happen. The trick, if it could be done at all, required a level of dexterity and co-ordination far beyond the capacities of the cack-handed and cock-eyed Brexiteers. Instead of gasps of amazement, there was always going to be the cacophonous din of tumbling tableware.

Yet there's another paradox: only a country that does not really know what the collapse of political authority looks like would play this game. To witness the wilful recklessness of seeking to plunge Britain into a Tory leadership contest at this moment of national crisis is to watch people playing with fire because they have never really been burned. Modern Britain has had its troubles but politically speaking it has been remarkably stable. A two-party system has survived. Political violence is rare. Even the nationalist movements in Scotland and Wales are civic, rational and democratic.

But what we see from the outside in the past three years is a country pushing its luck. There seems to be an assumption that the political system can discredit itself as much as it likes with no long-term consequences for the very idea of political order. All we outsiders, scarred as we are by very different memories, can say is: good luck with that.

There is, of course, a part of the UK that has had no such luck. Northern Ireland's Troubles are part of the wider story that Gookin was alluding to in the seventeenth century: the unsettling of Ireland that, as he suspected, would not be so easy to undo.

We talk casually of the Belfast Agreement of 1998, also known as the Good Friday Agreement, as a 'settlement', but the word has a much deeper resonance. The settling process has been going on for a long time now: we're just marking the centenary of the 1918 Westminster general election in which Sinn Féin won a majority of the Irish seats, leading to secession, guerrilla warfare, partition, independence and the resurgence and eventual ending of the Troubles.

This settling has not been easy work. It has been built on terrible human suffering. It has demanded of politicians (very much including British ones) patience, intelligence, planning, compromise, creativity and the acceptance of personal moral responsibility for the consequences of what is done and not done.

A big part of this process has been that most delicate, precious and powerful of feelings: trust. The settling of Northern Ireland has been possible because Britain and Ireland came to trust each other. By working together on the peace process (and, ironically, as very close allies in the EU), Irish and British leaders and diplomats came to believe implicitly in each other's good faith. One of the tragedies of Brexit is that this faith has been broken.

There is, in Brexitland, a sense of outrage that the Irish government has not taken Britain at its word when it says that there will never be a return to a hard border in Ireland. The message all along has been: trust us, it will be fine, no need for a legally binding guarantee. But would you trust Theresa May who swore by her red lines until she crossed every one of them and who insisted she would not call an election until she did? Does anyone on earth trust Boris Johnson, who was foreign secretary for much of this period and has ambitions to be the prime minister after Brexit? Could anyone have faith that David Davis would even understand what he had signed up to, let alone implement it?

But this is not just about individual politicians. The bigger question is: would you trust the settling of your nation to a process that is so utterly unsettling its own? Trust in political assurances requires some reasonable sense of predictability and security. You have to know that there are stable democratic institutions capable of keeping promises and seeing things through. Would anyone looking at the goings-on in Westminster over the past fortnight seriously believe that Britain is a settled democracy?

22 December 2018

Before we declare a Christmas truce in the Brexit wars, let's clear away one large piece of debris. In Britain, and even in Ireland, a narrative has taken hold: the border problem was not a big issue until Leo Varadkar replaced Enda Kenny as taoiseach in June 2017. The issue would all have been settled amicably if a callow new administration had not come to power in Dublin. Varadkar was insecure, looking over his shoulder at Sinn Féin and determined not to be outflanked. So the Irish became unreasonable, egged the EU on to take a hard line and created the backstop. They were too successful for their own good – the backstop has made an acceptable deal impossible. There will be no deal and it will all be Ireland's fault.

This narrative – popular among the Brexiteers, in the DUP, in the Tory party and in the right-wing press – feeds the larger story that nothing that has happened is their fault. It takes the self-pity that is at the heart of the Brexit project a stage further: bad enough being tyrannised by the Germans, but poor little England is now being bullied by the Irish. Nicholas Watt, political editor of BBC's *Newsnight* wrote recently of a conversation with a Tory grandee who told him: 'We simply cannot allow the Irish to treat us like this... The Irish really should know their place.'

This kind of language brings out the worst in us all, so let's try to keep this civil and factual. First, a little chronology. Leo Varadkar became taoiseach on 14 June 2017. Was the border question a crucial issue before then? Yes, it was.

Almost five months earlier, on 17 January, Theresa May made her now infamous speech on Brexit at Lancaster House, in which she told the Brexit ultras everything they wanted to hear. They agree with every word of it and want her to return to it.

And in this speech, May said: 'Nobody wants to return to the borders of the past, so we will make it a priority to deliver a practical solution as soon as we can.'

So, of course, the Anglo-Irish mood music was good at this stage because here was the British prime minister saying clearly that she was prioritising a 'practical solution' to the border question and that it would be delivered soon.

Also while Kenny was still in charge, another big thing happened. On 29 April 2017, a month after May triggered the Article 50 process for leaving the union, the EU issued its riding instructions to its chief negotiator, Michel Barnier.

The instructions were clear on the centrality of the border question to the withdrawal talks: 'Continuing to support and protect the achievements, benefits and commitments of the Peace Process will remain of paramount importance. In view of the unique circumstances on the island of Ireland, flexible and imaginative solutions will be required, including with the aim of avoiding a hard border…'

So both sides knew and accepted by the end of April 2017 that the border question was 'a priority' and of 'paramount importance'. And both sides fully understood that dealing with the border in the context of the peace process meant one thing above all: no physical infrastructure.

Don't take my word for this. Here is Theresa May in Florence in September 2017, in another speech that had the full backing of the Brexit ultras: 'We and the EU… have both stated explicitly that we will not accept any physical infrastructure at the border. We owe it to the people of Northern Ireland – and indeed to everyone on the island of Ireland – to see through these commitments.'

So what actually happened after June 2017? It was not the change of government in Dublin that suddenly made the border question central to the withdrawal process. What really happened is something much less dramatic: nothing. May had said that her government owed it to everyone on the island to see through the commitments she (and her government, including Boris

243

Johnson and David Davis) had made to 'everyone on the island of Ireland'.

But the British did damn all. Again, don't trust my interpretation on this.

The House of Commons all-party committee on Brexit noted just two weeks ago: 'In December 2017, we said that we did not see how it would be possible to reconcile maintaining an open border on the island of Ireland with leaving the Single Market and Customs Union… Since then, we have seen no realistic, long-term proposals from the Government that would address this.'

But it is not just that the British didn't follow through on their commitment to produce a 'practical solution' in 2017. They didn't even try. The staggering fact is that even though they knew that the border was the key to Brexit, they left it out of their Brexit planning.

In a report, the public accounts committee at Westminster noted dryly that, 'Some incredibly important issues have not yet even been considered by the [border planning] group; for example arrangements for the 300 crossing points across the land border in Ireland are currently outside the scope of the group.'

And this never really changed: the British have to date not produced a single credible proposal for how they intend both to leave the customs union and avoid any border infrastructure in Ireland. The only logical conclusion is that the British don't in fact believe that there is a technological solution. For if they did, why would they worry about the backstop? If the problem can be made to go away by the use of ingenious technology, then the backstop will never be used. Conversely, if you're so worried about the backstop being activated, it can only be because you don't believe your own high-tech 'solutions'.

So how could any Irish government of any hue simply take it on trust that the British would keep the commitments they had so freely given? It simply didn't matter who was in power in Dublin. If the British either would not or could not come up with credible proposals to deal with what they knew to be the single biggest obstacle to Brexit, there were only two things any Irish government could do. It could ask for a legally binding assurance.

Or it could 'know its place' and shut up about its own vital national interests.

TIMELINE

8 January 2019: In another defeat for Theresa May, MPs approve an amendment that limits the government's financial powers in the event of a no-deal Brexit.

9 January 2019: In a further setback to the prime minister ahead of the start of five days of Brexit debates, the Speaker of the House of Commons allows an amendment to the business motion by Dominic Grieve, which is passed by 308 votes to 297. This amendment means that if the government loses the 'meaningful vote' on 15 January 2019, the prime minister will then have to present a new 'Plan B' Brexit plan within three days. The House of Commons then commences the Brexit debates.

15 January 2019: Day five of the Brexit debates on the EU Withdrawal Agreement. The 'meaningful vote' takes place, with the government suffering a huge defeat, losing the vote by a majority of 230 (with 202 voting in favour of the prime minister's Brexit deal and 432 against).

5 January 2019

At some point in 2019, British troops will withdraw from Germany. This has nothing to do with Brexit. The British army announced in 2015 that over the course of 2019 its remaining field army units will return home from their bases in Paderborn, Sennelager, Bielefeld and Gütersloh. The so-called British Forces Germany headquarters will shut up shop, leaving only a small number of specialists to work with their German counterparts.

The moment will be poignant: the Second World War will be over and the same, in one sense, will be true of the Cold War. These bases were established in 1945 by the invading British Army of the Rhine and became semi-permanent during the long stand-off with the Soviet Union.

In itself, this withdrawal may be of minimal significance – certainly when compared with the prospect of a much larger British withdrawal from Europe. But it reminds us of the very long afterlife of the catastrophic wars of the first half of the twentieth century.

In 1919, Europe, the United States and the British empire imagined they were entering a post-war world. In 2019, we could all say the same, but not with any great joy. It is not just that we know from a century ago that 'post-war' can turn into 'inter-war'. It is that we actually need the memory of those wars to stay alive. They are still the best warnings we have about our collective capacity to manufacture catastrophe.

Politically speaking, the two most powerful words in the English language in recent years have been 'back' and 'again': Take Back Control; Make America Great Again. Yet the projects associated with these words – Brexit and Donald Trump's presidency – have been marked by a profound ignorance of history. They evoke the past as an idyll to which the people can return.

There was, allegedly, a Britain that once stood alone and controlled its own destiny. Not so, of course – at no point since Britain was formed in 1707 has it ever not been part of a much larger political and economic entity, Empire first, then the EU. There was, allegedly, a past in which America was 'great' – a simple concept that suppresses the history of slavery and racial oppression and of disastrous neo-imperial adventures like the Vietnam War.

Yet 'back' and 'again' are not in themselves the wrong words. Even as we look forward to 2019, we must survey a political landscape in which it is broadly true that if we do not go back to the searing memories of modern history, we may have to endure it all again.

The paradox of our time is that because we forget the past, we are in some ways slipping back into it. We forget that we have had gilded ages before in which the super-rich were able to think of themselves as a separate species of humanity. We forget that we have created environmental disasters before and that they have led civilisations to collapse.

We forget that we have seen demagogues ride to power on the promise of protecting Us from Them and that they have led both Us and Them to disaster. We forget that we have, in the First World War, for example, allowed our technology to far outrun our moral capacity to control it. And so we are in the midst of all of these things again.

In 2019, as in every recent year, there will be a lot at stake. The Brexit project will have to take some kind of shape very early in the year. The extraordinary indulgence in time-wasting has run out of road, and both relatively benign (a second referendum) and utterly malign (no deal) scenarios remain as live possibilities.

In the United States, the Mueller inquiry will have to report its findings on the depth or otherwise of collusion between Trump's campaign and Vladimir Putin's Russia. If Trump, in response, escalates his trade war with China, there could be severe global implications.

In the EU, the elections to the European Parliament in May will be arguably the most important in the history of the EU. If the far right continues its recent advances with an anti-EU, anti-immigrant nationalist agenda, the repercussions for the whole European project could be huge.

If the implementation programme for action on climate change agreed in December at Katowice – itself widely regarded as insufficient – does not take rapid hold, the chances of environmental catastrophe will continue to rise.

A lot will depend on 'back' and 'again'. What is the alternative to a reactionary and destructive use of these words? Many in Europe and the US see the alternative as just going back again to the way things were before Brexit, before Trump, before the rise of the far right.

Let's pretend that none of it ever happened. Let's see these phenomena as essentially freakish aberrations, temporary flaws in the pattern of a neoliberal global norm. In the case of both Brexit and Trump, this approach is superficially tempting because the chances are that in 2019 both of those projects will be undermined by the flaws that were present at their moments of triumph in 2016 – Brexit's false promises; Trump's very real Putinism. At a stretch, the same case could be made even in the EU – the corruption and incompetence of the far right becomes even more visible as it gains more power, so perhaps it will destroy itself.

But hoping that the reactionary projects blow themselves up and that the people who supported them come to their senses and go back to believing in the old status quo is delusional. The old status quo, as it existed roughly between the end of the Cold War and the great banking collapse of 2008, was unsustainable. It created economic inequalities incompatible with democracy; it fed a feral form of casino capitalism that was inherently unstable; and it could not deal with the great challenge of climate change.

So 'back' and 'again' has to mean instead a return to the memories of disaster and to the egalitarian values and serious governance that came from them.

There is a decent chance that 2019 may be the year in which we see, at least in the US and Britain, decisive moments of disenchantment with the reactionary hopes of 2016. But it will then be all the more vital that this disenchantment is not allowed to curdle into something even more toxic.

Disillusionment must be met, not with more illusions that there is a sustainable reality to which we can simply return, but with the sober hope for a better future that is the only guarantor that we do not repeat the past.

8 January 2019

We need to talk about political violence. In Britain's current crisis, it is hinted at, alluded to, occasionally threatened. It has a spectral presence, as for example last week, when foreign secretary Jeremy Hunt claimed that 'the social consequences… of not going ahead and leaving the EU on March 29th, as we've been instructed to do, would be devastating'. But it also has a very specific resonance: different ways of thinking about political violence are at the heart of the divide between Britain and Ireland and thus of the failure of the whole Brexit project.

In less than five years, Britain has experienced two attempted revolutions, two upheavals of the kind that, historically speaking, are typically associated with mass violence. One of these is the demand for Scottish independence, culminating in the referendum of 2014. The other is Brexit. Each occupies the emotion-soaked terrain of belonging and identity, that treacherous landscape of minefields and quicksand. And each has been remarkably peaceful. There was no serious violence in Scotland. Brexit has resulted in the murder of an MP, Jo Cox, and has indirectly fed a rise in attacks on 'foreigners'. But from any global or historical viewpoint, it looks unusually pacific.

If you're Irish and you say this to Scots or English people, they look at you in puzzlement. They measure these things by a different scale. Scots were deeply upset that people were abusing each other online during the referendum and that there were some instances of politicians being shouted at in the street. English people are devastated that they can't talk about Brexit at the Christmas dinner table without risking a row. I do not want to minimise the genuine unpleasantness of this discord, but – how shall we put this? – it's not Bloody Sunday or Bloody Friday or Enniskillen or Greysteel or La Mon or the Shankill Butchers.

To understand the roots of this difference, just consider what is blithely known in Britain as the Glorious Revolution of 1688. Look it up on Wikipedia and the first sentence reads: '"The Bloodless Revolution" redirects here.' This is the last great constitutional revolt within Britain itself and it is remembered as 'bloodless'. Which, for England, it mostly was. But in Ireland, the Bloodless Revolution is the Williamite Wars, a murderous international conflict fought on Irish soil, culminating in the Battle of the Boyne and the Battle of Aughrim. Not only was it extremely violent but that violence has been antagonistically encoded in Irish public memory.

Of course, the United Kingdom has in fact experienced a very bloody civil conflict within its own territory much more recently. But the British largely managed to categorise the Troubles in Northern Ireland as a foreign war of the kind they were used to rather than an internal affair. The Irish of all hues were, and still are, Over There. Even appalling atrocities on English soil such as the Birmingham and Guildford bombings never really altered the sense that the Troubles were, and remain, a matter of the bloody Irish killing each other as usual.

The British expect revolutions to be bloodless; the Irish don't. But as with so much else, Brexit plays strange games with these perceptions. Objectively, by far the biggest danger of violence resulting from this half-cocked revolution is in Ireland. Thus, for example, a thousand English and Scottish police officers are currently being given special training to prepare them to be sent to Northern Ireland to keep order in the event of a no-deal Brexit. But in the rhetoric of the Brexiteers, this reality is reversed: the threat of political violence in Ireland is non-existent and anyone alluding to it is scaremongering. But they themselves are free to threaten political violence in England if Brexit is stopped. History is turned on its head: Northern Ireland is apparently so stable that there are no risks but England is a powder keg ready to explode.

At work here is the paradox that the less you know about what internal political violence is really like, the freer you are to wave your rhetorical sword. It is the very belief that revolutions are naturally bloodless that allows Nigel Farage, for example, to boast to a cheering audience in Southampton that if Brexit is obstructed, he would personally 'don khaki, pick up a rifle and head for the front lines'. Playing soldiers is a childish game for English nationalists. They can threaten doom because they are actually conditioned by history to be blithely optimistic – in the land of bloodless revolutions, the blood will always be theatrical ketchup.

We in Ireland know different – as, in different ways, do most European countries. We have had no such luck as Britain has enjoyed for centuries, and thus we do not want to push our luck. Even twenty years after the Belfast Agreement, the North is nowhere near being over the trauma of the Troubles. The memory of blood is still in its blood. But the dark irony of this moment in the history of these islands is that we could again see something like the great divide of 1688, a revolution that is bloodless in England but for which Ireland has to pay the violent price.

15 January 2019

The 'meaningful vote' on the withdrawal
agreement is due today.

Today is supposed to be historic, one of the most epic moments in the long life of the Westminster parliament. So why does it not feel like that? The tabling by a British prime minister of an agreement on the terms of withdrawal from the European Union ought to feel much bigger than this. Some of the reasons are obvious enough: the sheer tedium of the journey; the tragicomic chaos that undermines the desired solemnity; the lack of any great drama attaching to the immediate outcome of the vote; the knowledge that this decisive moment will in reality decide nothing.

But there is a deeper contradiction at work: Brexit seeks to make history by unmaking history. Like all revolutions, it imagines a Year Zero, a point at which time's great clocks are set to the beginning and all unwanted histories are erased. In the imagination of its leaders and supporters, history both ended and began on 23 June 2016: a history of humiliation and submission was over and done with, and a new history of self-assertion and liberation began.

We have to remember what today was supposed to be like, what those who have brought their country to this pass had in their heads three years ago. After what Nigel Farage hailed as Independence Day when the referendum results came in, today should have been the formal declaration of *independence* by parliament. Presumably, when they pictured the scene, what they saw was an overwhelmingly united House of Commons, its members – apart from a few snarling Scots, malcontents and traitors – on their feet, tears streaming down their faces, singing 'Rule, Britannia' in lusty chorus. That's what making history is supposed to be like.

There are two problems, however. One is that, as with everything else, Brexit is self-contradictory in its idea of history. On the one side it proposes a revolutionary break with the past. On the other, the word that conjured it into being was 'back', as in Take Back Control. It is full, not just of nostalgia, but of pseudo-history. It is an old curiosity shop of fake antiques: the Dunkirk spirit, the Blitz spirit, Agincourt, Henry VIII, Winston Churchill, the Spanish Armada... When you listen to the ardent Leavers, what they say about a no-deal Brexit is not that they are really convinced it is a good thing but that the English will endure the suffering and get through it because that is what they have always done.

Fifty years ago, in 'A Poem in Praise of the British', the Scottish poet Douglas Dunn chillingly – and presciently – captured the strange afterlife of all this zombie history: 'The archivist wears a sword and clipped moustache. / He files our memories, more precious than light, / To be of easy access to politicians of the Right, / Who now are sleeping, like undertakers on black cushions, / Thinking of inflammatory speeches and the adoring mob...'

The other problem is, of course, that history can never be ditched. It can, perhaps, be transcended, which is what we on this island have been trying to do. But it cannot be erased. In the imagination of the Brexiteers, the great English balloon will ascend when the ropes connecting it to the ground of history are untied and the complications of the recent past are jettisoned like sandbags. Up, up and away! – floating above the entire past forty-six years of being merely a normal European country, into the blue skies of an exceptional destiny.

One of those commitments is the Belfast Agreement. To adopt a term from medical insurance, Northern Ireland is a pre-existing condition of the British state. It is just as much British history as Agincourt and Dunkirk are – and, right now, much more so. And it exerts a gravitational pull that cannot be escaped. Karl Marx said that we make our own history, but we do not do so in circumstances of our own choosing. The basic problem of Brexit is that it embraces the first part of this dictum while ignoring the second. The circumstances in which the history of these islands is being made include both forty-five years of common membership of Europe and thirty years of the Troubles. Those years cannot be wished away.

And so climax sags into anti-climax. With one bound our hero is not free: if you try to leap when one foot is snagged on the briars of pre-existing conditions, you fall on your face. And afterwards? Where can Britain go but 'back': back to its actual here-and-now of complexities, compromises and ambiguities not so different from anyone else's. There is still much history to be made, for Britain, Ireland and Europe. But it cannot begin with fantasies.

18 January 2019

The sense of anarchy deepens as a crisis of authority unfolds. Increasingly, it seems that none of this is about the European Union. It is about the other union, the UK and its argument with itself.

A t least the *Sun* thrives on chaos. The savage parliamentary mauling of Britain's withdrawal agreement with the European Union allowed Rupert Murdoch's pet tabloid to unveil on Wednesday morning a front page of grandly gleeful malevolence. Under the headline 'Brextinct' it conjured a creepy chimera of Theresa May's head pasted on to the body of a dodo. But the thing about such surreal pictures is that it is not easy to control their interpretation. From the outside, this one seemed to suggest much more than the immediately intended message that both May and her deal are politically dead. When, it prompted one to ask, did Brextinction really happen? Was this strange creature ever really alive or was it not always a grotesquely Photoshopped image of something else, a crisis of belonging that has attached itself to the wrong union? Do the events of this week point us, not towards the EU, but to the travails of a radically disunited kingdom?

The dodo, after all, may be proverbially dead but it has a vivid afterlife in that great trawl of the English unconscious, Lewis Carroll's *Alice's Adventures in Wonderland*. It is the Dodo, when various characters have fallen into a pool of tears, who suggests how they might dry themselves – the Caucus-race. 'There was no "One, two, three, and away", but they began running when they liked, and left off when they liked, so that it was not easy to know when the race was over. However, when they had been running half an hour or so, and were quite dry again, the Dodo suddenly called out, "The race is over!" and they all crowded round it, panting, and asking, "But who has won?"'

This seems, this week more than ever, a perfect description of the state to which British politics has been reduced – a lot of frantically anarchic running overseen by a defunct creature, the Brextinct dodo. And who has won? Carroll's Dodo, of course, decrees: 'Everybody has won, and all must have prizes.' Having emptied Alice's pockets to provide rewards for everyone else, the Dodo solemnly presents her with the only thing that's left: her own thimble. 'We beg your acceptance of this elegant thimble.'

The Brexit game is patently not worth the thimble to be presented at the end of it. Yet in Theresa May's humiliation on Tuesday there were prizes for almost everybody else: a glimpse of opportunity for her rivals in cabinet; a revival of their sado-masochistic no-deal fantasies for the zealots; the hope of a second referendum for Remainers; proof of the near-collapse of the Westminster order for nationalists; the hope of a general election for Jeremy Corbyn. But in truth nobody has won anything – it is a losing game all round.

For all of this is the afterlife of dead things. One of them is Brexit itself. When did Brextinction occur? On 24 June 2016. The project was driven by decades of camped-up mendacity about the tyranny of the EU, and sold in the referendum as a fantasy of national liberation. It simply could not survive contact with reality. It died the moment it became real. You cannot free yourself from imaginary oppression. Even if May were a political genius – and let us concede that she is not – Brexit was always going to come down to a choice between two evils: the heroic but catastrophic failure of crashing out; or the unheroic but less damaging failure of swapping first-class for second-class EU membership. These are the real afterlives of a departed reverie.

If the choice between shooting oneself in the head or in the foot is the answer to Britain's long-term problems, surely the wrong question is being asked. It is becoming ever clearer that Brexit is not about its ostensible subject: Britain's relationship with the EU. The very word Brexit contains a literally unspoken truth. It does not include or even allude to Europe. It is British exit that is the point, not what it is exiting from. The tautologous slogan Leave Means Leave is similarly (if unintentionally) honest: the meaning is in the leaving, not in what is being left or how.

Paradoxically, this drama of departure has really served only to displace a crisis of belonging. Brexit plays out a conflict between Them and Us, but it is surely obvious after this week that the problem is not with Them on the Continent. It's with the British Us, the unravelling of an imagined community. The visible collapse of the Westminster polity this week may be a result of Brexit, but Brexit itself is the result of the invisible subsidence of the political order over recent decades.

It may seem strange to call this slow collapse invisible since so much of it is obvious: the deep uncertainties about the union after the Good Friday Agreement of 1998 and the establishment of the Scottish parliament the following year; the consequent rise of English nationalism; the profound regional inequalities within England itself; the generational divergence of values and aspirations; the undermining of the welfare state and its promise of shared citizenship; the contempt for the poor and vulnerable expressed through austerity; the rise of a sensationally self-indulgent and clownish ruling class. But the collective effects of these interrelated developments do seem to have been barely visible within the political mainstream until David Cameron accidentally took the lid off by calling a referendum and asking people to endorse the status quo.

What we see with the lid off and the fog of fantasies at last beginning to dissipate is the truth that Brexit is much less about Britain's relationship with the EU than it is about Britain's relationship with itself. It is the projection outwards of an inner turmoil. An archaic political system had carried on even while its foundations in a collective sense of belonging were crumbling. Brexit in one way alone has done a real service: it has forced the old system to play out its death throes in public. The spectacle is ugly, but at least it shows that a fissiparous four-nation state cannot be governed without radical social and constitutional change.

European leaders have continually expressed exasperation that the British have really been negotiating not with them, but with each other. But perhaps it is time to recognise that there is a useful truth in this: Brexit is really just the vehicle that has delivered a fraught state to a place where it can no longer pretend to be a settled and functioning democracy. Brexit's work is done – everyone can now see that the Westminster dodo is dead. It is time to move on from the pretence that the problem with British democracy is the EU and to recognise that it is with itself. After Brextinction there must be a whole new political ecosystem. Drop the dead dodo, end the mad race for a meaningless prize, and start talking about who you want to be.

22 January 2019

Before Christmas I was talking to a middle-aged man in Magherafelt, Co. Derry. He was from a Catholic background and was active locally in the SDLP. Inevitably, the talk turned to Brexit and the economic harm it would do. But he pointed out that in the 1970s, the Republic was an economic 'basket case' while standards of living were much better north of the border, even for people like him. 'And yet,' he said, 'if someone had given me the chance to vote for a united Ireland, I'd have done it in a heartbeat. I'd have taken the hit. So I understand where people are coming from in England. It's not all about the economy, you know.'

He was right, of course, and there is no chance of escaping from the current crisis for these islands until we all recognise that economics arguments will not change many minds. In the 1990s every wannabe politician or spin doctor in the settled democracies watched the brilliant fly-on-the-wall documentary on Bill Clinton's campaign in 1992, *The War Room*. In it, the campaign manager James Carville sticks a sign on the wall, intended to focus the minds of the staff: 'It's the economy, stupid!' It became, of course, conventional wisdom. In his gripping book on the Brexit campaign, *Unleashing Demons*, David Cameron's chief strategist Craig Oliver writes, 'Our campaign was based on the simple proposition that electorates don't vote against their own pockets. That view is summed up best in the closest thing to an iron law in politics, James Carville's realisation when running the first Clinton presidential election campaign, "It's the economy, stupid!"'

The big problem is with the 'stupid' bit. It is, of course, never not the economy: people's economic conditions and expectations will always shape their lives and those lives will always shape their political attitudes. But it is not 'stupid' to vote for other reasons, too. Some people are indeed ignorant or deluded or misled about the economic consequences of their votes. And some people know very well that they are risking their own economic wellbeing but feel it is a price worth paying anyway.

Ireland is a perfect case in point. For about the first seventy years of Irish independence, the decision to leave the United Kingdom was – on a cold calculation – a mistake. Most ordinary Irish people were worse off than their UK counterparts – that's why so many of them emigrated to Britain. And yet very few of them would have voted to go back into the UK. We should remember this when we look across the water and wonder at the obvious willingness of so many people in England to trade economic self-harm for an idea (however misplaced) of national independence.

One of the fatal flaws of progressive centre-left politics as it developed under Clinton and Tony Blair was its contradictory attitude to all of this. On the one hand, the centre-left knew very well that it was not all about the economy – it embraced the importance of race, gender and sexual orientation. On the other, it came to believe that identity politics stopped where economics began. As the old working class was dismantled and the power of labour unions diminished, it was convenient to forget that economics and identity are and always have been deeply intertwined.

So it was easy to understand that a sense of belonging might be more important than money to minorities, but less and less understood that the same might be true for white working-class communities. Black pride or gay pride were good things, but the old forms of working-class pride – being in a union, for example – were outmoded and the people who clung to them would just have to get over themselves.

Brexit – like the election of Donald Trump and the rise of far-right identity politics in Europe – is a consequence of this contradiction. The anti-Brexit campaign rigidly obeyed the 'iron law' that, in the end, people do not vote against their pockets. And most of the arguments against Brexit still come down to dire warnings about jobs and living standards. Those arguments are necessary, but they are not sufficient.

There is a long-term crisis of belonging in the UK. Brexit is its most lurid symptom, but it is not a cure. Theresa May's appeal to the 'precious, precious union' is mere denial about the rise of English identity. The hard Brexiteers, under the cover of nationalism, want to unleash an even more virulent form of globalisation that will destroy what is left of working-class communities.

And yet these liars and fantasists have been allowed to own the most potent political emotions – collective pride, identity, belonging. The willingness to sacrifice economic comfort for a sense of the greater good or a higher ideal is not innately self-destructive. Nothing noble or decent is ever accomplished without it. The right has turned it into a sharp blade and told people to cut themselves with it. Those people think they are making a sacrifice when they are merely being sacrificed. The left has to speak, not just to their rational desire not to make themselves poorer, but to the bigger reasons why they don't think it's all about money.

TIMELINE

16 January 2019:	Theresa May wins a vote of confidence in the government.
21 January 2019:	May presents the government's 'Plan B' Brexit deal.
29 January 2019:	MPs debate the prime minister's 'Plan B' deal, which is then approved following two amendments.
14 February 2019:	The government's Brexit plan suffers a defeat in the House of Commons.
12 March 2019:	The prime minister loses 'meaningful vote 2'.
13 March 2019:	In a defeat for the prime minister, MPs vote to rule out a 'no-deal Brexit'.
14 March 2019:	MPs approve the amended government's motion, instructing the government to seek permission from the EU to extend Article 50.
5 April 2019:	The prime minister writes to European Council President Donald Tusk, asking to extend Article 50 until 30 June 2019.
10 April 2019:	Following a meeting of the European Council, EU27 leaders agree to grant an extension comprising two possible dates: 22 May 2019, should the withdrawal agreement gain approval from MPs the following week; or 12 April 2019, should the withdrawal agreement not be approved by the House of Commons.
27 March 2019:	The Commons debates and votes on eight

indicative votes, in an attempt to find a Brexit plan that wins the support of the majority of MPs. All options are defeated.

29 March 2019: On the day the UK was supposed to leave the EU, May loses 'meaningful vote 3' by 344 votes to 286.

12 February 2019

The UK is still supposed to be leaving the EU
at the end of March, but there is no real prospect
of the withdrawal agreement – or any other
realistic plan – getting through parliament.

Those ships have already sailed. Since last Friday, freighters leaving UK ports for Australia and New Zealand are sailing into the unknown. Their voyage will take fifty days, so they will arrive after 29 March, which means they have departed with no idea of what trading regime will apply when they try to land their goods.

From next Friday the same will be true of ships leaving Britain for ports in Asia. In its own weird way, Brexit is already replicating the conditions of heroic eighteenth-century imperial exploration. Every captain is a Captain Cook. These stout mariners may know where they are going in a literal sense, but they have no idea what awaits them. Quarantine? Tariffs? Demands for papers they do not have? They have left a place of legal certainty and are going into the trading equivalent of terra incognita. The sixty-seven trade arrangements the UK has with and through the EU could lapse overnight on 29 March.

In the abstract – if you're not a real exporter actually engaged in trading tangible things – there is something thrilling about this. A little bit of Brexit is about boredom. The great problem with the EU is its day-to-day tediousness. Viewed as a historical whole, it is extraordinary, even epic. But on the mundane level, it is a bureaucratic machine. Its language is fluent acronym-ese, its methods slow and consensual, its outcomes compromised, its treaties unreadable. Who, at some level, would not wish to run away and join a crew of jolly jack tars, setting out on the high seas with a yo-ho-ho and several bottles of rum to keep reality at bay?

In truth, this question of boredom is rather more complicated. One of the things we've all had to learn since June 2016 is precisely that we don't have to think about the boring stuff because the EU does it for us. Only when it is thrown into doubt do we realise how much tedium the EU has taken from us. Life is too short to spend it thinking about customs codes and VAT regimes and safety standards for light bulbs and roaming charges for mobile phones. The word 'frictionless' has bubbled up into the Brexit lexicon as a desirable future state. But what we've all been forced to remember is that we have come to take frictionlessness for granted, not just on borders but in everyday life.

And, of course, in business, too. If the EU is bureaucratic – and it is – it is because it has lifted vast burdens of bureaucracy from businesses and transferred them to itself. The more boring the EU has become, the less boring work has to be done in the back offices of companies. Most firms no longer even have customs departments. Most don't have to think regularly about technical standards. The EU is Tedium Inc. If it's not boring, it's not working.

Another word for 'boring' is 'predictable'. In our culture, it's a very negative word – who wants a predictable response or a pre-dictable plot twist? Part of the appeal of the reactionary politics currently in the ascendant round the world is the allure of the unpredictable. Bored by the predictability of bland centrist politics, many voters become like readers of a good thriller for whom the highest compliment is: 'Well, I didn't see that coming!'

And yet, those same voters also expect predictability in the food they eat, in the safety of goods in the shops, in the supply chains for the factories they work in, in their right to retire to the Costa del Sol and in a million details too dull to think about. They are at once sick of predictability and hooked on it.

Here we meet one of the inescapable paradoxes of Brexit. Its member states, including the UK, have outsourced the tedium of trade regulation to the EU. Brexit presents itself as a liberation from all of that dullness. But in fact it is a repatriation of boredom. What it takes back is not 'control', but all the bureaucratic monotony, the form-filling, the box ticking, the acronyms, the technical specifications, the 'sorry, mate, we don't have your WTF-666 declaration and the office is now closed until Monday'. It will not be a bonfire of red tape; the tape will simply become red, white and blue instead.

This is why Brexit itself has already become history's most boring revolution. Once, in the reverse alchemy of negotiation, you transmute its golden aspirations into the real world of international legal agreements, you end up with very leaden stuff. For many people in Britain, this huge event in their national life is already excruciatingly tedious. And who can blame them? It is the same damn thing every week, every promised climax collapsing into anti-climactic overfamiliarity.

In this atmosphere, the allure of danger is strong. The air rushing up your trousers as you plunge from a great height is, I imagine, very invigorating. The voyage into the unknown, away from the dreary dockyards of predictability, is exciting. Until, after a long time all at sea, you arrive at some dismal port only to be kept in quarantine, unable to land and unwilling to go back where you came from.

19 February 2019

When all of this is done – if indeed it ever is done – a question will puzzle historians. How did absurd characters like Boris Johnson, Jacob Rees-Mogg, and all those lesser swivel-eyed loons you think must have just wandered into shot but who turn out to be long-serving Tory MPs, come to exert such influence on the fate of nations? They will have to grapple with a strange phenomenon – the way the English love of eccentricity turned sour.

Just a decade ago, Henry Hemming produced a long book, *In Search of the English Eccentric*, warning that 'the English eccentric was about to become an endangered species'. If only. For not only is the English eccentric not an endangered species, he is flourishing right at the top of the food chain. Brexit can be thought of as an experiment in political re-wilding: instead of bringing back wolves or bears or lynx, it has reintroduced the English eccentric to the ecosystem of power.

When we outsiders see Johnson stuck on a zip wire with a Union Jack in each hand or Rees-Mogg bringing his nanny along to canvass voters on his behalf, we are initially indulgent: how delight-fully, comically, English. But then we remember that Johnson was the single most influential figure in persuading his compatriots to vote to leave the European Union in June 2016 and that Rees-Mogg is the leader of a faction that has brought Britain to the brink of a catastrophic no-deal Brexit.

How did this happen? Hemming tellingly linked his search for eccentrics to expressions that would come to shape much of the emotion behind Brexit: 'the nanny state', 'cultural globalisa-tion', 'political correctness', 'risk-resistant planning' and, of course,

'European standardisation'. His fear was that 'English society's irregularities were being ironed out one by one and with this the eccentric was being fined, imprisoned, or assimilated into everything I understood by the word "normal"'.

Wrapped up in this anxiety are two assumptions that helped both to create Brexit and to imply that it is a movement best led by eccentrics. One is that eccentricity is not just a personal oddity – it is an expression of the English national character and therefore a matter of profound political significance. The other is that this national character is under threat. It is being forcibly repressed by a newly homogenised normality. This 'ironing out' of the wrinkles of Englishness is happening, not just because of cultural globalisation, but specifically as a result of European regulation.

If you think like this, it makes sense to see Brexit as a reassertion of the true English character, a last-gasp rescuing of its distinctiveness from the incoming tides of Euro-blandness. And thus to see self-parodying eccentrics like Johnson and Rees-Mogg, not just as saviours of this endangered Englishness but as embodiments of it.

The idea of eccentricity has a long history as a signifier of English freedom. England's glorying in eccentrics (actually only those of the male and upper-class variety), so the story went, contrasted favourably with the conformism of slavish continentals and was thus a kind of personal tribute to the virtues of the English constitution. This idea had more than an element of religious prejudice: Protestants thought for themselves, while Catholics (especially the French) were mindless followers of authority. Eccentricity was the proof of the value England placed on individualism: only in England could you be free to behave in a manner that most of society regarded as odd.

Eccentricity was a revolt against the tyranny of conformity. The more it flourished, the more the English could distinguish themselves as a nation of free-thinkers.

Of course, this was always a myth. In the 1940s, George Orwell evoked a self-image of the English masses that was the opposite of eccentric: 'the gentle-mannered, undemonstrative, law-abiding English... the orderly behaviour of English crowds, the lack of pushing and quarrelling, the willingness to form queues.' Perhaps the English valued their eccentrics precisely because they were actually much more obedient and orthodox than they liked to acknowledge.

In any case, upper-class male eccentricity was meant to be free of damage – the invariable modifier of 'eccentric' in the English language was 'harmless'. And so it was: when your ruling class is running a vast empire and your practical industrialists are leading the world, you can afford a decorative eccentric or two. The eccentric Englishman was a self-conscious indulgence, a way of disguising the relentless reality of global domination. The English liked to see even their empire, not as a ruthless machine, but as an almost accidental side effect of curious gentlemen wandering off the beaten track.

Brexit has a way of reviving habits of mind that no longer conform to reality. The embrace of the eccentrics is one way of insisting that Britain is not what it actually is: a normal European country. Except this time there is a twist, the harmless eccentric has mutated into the harmful kind.

16 March 2019

*As she loses another 'meaningful vote' on the withdrawal
agreement and is forced to write to the EU asking for an
extension of the UK's membership beyond 29 March,
Theresa May's repeated humiliations evoke a
sympathy she does not deserve.*

Theresa May always made much of her devotion to the
cricketer Geoffrey Boycott. She campaigned unsuccessfully
for the former England and Yorkshire batsman to be awarded
a knighthood and implicitly compared herself to him: 'I have been
a Geoff Boycott fan all my life. It was just that he kind of solidly
got on with what he was doing.' But while this idea of modelling
herself on Boycott's dogged, undemonstrative persistence at the
wicket seems to capture May's own qualities, it has one big flaw.
Boycott actually scored the runs.

His relentless piling up of unspectacular incremental gains was
rewarded with centuries on the scoreboards and victories for his
teams. He may have been boring and metronomic but he won
matches. May has shown all of her hero's persistence, grit and dullness. But she has lost more dramatically than any previous British
prime minister. She managed to be 'not out' for a remarkably long
time, but she was never really in.

Perhaps, if we really must have a sporting simile for Theresa
May, we have to look to a different code. It seems apt that her
father and grandfather grew up in Wimbledon and that she began
both her married life and her political career as a Tory councillor
there. For May is perhaps the political equivalent of one of those
English players who was going to end at last the long drought

of home victories at Wimbledon and make English tennis great again.

They would be hyped up far beyond their merits and promoted to Centre Court, their matches simulcasted on to giant screens where the fans could see shots of Cliff Richard and some minor royals cheering them on from the arena. They would be carried along on a wave of patriotic enthusiasm to the later rounds of the tournament where they would hit four double faults in a row to lose the decisive set. May was never the Geoff Boycott of British politics, always the Tim Henman.

As she was pleading for her withdrawal deal and for her political life in the House of Commons on Tuesday, with the Tory benches behind her only half full, her hoarse voice sepulchral and faltering, it was possible to feel great sympathy for May. She looked and sounded so harried and hollowed out that it seemed as if all the accumulated humiliations and frustrations she had suppressed for two years with such remarkable powers of denial had risen up to take possession of her at last.

If there is anything to admire in May it is that she has carried on, and here she was, doing it again, even in what must have been the knowledge of certain and this time possibly terminal defeat. But May is not solid, merely stolid. 'Dull' and 'reliable' tend to go together. In May's case, though, they have never been conjoined twins. It is easy to think that just as visually impaired people are supposed to have sharper hearing, a lack of charisma must be compensated for by rocklike reliability.

May, indeed, always tried to make a virtue of this necessity, to suggest somehow that her lack of charm and absence of magnetism proved that she must be, in the mantra that defined her disastrous 2017 general election campaign, 'strong and stable'. But in fact May has proved, under pressure, to be wildly unreliable, forever making commitments and sealing deals only to unmake and unseal them again. She turned out to be that most unfortunate political hybrid: dull and unreliable.

The dullness matters, not because charm is much of a virtue, but because in her case it amounted to a deadly lack of imagination. May's world is intensely narrow. She is not so much a Little Englander as a Little Southeast-of-Englander. She is imaginatively bound within a little square: the pretty Oxfordshire villages where she grew up in her father's vicarages, Oxford University, the City of London and Westminster. When she went up to Oxford from grammar school, she was travelling less than ten miles from her parents' home. She met her husband Philip at an Oxford University Conservative Association disco. They were married by May's own father.

She went straight from Oxford to a job in the Bank of England. Her husband also worked in the City. In 1995, when she was thirty-nine, she was selected for the safe Tory seat of Maidenhead, so safe that even in the Tony Blair landslide of 1997 she was elected to parliament with more than 50 per cent of the vote. She moved to Sonning, a village on the Thames described by Jerome K. Jerome in *Three Men in a Boat* as 'the most fairy-like little nook on the whole river'. Jimmy Page and George and Amal Clooney are local residents – gritty it is not.

This lack of experience of a wider world matters. For one thing, it left May with a deep distrust of immigrants. If there is a defining question of May's career in the British Home Office and as prime minister, it is immigration. It was the issue on which she fell out with her principal internal enemy, the then chancellor George Osborne. It was May who promised to create a 'hostile environment' for undocumented migrants. She was largely responsible for the Windrush scandal in which elderly Caribbean migrants who had made long lives in Britain were harassed and in some cases deported.

It was under May's Home Office regime that the disastrous doctrine of reducing annual net migration to the 'tens of thousands' was promulgated. It should not be forgotten that this unattainable goal was a big factor in Brexit – it created a false narrative that immigration could be slashed and the only reason it was rising was because of freedom of movement in the EU. It also created the sense among voters that everything was out of control. May did not actually support Brexit but in this regard she did much to create the conditions for it.

Just as importantly, when she became prime minister she prioritised immigration over everything else. It was the deepest crimson of all her red lines and it shaped the withdrawal agreement more than any other factor. And what it betrayed was a visceral mistrust of people who, unlike herself, are not 'rooted'. When, at the height of her hubris in 2016, she railed that 'if you believe you are a citizen of the world, you are a citizen of nowhere. You don't understand what citizenship means', the cosiness of her enclosed world view showed its nasty obverse side. Dullness, in the sense of a lack of curiosity about people from beyond one's own circle of experience, shades easily into the rhetoric of exclusion.

May's surface sheen of colourless efficiency also hid something else. She doesn't look like an obsessional monomaniac. But she is one. What she was always obsessed with was political power. May decided when she was twelve that she was going to be an MP (it went without saying that this meant a Tory MP). By the age of seventeen, she had upped her ambition – she told her schoolmates and cousins that she intended to become prime minister. Her college friends at Oxford remembered her open irritation when Margaret Thatcher got to 10 Downing Street and so deprived May of her goal of being the first woman to hold the office.

This is not normal. There is something deeply odd about a child who decides in all seriousness that her project is to become prime minister, not as a passing fancy but as a life plan. The robotic quality for which May was so often mocked is really a machinelike focus on a single goal: to become and remain prime minister. And this, too, has had a profound effect on the course of Brexit. In the 2016 referendum campaign, it was obvious that May was fixated, not on what was best for her country, but on how she might exploit the opportunity if David Cameron was defeated. She said the minimum necessary to support Remain while signalling to the Leavers that her heart wasn't in it.

It was a breathtakingly cynical calculation driven by a raging lust for power – no less reprehensible, if somewhat more devious, than Boris Johnson's more overt cynicism. And, of course, it paid off. When Johnson and Michael Gove did their Laurel and Hardy act and pushed each other off the ladder, May ascended it by default.

But once in the highest office her overwhelming priority was to stay there. People mistake her willingness to endure humiliation for a lack of ego but her essential egocentricity was manifested, not just in the desire for a suitably massive Commons majority that lured her into calling an entirely unnecessary election in 2017, but in the weird conduct of that campaign as a cult of personality built around a leader who didn't have one.

This prioritisation of her own grip on office has shaped the whole Brexit debacle. May was certainly faced with an extremely difficult task, but she could have done it differently. She could have thought about how to bring together a divided country and limit the damage to people's lives and livelihoods. Instead she focused relentlessly, and with all that stubborn persistence, on her own life and livelihood. She directed Brexit entirely around the path of least resistance, which lay firstly through telling the zealots what they wanted to hear and, after the 2017 election, through keeping the DUP sweet as well.

She tried to stay in power by telling everyone – including at times the EU and the Irish government – what they wanted to hear. The inevitable result was not so much heroic endurance as a blind determination to keep muddling on even as the Brexit deadline she herself had set got ever closer. May does not, then, quite cut it as a tragic figure. She had the overweening ambition of a mini-Macbeth, and, like him, she was destroyed by the attainment of the very power she craved. But she ended up much more as a sad servant than a tragic master. She gradually became a political paradox: a leader held in office only by her willingness to endure the disrespect, defiance and disobedience of those she supposedly led.

Declaring her candidacy for the Tory leadership in June 2016,

May defined herself as 'the daughter of a local vicar and the grand-daughter of a regimental sergeant major'. She did not mention that both of her grandmothers were maids in Victorian big houses and that her other grandfather was a butler. The public persona she tried to project was somewhere between the vicar and the sergeant major, at once moral guide to her nation and creator of good order in the ranks. But she ended up much more like a servant in the crazy, rambling, neo-Gothic big house of Brexit, endlessly trying to tidy away its mad clutter of contradictions, polishing its hopelessly tarnished silver and trying to be Jeeves to its absurd Bertie Woosters. In the end, for serving such a bad cause so relentlessly, her ignominy serves her right.

19 March 2019

The chaos at Westminster affords a preview of
England standing alone with its demons.

'The alleged aptitude of the English for self-government,' wrote Bernard Shaw in his preface to *Androcles and the Lion*, 'is contradicted by every chapter of their history.' Shaw was, of course, parodying British imperialist rhetoric and its insistence that lesser peoples – including his own nation, the Irish – were not ready to govern themselves. He was being naughtily provocative, which only the most irresponsible of commentators would dare to be in these grave times.

But there is nonetheless some tinge of truth in his words. Aptitude for self-government is not what comes to mind when one looks in from the outside at the goings-on in Westminster last week, when, as Tom Peck so brilliantly put it in the London *Independent*, 'the House of Commons was a Benny Hill chase on acid, running through a Salvador Dalí painting in a spaceship on its way to infinity'.

Let's just say that if Theresa May were the head of a newly liberated African colony in the 1950s, British conservatives would have been pointing, half ruefully, half gleefully, in her direction and saying 'See? Told you so – they just weren't ready to rule themselves. Needed at least another generation of tutelage by the Mother Country.'

There is a surreal kind of logic to this. If, as the Brexiteers do, you imagine yourself to be an oppressed colony breaking away from the German Reich aka the European Union, perhaps you do end up with a pantomime version of the travails of newly independent colonies, including the civil wars that often follow national liberation.

And without wishing to rub it in, Shaw's quip does point up two of the deep problems that underlie, and undermine, the whole Brexit project. First, the problem of this imagined effort at self-government is the 'self' bit. What is the self of the British polity? As in all nationalist revolts, the easy bit of 'Them against Us' is Them: in this case the EU. The hard bit is Us. Brexit appeals to a collective British self but it is itself the most dramatic symptom of the unravelling of that very thing.

The anarchy at Westminster is the political expression of anarchy in the UK, the sundering of a common sense of belonging. Brexit is a fabulous form of displacement – it acknowledges a profound and genuine unhappiness about how the British are governed but deflects it on to Europe. It has merely marked out in bright red ink the fault lines that have long been less vividly present – the drifting apart of England and Scotland; the economic and cultural divide between what Anthony Barnett calls 'England-without-London' and the rest of the UK (Wales being the obvious anomaly); the social and geographic rifts between the winners and losers of the long Thatcherite revolution. Brexit, in a worst-of-all-worlds moment, brings all of these divisions to a head while doing absolutely nothing to address them. It reveals a polity that cannot create consensus because it lacks a foundation in social consent.

The other, closely related, problem is the English nationalism that is at once such a powerful force in Brexit and so poorly articulated. As every former colony knows, nationalism is a great beast for carrying you to the point of independence – and then it becomes a dead horse. Shaw wrote to his friend Mabel FitzGerald (mother of the future taoiseach Garret) in December 1914: 'Even the subject nations like Ireland must never forget that the moment they gain home rule, the horse will drop down under them, and reveal, by a sudden and horrible decomposition, that he has been dead for years.'

Brexit is a dead horse, a form of nationalist energy that started to decompose rapidly on 24 June 2016, as soon as it entered the field of political reality. It can't go anywhere. It can't carry the British state to any promised land. It can only leave it where it has arrived, in a no man's land between vague patriotic fantasies and irritatingly persistent facts. But equally, because of the referendum result, the British state can't get down off the dead horse and has to keep flogging it.

Hovering over this whole idea of English self-government is the myth of standing alone. All independence movements have at their core the meaning of Sinn Féin – 'Ourselves Alone'. Standing alone is also one of the great motifs of the English self-image, brilliantly visualised in David Low's famous cartoon of June 1940, after the fall of France, showing a Tommy standing on the cliffs of Dover shaking his fist at the Luftwaffe bombers overhead with the caption 'Very well, alone'. But Britain was not alone then (it had a vast empire) and it has never been alone. In its entire history since 1707, it has always been part of a larger multinational entity. Yet a fantasy of glorious, defiant aloneness is at the heart of Brexit's wish-fulfilment. It is a great warning about being careful what you wish for. What we are seeing at the moment is a sneak preview of England standing alone. It is not surprising that it is a preview of a horror show. For when you really are alone, what are you alone with? You are alone with your demons.

23 March 2019

As we take our seats yet again on the great Brexit merry-go-round, I have been thinking of the elegant, high-backed chairs in a dining room fifteen miles south of Belfast. They are in Mount Stewart, the big house on Strangford Lough.

But you can see them in paintings of the Congress of Vienna of 1815 – the posteriors of the men who redrew the map of Europe after the defeat of Napoleon graced their seats. One of the men in the pictures is Robert Stewart, Lord Castlereagh, the British foreign secretary who was one of the dominant figures in deciding Europe's future. Though he was born in Henry Street in Dublin, Mount Stewart was the family pile. So he took the chairs home from Vienna to Co. Down as a memento.

What they bring to mind now is unintended consequences. They remind us that revolutions can leave legacies for the long term that no one imagined. What is the long-term legacy of the Russian Revolution? Not so much contemporary Russia as contemporary China and its strange mixture of Leninism and hyper-capitalism.

And what is the long-term legacy of the French Revolution? A place called Germany. There was no such place in the eighteenth century, just hundreds of independent city states and principalities whose people were Germanic in culture but had no sense of belonging to a single political nation. The French Revolution created Napoleon, who realised that these micro-states were easy pickings and invaded them.

Here we have the most consequential of unintended consequences. France was the dominant power in Europe, and Germany did not exist. Napoleon invaded the Germanic states and accidentally summoned Germany into existence. He reorganised the statelets into confederations. Resistance to him created a pan-German nationalism.

After Napoleon's defeat, at the Congress of Vienna, the men sitting on those Mount Stewart chairs created the German Confederation, which would eventually lead to German unification in 1871. France's position as the dominant Western European continental power was thus ended by Napoleon. And Britain, which encouraged the creation of a strong Germany, went to war with it twice in the twentieth century.

So what will be the unintended consequences of Brexit? This may be a particularly foolish question when we don't really know what the intended consequences are, never mind the unintended ones. The absence of a clear and realistic set of goals has characterised the project from the beginning. Since so little has been planned, so much left to chance, is there even a difference in this case between effects that were and were not foreseen? Perhaps not. Perhaps none of Brexit's consequences will have been fully intended.

But we can guess at some of the ones that run directly counter to the aspirations of those who have created Brexit. One of them will be a strange echo of the French Revolution's accidental creation of Germany. And this will be doubly ironic.

In the first place, the anti-EU sentiment that would fuel Brexit really began to gather in England in the wake of German reunification in 1990. The fear that the Germany that had so aggressively pursued dominance of Europe in the twentieth century was now reborn and would return to its old ways revived the paranoid suspicion that the EU itself was really a German front.

The notion that Germany was in effect reversing by stealth the result of two world wars and achieving by economic means the dominance it had been denied on the battlefield had long been there. But its rise as a potent political myth in England was itself an unintended consequence of the fall of the Berlin Wall.

The irony here is that Brexit will help to create the very thing its political proponents feared. When Boris Johnson told voters a month before the referendum in 2016 that the EU was 'pursuing a similar goal to Hitler in trying to create a powerful superstate', he was manipulating English anxieties about the dark Teutonic truth behind the EU's tediously consensual deal-making. Yet, while Brexit will not actually turn this conspiracy theory into a reality, it will unquestionably create a much greater degree of German dominance on the continent.

One of the reasons most small EU countries are especially unhappy about Brexit is that having the British at the European table has helped to disperse power among a larger number of big players. It is easier for smaller countries to use their diplomatic skills to create coalitions on questions of vital interest to themselves when they can play on rivalries and disagreements between the major states, including the UK.

We can see this most clearly from a negative example: without the UK in the eurozone, Ireland was much more vulnerable in the banking crisis to bullying by the ECB.

If and when Britain leaves, Germany will, merely by default, become much more dominant. The balance of power that Castlereagh did so much to create at the Congress of Vienna will have tilted towards Berlin. But there is another irony, too: the Germans don't really want this dominance. Scarred by the experience of defeat, they don't trust themselves with it. This unintended consequence is also, even for its apparent beneficiary, an unwanted one.

It is weirdly apt that British influence on the Continent was largely the creation of two Irishmen: the Duke of Wellington and Castlereagh. For the collapse of that influence as a result of Brexit will also have unintended consequences for Ireland.

Those chairs in Mount Stewart represent in tangible form an immensely important intangible: the prestige of Britishness. That prestige once came from hard power – military prowess and industrial strength. In our time, it has been maintained by soft power – the notion that Britain still cuts a great figure in the world, maintained through popular culture, an image of vibrancy and openness and a reputation for competence and reliability.

We have to keep in mind that for us in Ireland this soft British power is a domestic matter. The allegiance of a very substantial minority on our island has been shaped by history, culture and economic interests. But it has been maintained, even as Britain ceased to be a world power, by a sense of British prestige. However Brexit now turns out, this prestige has melted before our eyes. Britain will no longer be a player on the Continent, and the fantasy that it will therefore emerge again as a global power will be cruelly exposed.

What glamour will attach to Britain then, and what will the British identity of so many people on the island of Ireland then mean? When Britain is no longer taken seriously at the table, are they just left with the old chairs?

26 March 2019

When even the Spectator *is playing 'Give Ireland Back to the Irish',*
how can people in Northern Ireland hold on to a British identity?

The health of Britishness is a vital Irish national interest. In surveys, a little under half of people in Northern Ireland say they feel strongly British. And though you might not know it from some of the crudely nationalist rhetoric that has bubbled back up to the surface, the people of the Republic overwhelmingly recognise their right to this identity. In 1998, 94 per cent of us voted to drop the territorial claim to the North and replace it with an aspiration to unite in harmony and friendship all the people who share the island in all the diversity of their identities and traditions. The number of people who actually voted against this radical revision – 85,748 – would almost fit into Croke Park.

Let's be clear what this means. It means not just that Britishness is a part of Ireland's present but that it belongs in Ireland's future. We collectively dropped the old nationalist myth that the British-ness of a large minority on the island is 'false consciousness', a mirage that will evaporate when Ireland is united. A diversity of identities is not a woeful legacy of imperial manipulation. It is part of an open-ended condition of plurality. This is what we signed up for in 1998: a capacious and complex sense of belonging that includes a right to Britishness.

And this is where we are in terrible trouble. The lovely phrase in the Belfast Agreement proclaims the birthright of everyone in Northern Ireland to be 'Irish or British or both as they may so choose'. Implicit in it is the idea that Britishness is a choice that will always be available to those who want it.

Twenty years ago, who had been denying that free choice? The IRA. The unspoken but resonant rebuke was to a violent and bullying form of Irish nationalism that had denied the legitimacy of a British identity on the island. What nobody imagined was that the choice would be threatened from the other political and geographical direction. Yet this is what has come to pass: in the deep crisis of the British state, the right to be British is looking ever more tenuous.

To grasp a small straw in the wind, listen to the *Spectator*'s Coffee House Shots podcast, presented by its editor Fraser Nelson. It is a very good sounding of Tory and pro-Brexit sentiment. Last week, it discussed the way the DUP's insistence on aligning the rest of the UK with Northern Ireland essentially ties the British into a soft Brexit. And what record did the *Spectator* play at the end? Paul McCartney's naive Brits-out agitpop song from 1972, 'Give Ireland Back to the Irish'. Banned from the UK airwaves in 1972, it is now in Tory circles an acceptably provocative way of hinting that perhaps all the 'Irish' (including the DUP) should bugger off and leave us to our own grand project of national liberation. This is just one tiny moment, but it is telling because it arises from a much deeper shift in English sentiment.

You can't choose a product that is not on offer. Britishness, like every other national identity, is manufactured – but what if they stop making it? Something very profound is happening to the political economy of Britishness: the demand in Northern Ireland is still pretty high but the supply is in real danger of drying up. The message is: Britishness is out of stock but have you tried Brexitness, which provides all the same thrills of tribal belonging? The DUP has bought the substitute product. But it does not do the same job at all. It is not an identity, just an identity crisis.

There is no joy in any of this for Irish nationalism. The simplistic notion that a quick transition to Irish unity will solve the problem is utterly unconstitutional. The Irish constitution requires a profound reconciliation between diverse identities. That in turn requires people to be secure and confident in their sense of belonging.

The crisis of the British state so evident in the collapse of the political order at Westminster has destroyed the security and confidence of Britishness. They will not return any time soon. The question for all of us on this island is: what else can make those who see themselves as British feel at home in Ireland? If we are to share this space decently, it is in all our interests to approach that question tenderly, openly and generously.

TIMELINE

1 April 2019:   In the second day of indicative votes, all four of the selected options are defeated.

2 April 2019:   May announces she will seek a further extension to the Article 50 process.

5 April 2019:   Theresa May formally writes to Donald Tusk, requesting a further extension to the Article 50 process to the end of June 2019.

10 April 2019:   The European Council meets. The UK and EU27 agree to extend Article 50 until 31 October 2019.

May 2019:   The UK votes in the European Parliament elections, with the Brexit Party emerging with the biggest number of seats in England.

24 May 2019:   Theresa May announces she will resign on 7 June. In a statement outside Downing Street, she admits: 'It is, and will always remain, a matter of deep regret to me that I have not been able to deliver Brexit.'

23 July 2019:   Boris Johnson wins the Conservative Party leadership contest by 92,153 votes to Jeremy Hunt's 46,656.

6 April 2019

In two series of 'indicative votes', all possible options have been defeated. As May announces she will seek a further extension to the Article 50 process and offers to sit down with the leader of the Opposition to finalise a deal that will (improbably) win the support of MPs. Flann O'Brien's The Third Policeman – *with its unending, hellish plot – is the Brexit Code.*

In 2005, viewers around the world were sucked into a meandering TV drama called *Lost*, in which it was never quite clear what was going on. Then the writer let it be known that, in the third episode of the second series, there would be an important clue. The clue was that one of the characters was seen reading Flann O'Brien's novel *The Third Policeman*, written in 1940, in which the reader begins to realise what the nameless narrator does not: that he is in hell.

This made sense of *Lost*. But I can now reveal that *The Third Policeman* is also the secret key to another long-running drama in which everyone is lost, no one quite knows what is going on and everything begins to look a lot like hell: Brexit.

Here is the history of Brexit in twelve passages from *The Third Policeman*.

1. The Leave campaign's promises

Early in the book, the narrator encounters an 'eccentric queerly-spoken' and 'tricky-looking' man. He is a ruthless robber but he takes a shine to the narrator and offers him a grandiose gift. 'He put his hand into a pocket at his crotch and took out a round thing. "Here is a sovereign for your good luck," he said, "the golden token of your golden destiny." I gave him, so to speak, my golden thank-you but I noticed that the coin he gave me was a bright penny.'

This is, of course, a foretelling of Boris Johnson and the other tricky-looking fellows; the Leave campaign's promise in 2016 of both £350 million a week for the National Health Service; a golden destiny and the promise of a shiny sovereignty that turned out to be really a bad penny.

2. The Leave campaign's illegal breach of spending limits, purloined Facebook data and use of secretly targeted digital propaganda

'Apparently there is no limit,' Joe remarked. 'Anything can be said in this place and it will be true and will have to be believed.'

3. The consequence of having no feasible plans for what would happen after the referendum

In *The Third Policeman*, the notebooks of the 'savant' De Selby, with whose obscure works and bizarre experiments the narrator is obsessed, contain rough sketches of his designs for houses. 'These structures were of two kinds: roofless "houses" and "houses" without walls.' One French commentator on De Selby suggests that he may have drawn these absent-mindedly as doodles. 'The next time he took it up he was confronted with a mass of diagrams and drawings which he took to be plans of a type of dwelling which he always had in mind and immediately wrote many pages explaining the sketches.'

The Brexiteers likewise looked at their own absent-minded political doodlings and wrote infinite pages (mostly in highly remunerated columns for the Tory press) justifying their plans for a great Brexit house with no roof or no walls.

4. The backward glance to empire and the Second World War

De Selby became fixated on the idea that, if you look at yourself in the mirror, you are seeing an image of yourself as you were a fraction of a second before.

Thus, by constructing a series of parallel mirrors, he claimed to have been able to recede to an image of himself as a 'beardless boy of twelve' with 'a countenance of singular beauty and nobility'.

So entranced was he with the idea that he eventually 'refused to countenance a direct view of anything' and looked at everything through a rear-view mirror.

Equally, the Brexiteers looked in the mirror and saw a singularly English vision of past beauty and nobility. Like De Selby, they refused to countenance a direct view of anything that might be called contemporary reality and walked backwards with a flattering mirror in front of their faces.

5. The triggering of Article 50 with no road map for negotiations

De Selby is convinced that there is no need for a sense of direction because a good road will have a 'certain air of destiny, an indefinable intimation that it is going somewhere, be it east or west'. When Theresa May triggered Article 50 in March 2017, she had absolutely no sense of direction, yet was certain that Britain was nonetheless on the road to destiny. When David Davis turned up in Brussels to begin negotiations (the easiest ever conducted, he predicted) with scarcely a piece of paper in front of him, he was following De Selby's teachings: 'If a friendly road should lead you into a complicated city with nets of crooked streets and five hundred other roads leaving it for unknown destinations, your own road will always... lead you to safety out of the tangled town.'

6. The increasingly ludicrous hype

The actual negotiations made it ever more obvious that the only really achievable Brexit was a kind of second-class membership of the European Union and that the whole exercise was thus inherently futile. But this resulted, not in calm reflection, but in an ever-increasing volume of noise: Global Britain! Vassal state! D-Day! Independence Day! British pluck! Colony! Bloody

Germans! WTO rules! Brexit means Brexit! Saboteurs! Enemies of the people! Go whistle for your money!

This, too, is foretold in *The Third Policeman*.

The narrator recalls the hammering noises that were heard while De Selby was conducting supposedly delicate experiments: 'no commentator has hazarded a guess as to what was being hammered and for what purpose'. But one of them 'has put forward the suggestion that loud hammering was a device resorted to by the savant to drown other noises which might give some indication of the real trend of the experiments'.

7. The promised trade deals with other countries fail to materialise

De Selby believes that 'A journey is an hallucination'. It is all in the mind. Thus, when he has to undertake a 'journey' from Bath to Folkestone, he shuts himself in his room with a series of postcards depicting the places that he would traverse were he actually to travel this route, 'together with an elaborate arrangement of clocks and barometric instruments'.

After seven hours, he emerges 'convinced that he was in Folkestone and possibly that he had evolved a formula for travellers which would be extremely distasteful to railway and shipping companies. There is no record of the extent of his disillusionment when he found himself still in the familiar surroundings of Bath.'

Effectively, the British government and the Brexit-supporting press shut themselves up in their own room for two years and concentrated very hard on visualising all the milestones on the journey towards the glorious post-Brexit global future.

In this room, they were travelling to the old white colonies (the United States, Canada, Australia, New Zealand) and to China and India to sign fabulously advantageous trade deals.

They were waving blue passports with proper British insignia as they passed unimpeded through foreign airports to be greeted with renewed respect and affection by the friendly natives who had always longed for their return.

They were sailing their new aircraft carrier, the *Queen Elizabeth II*, into the South China Seas (as the witless defence secretary Gavin Williamson promised) to remind everyone who is in charge. (I cannot remember whether it was De Selby or Williamson who said: 'Brexit has brought us to a great moment in our history. A moment when we must strengthen our global presence, enhance our lethality and increase our mass.')

We do not yet have the record of the full extent of their disillusionment when they opened the door and found themselves still in Bath.

8. The backstop

'The savant spent several months trying to find a satisfactory method of "diluting" water.' Could there be a clearer foreshadowing of the problem of the Irish backstop?

The backstop is the insurance policy placed in the withdrawal agreement to ensure that there could be no imposition of a hard border on the island of Ireland.

The British government agreed to it in December 2017 when Boris Johnson was foreign secretary and David Davis was Brexit secretary. And then they spent more than a year trying to dilute it.

'We stand by Ireland,' warned Guy Verhofstadt. 'There is no majority to reopen or dilute the withdrawal agreement in the European Parliament, including the backstop.' But the British carried on thinking up various ways of diluting water. Amazingly, they couldn't do it.

9. The indicative votes

'Do you not see that every reply is in the negative? No matter what you ask him he says No.' Early in *The Third Policeman*, the narrator encounters the man he has murdered, Old Mathers. When he asks Mathers questions, the answers are 'I am not', 'No', 'I do not'. Eventually Mathers explains that having been led into bad ways in his youth by agreeing to the suggestions of others, he decided to keep himself out of trouble by resolving to 'say No henceforth to every suggestion'. He holds that '"No" is, generally speaking, a better answer than "Yes".'

In one of its more arcane moments of delusion, the House of Commons became fixated on something called the Malthouse Compromise, which was really another way to dilute water. But when that evaporated, the parliament settled on what should surely have been called the Mathers Compromise. It realised that the safest way to answer every question thrown up by Brexit is in the negative: no, we do not, none of the above. It has now twice gone through lists of possible outcomes and rejected each of them one by one. Brexit was always a negative reply – the British (or more accurately the English) said what they do not want, but have not really been given a chance to say what they do.

10. The mirage that keeps receding into the distance

The epigraph to the novel is a quote from De Selby: 'It ill becomes any man of sense to be concerned at the illusory approach of the supreme hallucination known as death.' This should rightly serve to remind us to keep everything in perspective: it ill becomes any man or woman to be concerned at the illusory approach of the supreme hallucination known as the end of Brexit.

The Third Policeman does not really end. In this hell, the narrator thinks he has escaped but we find him on the last pages approaching again the place he has just been, with no memory of it all, doomed to repeat the same terrible adventures forever.

When will Brexit be over? 'The wisest course on this question,' writes the narrator, 'is probably that taken by the little-known Swiss writer Le Clerque. "This matter," he says, "is outside the true province of the conscientious commentator inasmuch as being unable to say aught that is charitable or useful, he must preserve silence."'

9 April 2019

The distance between the gloriously bonkers opening ceremony of the London Olympics and the sourness of Brexit is not as great as it seems.

In his very funny and very sad novel about the years leading up to Brexit, *Middle England,* Jonathan Coe captures a moment that now seems strangely distant.

Looking at the gloriously bonkers opening ceremony for the Olympic Games in London in July 2012, Coe's protagonist, Doug, is initially sceptical. But he 'watched it with a mounting sense of admiration that was soon bordering on awe. The scale of the spectacle, the originality of it – the weirdness, at points... This eccentric hymn to Britain's industrial heritage was the last thing he had been expecting, but there was something hugely affecting and persuasive about it...what he felt while watching it were the stirrings of an emotion he hadn't experienced for years – had never really experienced at all, perhaps, having grown up in a household where all expressions of patriotism had been considered suspect: national pride. Yes, why not come straight out and admit it, at this moment he felt proud, proud to be British, proud to be part of a nation which had not only achieved such great things but could now celebrate them with such confidence and irony and lack of self-importance.'

It's a question English people often bring up in conversation: how did we go from that to this? How do you get from the joyously quirky celebration of Britishness in Danny Boyle's brilliantly choreographed spectacle to the rage and sourness of Brexit in less than four years? The question is freighted with sorrow and bafflement. July 2012 and June 2016 seem to belong to different epochs and to different cultural universes. But perhaps we cannot quite understand what is happening to our neighbour if we do not allow for the fact that the gulf is not quite as great as it seems. Perhaps the self-mockery of 2012 is also, in another guise, the spectacle of a country making a mockery of itself after 2016.

In the updated 2014 edition of her classic book *Watching the English*, the social anthropologist Kate Fox astutely noted that the thing that made the 2012 Olympic ceremony so delightful was its essential haughtiness – not giving a damn whether the global audience of billions got any of the jokes: 'The majority of English people loved it, and didn't much care whether the rest of the world understood it or not. In fact, many were probably secretly pleased that they didn't. The degree of self-mockery, self-denigration, obscure self-reference and self-indulgent eccentricity exhibited in that ceremony required a breathtaking disregard for the opinion of others – in this case billions of others – which can only stem from a deep sense of superiority.'

Fox was not thinking of Brexit, which was still just a twinkle in Nigel Farage's beady eye. But her analysis is nonetheless prescient. 'I suspect,' she wrote, 'that English self-mockery is rooted in a rather smug complacency, if not outright arrogance.' For the thing about self-mockery on this heroic scale is that you can only really afford it if you actually think you are pretty damn great. Self-mockery is the glory of modern English culture, the heart of that strain of comic genius that runs from Tony Hancock and The Goons through Monty Python all the way to Fleabag and Alan Partridge. The English have put enormously serious effort into seeming to take nothing about themselves seriously.

Their national language is not English. It is irony. A character in Alan Bennett's *The Old Country* says that his compatriots are 'conceived in irony. We float in it from the womb. It's the amniotic fluid… Joking but not joking. Caring but not caring. Serious but not serious.' Irish people are close enough to get this, but we are the only foreigners who do. For continental Europeans or North

Americans, there is always the uneasy question: are they being serious or not? And the English have always liked it that way – it keeps outsiders nicely confused and therefore at a disadvantage.

In the Olympic ceremony in 2012, these habits and attitudes were displayed at their most endearing. But it turned out that there is a much thinner line than anyone suspected between self-mockery and becoming a mockery of yourself. As the tragicomedy has unfolded, it is as if the quotation marks that surround everything in the ironic English frame of mind have simply been erased. What Fox called the 'self-mockery, self-denigration, obscure self-reference and self-indulgent eccentricity' of 2012 are now the daily stuff of politics. Even in the midst of a profound national crisis, everything remains 'serious but not serious'.

We love the English for their self-mockery, but the truth is they can't afford it any more. The humour has become far too close to the bone. The hidden message of the comic self-denigration was always: we are so sure of ourselves that we can pretend to find ourselves ridiculous. But it's not a pretence any more. Send in the clowns? Don't bother, they are here, right at the heart of the state. The British state really has become ridiculous. It is one long closing ceremony for games that refuse to end. The habit of ironical complacency cannot be shaken off even in a crisis that has long since gone beyond a joke.

7 May 2019

Even as Ireland has such a central place in the
Brexit saga, Irish history appears to be a mystery
to much of Britain's intellectual elite.

The book is very good so I will spare the author's blushes and not name her. It's a study of British culture in the eighteenth century and it has just recently appeared from one of the most prestigious academic publishers in the English-speaking world. The writer is a senior lecturer in eighteenth-century cultural history at one of England's best universities.

The book itself is dazzlingly erudite, the work of a top-of-the-range scholar. And here is the sentence that made me dizzy: 'The Act of Union in 1707 united Scotland with England, which by that time also included Wales and parts of Ireland.'

And parts of Ireland. Which parts of Ireland were in England in 1707? West Cork, perhaps, or the Gold Coast of Co. Down? And why only parts? What country were the other parts of Ireland in back then? For the record, if we really must: no part of Ireland was in any sense included in England – not now, not then, not ever.

In 1707, the Kingdom of Ireland was one of three distinct kingdoms under the 'personal union' of crowns held by the British monarchy, the other two being England and Scotland. It had its own parliament, albeit one that excluded Catholics. It remained a separate political entity until 1801 when the Act of Union came into force. Even then Ireland was in no sense part of England. It merged with the Kingdom of Great Britain to form the United Kingdom of Great Britain and Ireland – not, note, of England and

Ireland. And the 'parts of Ireland' stuff didn't happen until actual partition in 1920.

One can just about understand that a historian, trying to summarise the history of the union in a sentence, might garble the chronology and lose all the nuances. At the very outmost reaches of generosity, one might even understand the error of saying that Ireland as a whole was included in England – it was after all effectively ruled from London. But this is much weirder than that.

The idea of 'parts of Ireland' being in England and other parts not is just baffling – unless we make one assumption. For surely what is happening here is that our historian is dragging up from the depths of her consciousness some vague notion that there is this place called Northern Ireland and it is still 'included' in England, so it must have been so in 1707.

And this is not just one historian. A prestigious scholarly book like this is read by many experts before it is published. The publisher would, at a minimum, get two independent experts in the field to read the manuscript as part of the peer review process, plus the overall editor and the copy editor – so that's at least four very smart people. But even before that, academics will ask colleagues to read the manuscript. In this case, the author acknowledges by name those who read it and 'offered generous and insightful advice' and those who also 'offered commentary, suggestions or guidance'.

I counted twenty people in these two categories. They are big figures in academic life in England, Scotland and the United States – including some of the most distinguished historians of British politics, art, literature and science.

So with the author, the editors and the peer reviewers, there are at least twenty-five super-educated people, most of them professional historians, who read that in 1707 'England... also included Wales and parts of Ireland' and did not cry out in amazement. This egregious piece of nonsense got through the intellectual equivalent of high-level airport security screening and set off no alarms.

Now, okay, this is one half-sentence in one book. Five years ago, it would barely have seemed worthy of complaint. But in the great upheaval of British politics since 2016, we've all had a crash course in ignorance. It has become increasingly clear that the nature of what Theresa May calls the 'precious, precious union' is in fact increasingly unclear to much of the political and intellectual nexus in Britain. If not knowing the most basic stuff about the contemporary politics of the place you are in charge of is okay, why should anyone, even professional historians, know about 1707 and 1801 and 1920?

I don't think this is true in Ireland. I don't think a claim that, say, in 1707 some parts of Scotland were already in England, would go unchallenged in Irish public discourse, let alone among professional historians. But this doesn't save us from the consequences of ignorance. The political tectonic plates of these islands are shifting and we cannot insulate ourselves from the shocks. The union may be coming towards its end and all of Ireland, not just 'parts', will be 'included' in its death throes, whether we like it or not. The least we might ask is that, if our histories are again to be bound together, there is a minimal understanding of what those histories are.

4 June 2019

*But there is also a dark side to Irish identity and
it feeds (paradoxically) into English xenophobia.*

O n either side of the accession to power of Margaret Thatcher,
two great songs acted as harbingers of the long, slow death
of the British state. Both used the Queen to personify it.
In 'God Save the Queen', Johnny Rotten/John Lydon snarled the
prophetic lines: 'There is no future / In England's dreaming'. In
'The Queen Is Dead', Morrissey wailed 'The Queen is dead, boys /
And it's so lonely on a limb'. Both Lydon and Morrissey were
children of the new Anglo-Irish, the hybrid people who were, for
most of us in Ireland, our first cousins barely removed. Lydon
spent his childhood summers on a farm in Co. Cork. Both of
Morrissey's parents are from my own patch of Crumlin in Dublin
and his siblings were actually born in Dublin.

Perhaps there was something in this outsider/insider position,
this hovering between London and Cork, Manchester and Crumlin,
that made them so acutely aware of the fragility of British identity.
They were divided kids. Lydon claimed that 'My Irish half provided
my sense of devilry', but he had an English half, too. Morrissey
sang 'Irish blood, English heart, this I'm made of'. These divisions
were politically and creatively fruitful – if you have more than one
identity, you know that no identity is fixed or sacred.

And they're both Brexiteers now. Lydon supports Brexit in a
vaguely populist way – he's a man of the people, so if the people
are for it, he's for it, too. But Morrissey has been sporting, for his
recent TV and stage performances, the badge of the far-right For
Britain party. Its website trumpets his support: 'We've had another

clear endorsement from Morrissey... he has thrown his weight behind our party... Morrissey is on board, join him!'

We should not draw too many broad conclusions from Morrissey's outré gestures. But it is striking that For Britain itself was founded and is led by a woman with Irish blood and an English heart, Anne Marie Waters. She is an anti-immigrant immigrant, born and raised in Stoneybatter in Dublin. Her associate 'Tommy Robinson' (Stephen Yaxley-Lennon) is half Irish, one of a small but significant cluster of Irish or Anglo-Irish figures on the far right of English politics.

What is going on here? A perfectly good answer is: who cares? These people may be vile, but they are (for the moment) on the lunatic fringe. (Robinson got 2 per cent of the vote in the European Parliament elections.) But Morrissey is a figure of real cultural power and his transformation from critic of Britishness to icon of far-right British nationalism does tell us something important about both identity politics and Irishness.

The Irish experience, shaped equally by the sectarian divide at home and by mass emigration, is an experience of divided identity. And, crudely, there are two ways you can deal with this condition. One is both/and, the other either/or. You can embrace the richness of a dual (or indeed multiple) heritage and use the insider/outsider position creatively. Generations of Irish artists in England did this – and Morrissey used to be one of them. 'The Queen Is Dead' is a provocation in the great tradition of Wilde and Shaw.

But dual identity can also lead to cognitive dissonance, the unbearable state of having attitudes and beliefs fundamentally incompatible with each other. If you can't hack both/and – if, in this case, the Irish blood is not flowing easily through the English heart – you go for either/or. You overcome the cognitive dissonance by adopting an exaggerated version of one or other identity. There's a very powerful strain of this in modern Irish history. Without figures with dual British/Irish identities (from Patrick Pearse to Maud Gonne to James Connolly to Erskine Childers) deciding to be hyper-Irish, that history would probably look very different. But the traffic has also gone the other way – think (as Thomas Kilroy does in his brilliant play *Double Cross*) of ultra-English Irishmen like Brendan Bracken and William 'Lord Haw Haw' Joyce.

Unfortunately, one of the obvious ways of transitioning into hyper-Englishness for Irish people is racism. There is, on the face of it, a crippling contradiction in the far-right politics now embraced by Morrissey. If its non-negotiable core value is fear and loathing of immigrants, how can the son of Irish immigrants be its poster boy? The great solvent is whiteness. What does not need to be stated openly is that what is really at stake is neither your Irish blood nor your English heart. It is your white skin. This may be the last resort of those who can't hack a dual identity, but it's also the first resort. As one of the characters in Tom Murphy's great play of 1961, *A Whistle in the Dark*, set among Irish immigrants in Coventry, puts it: if it wasn't for the Muslims, our skins would look a lot darker to the English.

We need to remember that this is one way Irishness can go in an age of multiple identities. It takes some courage and some creativity to be comfortably more than one thing, which is what we have to be. If those qualities sour into either/or identity politics, we will be left with no heart and a great deal of blood.

11 June 2019

*Michael Gove, a candidate for the leadership of the
Conservative Party, admits that he used to use cocaine.
This helps explain the hostility to the Good Friday Agreement
that is an undercurrent in pro-Brexit discourse.*

So now we know: it was the drugs. Michael Gove, a key figure in the creation of Brexit and a contender to be the next British prime minister, was dosing himself with cocaine before writing his columns and pamphlets 'about 20 years ago'. That is when he published a long polemical essay called *The Price of Peace*. It is an important document. Gove is what passes for the intellectual driving force behind Brexit. *The Price of Peace* is an attack on the Belfast Agreement. If you want to understand the inherent hostility to the peace process that is at the heart of the Brexit project, you have to read it.

But now, you can read it as a set of symptoms. Which of us, at some point in our lives, has not had to utter those mortifying words prompted by some painful memories of offensive nonsense spouted the night before, 'Oh God, I'm so sorry. It was the drink talking'? We can now, surely, look forward to the Brexiteers' shame-faced apology for the drivel they have spouted about Northern Ireland – that wasn't really Michael, it was just Charlie talking.

The short-term physiological effects of cocaine use include dilated pupils and increased body temperature, heart rate and blood pressure. Knowing what we now know, it is easy to see at least some of these effects in Gove's polemic. Dilated pupils? Check. Gove's vision was undoubtedly askew. He could not see the big picture of conflict resolution but only an assault on all things moral and British (terms that are, of course, synonymous): 'The Belfast Agreement has, at its heart… an even greater wickedness. It is a capitulation to violence, a validation of terrorism which has led "demilitarisation" – the removal of the British army from our sovereign territory – to be rendered as the equivalent to "decommissioning" – the placing beyond use of illegally-held criminal arsenals. The moral stain of such a process will prove hard to efface. It is a humiliation of our army, police and parliament. But, worse still, it is a denial of our national integrity, in every sense of the word.'

Overheated rhetoric and rising blood pressure? Check. Michael/ Charlie insisted on drawing parallels between the Belfast Agreement and the appeasement of the Nazis in the 1930s. The word 'appeasement' appears eight times in the pamphlet, culminating in this coked-up rant: 'The men who opposed Munich found the Government of their time capable of manipulating the Royal Family to bestow a special sanction on a flawed policy. Those who warned of the consequences of appeasement in the Thirties were derided as glamour boys, renegades and warmongers. But if it were not for their opposition then who would there have been to rescue the nation from folly?'

This, of course, exhibits another classic symptom of cocaine use: a ludicrous grandiosity. In the throes of a cocaine rush, users may feel what the online Urban Dictionary calls 'cocainomania', defined as a 'false sense of grandeur under the influence of cocaine'. It cites an example of proper usage of the term: 'Dave thinks he's all powerful when he's coked out. He's got some serious cocainomania.' Or, as we might now say: 'Michael thinks he's Winston Churchill when he's coked out.' Because his pose in *The Price of Peace* is as a lone voice who may now be derided by flabby liberals as a warmonger, but who will in time be recognised as having rescued the nation from the folly of appeasing the IRA.

In high doses, say the medical experts, cocaine use can lead to extreme paranoia. One suspects that Gove may have done a few extra lines before writing *The Price of Peace* because the paranoia is turned up to eleven. It goes off the scale as Michael/Charlie identifies the creation of the Northern Ireland Human Rights Commission as the end of British civilisation as we know it: 'Creating a culture of children's rights would allow sons to sue fathers and mothers pursue daughters for slights real or imagined... Creating new rights to eradicate "disablism" would mean that institutions such as the police, fire service or army would no longer be able to discriminate in favour of the able-bodied... Creating new rights for transsexuals again allows common sense to be supplanted by legal intrusion. Will new rights to marry, adopt and enter any job of their choosing be extended? And if so, at what cost to the dignity, stability and durability of our tested notions of married life?'

For Michael/Charlie, the Belfast Agreement was, in his words, a Trojan horse carrying into the citadel of Britishness the enemies that would burn down Britain and leave the fire brigade unable to put out the flames because it is full of disabled transsexuals (sniff). It would create the dystopian nightmare of children suing their parents (sniff), wheelchair users in the army (sniff) and the stability and durability of married life, embodied presumably by such fine characters as Gove's then buddy Boris Johnson, forever gone (sniff, sniff).

At least now we know – it was Class A thinking from a Class A mind. These insights from the Boy from the White Stuff are not to be sniffed at.

14 June 2019

*The language of humiliation has become deeply
embedded in the language of Brexit and arises
again in the Tory leadership contest.*

Launching his bid for the Tory leadership this week, Dominic Raab announced, histrionically: 'We've been humiliated as a country.' For those of us who do not live on planet Brexit, this might have been mistaken for a belated reaction to the genuinely demeaning spectacle of Donald Trump's state visit a week earlier. But, of course, like almost all of his fellow contenders to be the next prime minister, Raab was playing his part in a strange performance in which the national honour has been so horribly besmirched by the European Union that it can be salved only by taking the pain of a no-deal Brexit.

Perhaps if you keep acting out phoney feelings, you end up not being able to recognise the real thing. Brexit Britain has been wallowing in a hyped-up psychodrama of national humiliation. It is, indeed, one of the very few things that Remainers and Leavers still share, even if they feel mortified for very different reasons. In relation to the EU, this sense of humiliation is wildly overplayed. But when Trump comes to town and really does degrade Britain, the sense of wounded dignity that ought to be felt seems curiously absent.

Trump's state visit sure looked like an episode of national humiliation. From the gratuitous insults tweeted about London mayor Sadiq Khan and the blatant interference in internal UK politics, to the sweeping demands as to what must be on the table in a prospective trade deal, to his openly patronising attitude to the serving prime minister, he acted like he was visiting one of his own resorts rather than a respected foreign country. And, even worse, the British state literally made a show of itself for him, rolling out its monarchy and its military as performers to entertain the emperor and his royal family of Trumps.

Now, in a way, this is fine. Humiliation is not an objective reality. It is calibrated against one's sense of one's own status. If you're used to travelling business class, you may feel humiliated by having to sit in economy; but if you've always sat in economy, it's just normal. So perhaps the willingness to suck up Trump's domineering boorishness is a sign of realism, even of maturity – this is what's it's like to be a medium-sized country dependent on a superpower. Standing on one's dignity is an indulgence Britain can no longer afford.

Fair enough. But then how come the idea of national humiliation has loomed so large in Brexit? Shortly before the missed departure date of 29 March, a Sky Data poll asked: 'Is the way Britain is dealing with Brexit a national humiliation?' Ninety per cent of respondents said yes. This idea of collective abasement is everywhere in the Brexit narrative. A random sample of headlines from across the spectrum tells the story: 'Brexit and the prospect of national humiliation' (*Financial Times*); 'Voice of the Mirror: Theresa May's Brexit is a national humiliation'; 'A national humiliation: Never was so much embarrassment caused to so many by so few' (*Daily Telegraph*); '"Humiliating to have to beg" for EU exit, says Arlene Foster' (*Irish Times*). And so, endlessly, on.

There is something hysterical in this constant evocation of humiliation. It is a cry of outraged self-regard: how dare they treat us like this?

Yes, of course, the Brexit debacle has reduced Britain's prestige around the world. And the withdrawal agreement negotiated by Theresa May is indeed a miserable thing when compared with the glorious visions that preceded it. But Britain has not been humiliated by the EU – the deal was shaped by May's (and Arlene Foster's) red lines. Britain did not get what the Brexiteers fantasised about, but it did get what it actually asked for. That's not humiliation.

There is, of course, a long British tradition of phoney affront. When Britain was an aggressive imperial power, it was always on the lookout for intolerable slights to the national honour – think of the War of Jenkins' Ear in the eighteenth century, when an assault on an English smuggler was the excuse for war with Spain. Perhaps when you are truly powerful there is even a certain pleasure in imagining the opposite. As the poet and critic Wayne Koestenbaum has written: 'Humiliation is bliss if the experience of largeness or magnitude has become overwhelming and unpleasant and you need relief.'

But a feeling that provided relief from the overwhelming greatness of empire becomes ridiculous when you are no longer a great power. It becomes a mere posture. This is what happened to the idea of national humiliation in the Brexit mentality. At its heart, Brexit depends on the idea that Britain cannot be an ordinary European country and, therefore, that equality within the EU is inherently humiliating. The EU traps a business-class country in economy class, where it must writhe in resentment, hemmed in between lesser nations and tormented by visions of the silver service and fine wines it should be getting instead of 'chicken or beef'.

And yet we have the apparently untroubled self-abasement towards Trump. National humiliation, it seems, depends on which nation or group of nations is inflicting the offence. Mere equality with France and Germany and Spain is intolerably demeaning. Subservience to a loutish US president is not. Honour is impugned when the EU negotiates realistically but not when Trump casually abuses elected English politicians and interferes in the selection of the next prime minister.

Britain is humiliated by the EU because it expects to be superior. It is not humiliated by Trump because, for all the illusion of a special relationship, it accepts that it is a junior partner. In one context, dominance is demanded; in the other, subservience is accepted. So much for honour. 'What,' Shakespeare's Falstaff asks, 'is honour?', and he answers: 'a word'. And so is its opposite, humiliation. But a dangerous word. It may have no substance, but it has the power to harm. It brings down with it an acid rain of corrosive emotions: the need, at all costs, not to lose face, the indulgence of self-pity, the demented idea that national pride can be restored only by the endurance of great pain.

It needs to be banished from the Brexit discourse. Acknowledging reality is not humiliating. Accepting that you have made a mistake is not humiliating. If this poisonous word can be avoided when it has no meaning, perhaps it can be used when it really is called for.

18 June 2019

It is becoming inevitable that Boris Johnson will win the
Tory leadership contest and become prime minister.
How does such an egregious liar rise so far?

If lies were flies, the swarm around him would be so thick that
Boris Johnson would be invisible. His gruff, mock-jovial Etonian
tones would be drowned out by their incessant, deafening hum.
There is ordinary political lying – evasions, circumlocutions, omissions, half-truths. And then there is Johnsonian lying – bare-faced,
full-throated, unabashed. I wonder is this the real mark of how far
British political life has fallen: people are so sick of the first kind
of dishonesty that they actually find Johnson's upfront mendacity
refreshing. Is this the only kind of authenticity some of them
can now imagine: the honest liar whose fabrications are unadulterated by any vestigial belief that truth even exists?

When Johnson was Brussels correspondent of the *Daily Telegraph*, his colleagues from the rest of the British media made up
a version of Hilaire Belloc's 'Matilda' in his honour: 'Boris told
such dreadful lies / It made one gasp and stretch one's eyes. /
His desk, which from its earliest youth / Had kept a strict regard
for truth, / Attempted to believe each scoop / Until they landed
in the soup.' He got away with it, of course, because mostly what
he lied about, in public at least, was the European Union. Even
for once-respectable Tory papers such as the *Telegraph*, the EU has
always been a free-fire zone. The rules of engagement are different
– minimal respect for facts is not required.

I went back and read Johnson's *Telegraph* column of 16 March
2016. It is important because it is the one in which he announced

that he was backing Brexit in the referendum. We now know that Johnson had in fact submitted two columns – the other one arguing passionately for Remain – because he had not, at deadline time, decided where the greatest advantage lay for his own career. Had the other column been printed, Brexit would not have happened: polls show that Johnson was by far the most influential figure in the referendum campaign. On such idiocies the fate of nations turns.

The core of the column that did appear is the intolerable craziness of EU legislation: 'Sometimes these EU rules sound simply ludicrous, like the rule that you can't recycle a teabag, or that children under eight cannot blow up balloons, or the limits on the power of vacuum cleaners. Sometimes they can be truly infuriating – like the time I discovered, in 2013, that there was nothing we could do to bring in better-designed cab windows for trucks, to stop cyclists being crushed.'

The EU says you can't recycle a teabag – lie. The truth is that some local councils in Britain itself had introduced this restriction: nothing to do with the EU. Children under eight cannot blow up balloons – lie. EU safety rules simply say that packets of balloons should carry the words: 'Warning: children under eight can choke or suffocate.' Limits on the power of vacuum cleaners – half true. The EU did have such limits, for good environmental reasons, but they were subsequently overturned by the European Court, which Johnson hates. Johnson as mayor of London being prevented by the EU from requiring safer cab windows to protect cyclists – a flaming beacon of deceit. In 2014, when he was mayor, Johnson actually made precisely the opposite complaint, that the British government was failing to back EU proposals for safer cab windows: 'If these amendments, supported by dozens of cities across Europe, can succeed, we can save literally hundreds of lives across the EU in years to come. I am deeply concerned at the position of the British government and urge them to embrace this vital issue.'

How does he continue to thrive on lies? In part because of a disgraceful dereliction of duty on the part of the *Telegraph*, which pays him almost €300,000 a year but refuses to hold him to the most basic standards of professional journalism. In April, when the paper was forced to retract a false claim by Johnson that polls showed a no-deal Brexit to be the most popular option, it added that Johnson was 'entitled to make sweeping generalisations based on his opinions' and that his column 'was clearly comically polemical, and could not be reasonably read as a serious, empirical, in-depth analysis of hard factual matters'.

Comically polemical says it all. Johnson has managed to claim the privileges of the Fool while seeking to play the King. He operates in the space between politics and buffoonery and shifts from one side to the other whenever it suits him. When he is lying, he is making political statements that shape the views of millions. When he is called out on the lies, they are just jokes.

In this, Johnson embodies more than anyone else the weirdly performative nature of Brexit as a jolly jape with real and awful consequences. It is simultaneously tragic and farcical. No one better captures this than BoJo the clown who doubles as Johnson the ringmaster. There is a horrible logic to the man whose own newspaper insists he 'could not be taken seriously' rising to lead his country in its most profound crisis for many decades. Who better to speak for a reckless and decadent ruling class for whom everything is desperate but nothing is serious?

25 June 2019

Why England and Ireland take vastly different
approaches to the Continent.

E arly on Sunday morning I was standing on the Via Cavana in Trieste having my photograph taken for *Il Piccolo della Sera*. This is of no earthly interest to anyone except that *Il Piccolo della Sera* was the newspaper for which James Joyce wrote, in perfect Italian of course, his most extensive incursions into journalism.

They were, for the most part, explanations of contemporary Irish politics and replies to the misrepresentations of the English press. I have always thought it a little odd that the most important commentaries on Irish affairs by arguably the most important Irish writer appeared in the local paper of a provincial Austro-Hungarian port city. But when you're actually in Trieste and when the same newspaper wants to talk to you about Brexit, it doesn't seem odd at all. It just seems European.

One of the things we are experiencing at the moment is a gulf of comprehension between large parts of the English establishment (the Brexity parts) and Ireland.

It has many facets, but one of them has to do with a difference in cultural genealogy. Most of the great works of modern English literature and art were created in England or, at very least, within the empire. But on the other hand, it is very hard to think of modern Irish literature and art without thinking of continental Europe.

John Synge and W. B. Yeats, the great collaborators (with Augusta Gregory) in the creation of the Abbey, didn't meet in Sligo or on the Aran Islands – they met in Paris. So did Joyce and Samuel Beckett. Most of Eileen Grey's great design work was done in

France. Kate O'Brien really became a writer in Spain, as did Colm Toibín. And so on.

When Joyce and Nora Barnacle left Dublin in 1904, they didn't go to London or New York. They made their way to Trieste, where, on their very first night, Joyce got himself arrested after being caught up in a brawl with English sailors.

Even today, it is a frontier city, on the edges of three countries – Italy, Slovenia and Croatia. But in the years that Joyce lived there (most of the period between 1904 and 1915 and again briefly in 1919 and 1920), Trieste was even more multicultural – Italian, Austrian, Slavic, Jewish, Greek.

Joyce was close to the Jewish community – his great friend, the writer Italo Svevo, became one of the models for Leopold Bloom. He taught English to wealthy Greek merchants and attended services in the beautiful Greek Orthodox (now Serbian Orthodox) church of San Nicolò. He feasted on this stew of languages and cultures.

It is, for all sorts of reasons, impossible to imagine the great anatomies of early twentieth-century London being produced in such a place. But when we think of *Dubliners*, with its minute etching of the physical and mental topography of the city, we have to remind ourselves that most of it was written, not in our capital, but in a second-floor flat in Via San Nicolò.

It was on the third floor of a house in Via Nuova that Joyce rewrote *Stephen Hero* as *A Portrait of the Artist as a Young Man*. In a second-floor room on Via Donato Bramante, he began work on perhaps the greatest of all Irish artistic achievements, *Ulysses*.

Joyce is inscribed on this city but it is also inscribed on his Dublin – it was Trieste that gave Joyce the sheer cosmopolitan energy that he infused back into the native city he had left in disgust, making it not the dull provincial nowhere he had fled but, in his re-imagining, a European metropolis.

I've been vaguely aware of all of this ever since I first read Joyce as a teenager, but it is particularly striking to encounter it physically while at the same time trying to explain Brexit to Italians.

It brings home the fact that, while Ireland and England are much more alike than we Irish like to admit, there is a gulf between us when it comes to attitudes to Europe.

Some of it has to do with political history – English nationalism defined itself in part against France; Irish nationalism looked first to Spain and then to France as places of refuge and sources of salvation. (Germany, too, in 1916 and – for the fanatics of the IRA – in the years of the Second World War, but we don't like to talk about that.) Some of it is religious – its Protestantism divided England from Catholic Europe; Irish Catholicism felt, of course, part of it.

But some of it goes beyond those dreary tribal identities. Perhaps, being obviously small, Ireland could find in the expansiveness of the Continent a relief from claustrophobia. And paradoxically, in that release lay the possibility of looking back on Ireland itself, as Joyce did so wonderfully, without rancour but with a good-humoured forgiveness. What he did in the early years of the twentieth century, his country men and women did after EU membership in 1973 – being European gave us relief and release from being too much enclosed in our own company and thus allowed us to get over ourselves. That, sadly, has not been quite the case for our nearest neighbours.

2 July 2019

*In the Tory leadership contest an idea that was confined
to the lunatic fringe just three years ago – the embrace of a
no-deal Brexit – has become a statement of principle.*

Nothing will come of nothing. Perhaps the greatest work of the English imagination, William Shakespeare's *King Lear* is about the breakup of Britain. It begins with a feckless act of misrule and some capricious egotism and it ends in catastrophe. And at its heart is nothing at all. When Lear's daughter Cordelia refuses to play along with his narcissistic demands for flattery, he asks what more she has to say. 'Nothing, my lord.' The word bounces back and forth between them, uttered five times in four lines. Lear warns that 'Nothing will come of nothing'. He does not yet know what he is saying: that this dark non-thing will grow and grow until it blots out everything – all meaning, all possibility, all of the future.

Brexit is nothing. It was always a negative proposition. Most British leaders, even those who wanted to stay in, never created for their people any positive vision of the European Union. It was spoken of grudgingly and engaged with defensively. The Remain campaign in 2016 essentially presented staying in as the lesser of two evils: the EU is bad but leaving it would be even worse. And David Cameron's egotistical capriciousness allowed the Leave campaign to offer a pure negative: vote for what you don't want (EU membership).

It was not required to put forward any clear sense of what would happen after it won. It pointed to the exit sign but shed no light on what lies outside the door. Insofar as it offered any vision

– £350 million a week for the NHS, sunny uplands, global Britain, easiest deal ever, have cake/eat cake, Brexit means Brexit – it was a thing of airy nothing.

And nothing does in the end come of nothing. Three years ago, very few of the Brexiteers, let alone those who voted for them, really imagined that Britain would simply leave the EU with no agreement on a future relationship. Few suggested that affiliation would be anything other than close. Yet here we are now with both contenders for the leadership of the Tory party, Boris Johnson and Jeremy Hunt, proposing a no-deal Brexit as a serious possibility that must be kept on the table. The lunatic fringe of 2016 is now at the centre.

This madness has a Lear-like logic. Brexit is a nothing that pretended to be a thing, a departure that posed as a destination, a breakup masquerading as a relationship. It knows only what it is not. It is rooted in a crisis of identity within the UK and thus there is an absurd rationale in Brexit ending up with a supposed policy that is merely an absence: no deal. The Brexit discourse has now arrived at the point where it has to present that nothing as if it were a something, as if failing to create an alternative to EU membership is in fact the alternative.

This is, in its own mad way, a version of that great British tradition, heroic failure. If the Light Brigade could be heroes for not charging in the right direction, it is always possible to imagine not being able to do a deal as a heroic act. Impotence, in this strange mindset, becomes potent. The collapse, you can convince yourself, is what you were always trying to construct.

Swept along on this crazy current, anarchism (the Tory anarchism that fuses the recklessness of a hollowed-out imperial ruling caste with a neoliberal disdain for the state) becomes nihilism. The last word of the Sex Pistols' 'Anarchy in the UK', which increasingly functions as the soundtrack of Brexit, is an exultant, orgiastic 'Destroy!'. If you cannot govern, you can always misgovern. If Brexit cannot be shaped as a constructive project, it can work wonders of destruction.

If Conservatism is dead (and it is) Destructivism is the next best thing. Wreck the industrial economy by forcing the closure of all those car and aerospace plants with their just-in-time processes and integrated supply chains. Pull down the 'precious, precious union'. Blow up the Irish peace process. Remember these are not abstract threats – polls of Tory members show that they are indeed all acceptable to most of them as prices to be paid for Brexit. They are even, in this mood of nihilistic ecstasy, quite prepared to destroy their own party.

Philosophers and physicists tell us that the most fundamental question is, as Gottfried Leibniz put it: 'Why is there something rather than nothing?' Brexit, in the end, is going to have to resolve itself into something rather than nothing. At some point, the two negatives of Brexit (no plan, no deal) have to make a positive. England in particular is going to have to think about what it is rather than revelling in what it is not. What we do not know is how much pain it will wish upon itself in the meantime.

9 July 2019

*Chris Cook's breathtaking account of the Brexit
negotiations from the British point of view holds
up an unflattering mirror to the state.*

The word of the moment in England seems to be 'spaff' or its variants, 'spaffed' and 'spaffing'. The *Oxford English Dictionary*, even in its regularly updated online version, has not caught up with it yet, but it is nonetheless fashionable in political and media discourse. When words bubble up from obscurity like this, they often tell us something about the zeitgeist, and spaffing is very Brexity.

It is a public schoolboy term for male ejaculation. One of the earliest examples I can find in print is from an account in the *Telegraph* of a visit to a sperm bank: 'I decided to spaff into a cup back in 2014.' It has since come to mean any form of careless waste. Old Etonian Boris Johnson speaks, with exquisite bad taste, of money spent on police probes into historical child abuse allegations being 'spaffed up the wall'. It seems apt, both that English public discourse would need a word to describe the pleasures of pointless self-abuse and that it would find it in the puerile vocabulary of its male elite.

I find a particularly interesting example, though, in Chris Cook's riveting new account of how the British screwed up their negotiations with the EU, *Defeated by Brexit*. It is January 2017 and it is finally dawning on Theresa May and those around her that the Irish/UK border really is a problem. May's joint chief of staff Fiona Hill instructs Britain's most senior civil servant, the cabinet secretary Sir Jeremy Heywood, to commission experts to come up with technological solutions. Her actual instruction is: 'spaff some money on some geeks.' Eloquent in so many ways.

Cook's book is the first coherent account we have of the Brexit negotiations as seen by the politicians and civil servants involved on the British side. It is careful and considered and all the more devastating for its deadpan tone. It goes a long way towards answering a question over which generations of historians will argue. Was May merely the fall guy for an inevitable failure or was she utterly incompetent? The answer is, of course, both – May was doomed to fail but she and her government sure managed, to adapt Samuel Beckett, to fail better.

It is worth saying that the EU made mistakes, especially in the period between the Brexit referendum in June 2016 and May's triggering of the Article 50 withdrawal process in March 2017. Brussels pressured her to invoke Article 50 quickly, which meant of course setting the clock ticking before she had created any clear consensus about what Britain could realistically hope to achieve. It also refused to engage in 'pre-negotiations' that might have allowed for some informal testing out of those possibilities. These were tactical victories for the EU side but strategic mistakes – they contributed to what we are obliged to call the spaffing up the wall of the previous two years of negotiation. But given the perfect storm of political incompetence and administrative incapacity on the British side, this contribution was in truth quite small.

Cook's informants within the diplomatic service tell him that, a year before the referendum, their Irish counterparts were already cornering them at EU meetings and demanding 'answers about what would happen in the event of a Leave vote'.

But the British did not merely not have the answers – they were not allowed to have them. According to one official, 'the instruction' to Whitehall from David Cameron's government 'was clear: Don't do any preparation.' Another official explains: 'Our contingency for losing [the referendum] was not losing.'

When they did lose, May came to power and established the 'department for exiting the European Union' under David Davis, described by Chris Patten in a foreword to Cook's book as 'breezy, open, amiable, lazy and incompetent'. Mandarins who had actually worked on European issues were actively excluded on the grounds that they might have 'gone native'. (Now there's another resonant term.) The result, according to Cook's analysis of the cohort of senior officials working on Brexit, is not merely that nearly all of them were 'generalists' with little knowledge of the EU or trade, but that, astonishingly, their average age is thirty. 'A third of the department were born since the passing of the Maastricht Treaty in 1991.' Is it surprising that the gallant youth of England, sent to charge the heavy guns of Brussels with their flashing sabres, got mown down?

And then there was May. She simply refused all entreaties from her officials to make a decision on the most obvious question: did the UK want to remain in the customs union? 'Stop bringing me binary choices,' she snapped at them. 'This is not going to be a binary choice.' She decided in mid-2017 that no-deal was impossible – but then decided not to tell anybody. Above all, she indulged a fatal miscalculation by some of her cabinet who continued to believe, as one minister tells Cook, 'that the Irish were really bluffing about this'. On the ideas floating around in Whitehall for the border, one official asks Cook: 'Has someone told you about facial recognition for pigs?' His mind-blowing book is a spiffing tale of a state spaffing away its culture of competence.

17 July 2019

*Meanwhile, another book, by Rod Liddle, articulates the myth
of betrayal that has taken hold among the Brexiteers.*

'Never,' Rod Liddle writes in his jeremiad on the 'betrayal'
of Brexit, 'have so many blameless people in this country
been held in such contempt, or been subject to such
vilification by an elite.' Really? Who wrote in 2014 of Britain as
'a nation of broken families clamouring about their entitlements
siring ill-educated and undisciplined kids unfamiliar with the concept of right and wrong'? Who described with relish 'the hulking
fat tattooed chavmonkey standing in the queue at Burger King'?
Who characterised the British masses as inhabiting 'a dumbed-
down culture', being in thrall to 'the background fugue of idiocy,
the moronic inferno, of celebrity fuckstories', and spending their
time 'watching TV, masturbating to pornography on the internet,
getting drunk'? That would be Liddle in his last book, whose title,
Selfish Whinging Monkeys, may just possibly have had a slight whiff
of contempt and vilification.

But that was then, this is now. Liddle's 'chavmonkeys' have
been redeemed by the Brexit referendum. Their 'fugue of idiocy'
is now a swelling symphony of reasserted sovereignty, their
'dumbed-down culture' a fount of wisdom. The man who saw 'a
moronic inferno' now champions the people against the 'stereo-
type of the decrepit moron Leave voter'. For now, apparently, it
is liberal Remainers who commit the unforgivable sin of calling
those voters stupid, 'uneducated thickos' – and racists to boot.
The evidence for this contention, as for everything else in Liddle's
polemic, is vanishingly thin. Yet the claim is central to his diagnosis

of 'a grotesque and unprecedented betrayal of the country' by the BBC, parliament, the judiciary, the civil service, Theresa May's government and of course 'Irish spite', embodied in that 'oily little shit', the taoiseach Leo Varadkar.

Liddle recalls that on the morning of the referendum result in 2016, he posted a one-line message on his Facebook page: 'Betcha we don't leave.' He now adds that he and his wife agreed that 'they won't let it happen'. Thus his narrative of Brexit betrayed is not a response to events since that (for him) glorious morning. It is the chronicle of a death foretold. And in a sense, this intuition of inevitable failure was quite right. Failure was baked in. The promise of a Brexit that delivered all the benefits of EU membership with none of the costs could not survive contact with reality. Brexit was not 'betrayed'. It was dead on arrival.

What makes Liddle's book so dishonest is that he seems well aware of this, but persists with his preprepared tale of treachery nonetheless. He accepts that Donald Tusk 'had a point' when he spoke of a special place in hell for those who urged people to vote Leave without having a plan for Brexit. He concedes that the Leave campaign was 'utterly lost' in the aftermath of its victory: 'There was no sense of direction, no notion of a strategy, no notion as to how to proceed from here.' How can a non-existent project, one that is already 'utterly lost', be betrayed? Can a strategy that has never been created be thwarted by traitors?

Tellingly, Liddle specifies the moment of perfidy. The conspiracy, as he sees it, began as soon as 'the establishment' started talking about a 'hard Brexit' and a 'soft Brexit', 'whereas hitherto we had simply been talking about Brexit'. In other words, the betrayal started as soon as 'Brexit' acquired any actual content. Once 'Brexit means Brexit' became 'Brexit means this or that', it was being sold out. There is here a kind of truth – the pure, unbetrayed Brexit could exist only in the abstract. To give it concrete meaning was to sully it. Nowhere does Liddle ever tell us what he himself actually thinks Brexit means in the real world. How could he, since by his own definition that would be an act of betrayal?

Of a piece is Liddle's suggestion that Brexit was betrayed because its implementation was allowed to pass into the 'hands of politicians... and away from the people who had voted'. How exactly does he think 'the people who had voted' were supposed to negotiate the mutual rights of citizens, the divorce bill, the UK–Ireland border and a vastly complex trade deal? Even conceding that the people who were, in Liddle's pre-Brexit rantings, so sunk in idiocy five years ago, are now intellectual giants, how might this process be managed? Might the people, perhaps, elect delegates to some kind of representative assembly which in turn would choose an executive?

Liddle is as untroubled by facts as by logic. He repeatedly cites the figure of £9 billion as the UK's annual net contribution to the EU – it is £7.9 billion. The House of Commons library report of 24 June on the net contribution says the £9 billion does not take account of EU funds given to non-governmental agencies in the UK (universities and so on). He thinks Ireland was 'forced' by the EU to hold another referendum on the Nice treaty in 2001 – it wasn't. He thinks the DUP speaks for 'the Northern Irish', even though it gets a third of the vote and does not represent the strongly anti-Brexit majority. He claims Britain could have negotiated a trade deal with the EU before it discussed a withdrawal agreement, even though the EU can't do a trade deal with Britain until it has actually left. His understanding of the border question – blockchain can solve 'almost all' the problems – is childish. He even seems oblivious to the basic history of the UK: 'Our boundaries have not shifted much over the years.' (So Ireland neither joined the UK in 1801 nor left it in 1922?)

At the heart of Liddle's new pose as defender of the people is his righteous rage against 'the allegations that Leave voters were all racists'. His only actual source for this 'allegation' is Diane Abbott, who Liddle quotes as saying that 'people who intended voting Leave "want to see less foreign-looking people on their streets"'. Abbott did not say this about people who intended to vote Leave. She said it on *Question Time* in April 2017, long after the vote. She did not say it about Leave voters as a whole – she actually said: 'The people that complain about the freedom of movement will not be satisfied because what they really want is to see less foreign-looking people on their streets.' And she also added that she would 'never say that people voted to come out because they were racist'. This is the sole foundation for Liddle's core argument.

Equally disingenuous, though, is his contention that racism and xenophobia played no role at all in the Leave vote. The grossly misleading posters showing brown-skin hordes supposedly queueing to get into the EU were 'a matter of taste rather than accuracy'. He acknowledges that the use by the official Leave campaign of Turkey's allegedly imminent membership of the EU was 'a little bit speculative'. But, he adds, it did not affect 'a single vote, apart maybe from some Kurds'. He does not tell us how he knows this or whether he has explained to Nigel Farage, Boris Johnson and Dominic Cummings how they wasted so much money and effort in appealing to a non-existent xenophobia.

It is just as well that it does not exist. If it did, people might misunderstand the benign nature of Liddle's questions about whether immigrants can have proper feelings for 'the nation': 'If you are a fairly recent arrival in this country, does its long existence as a nation state matter very much to you? Do you have a stake in our history? Is the UK's history as an independent country as impinging as it might be on someone whose family has lived here for countless generations?' He insists on giving one despised anti-Brexit campaigner her full name: 'Gina Miller, née Singh' though he never refers, for example, to 'Theresa May, née Brasier'. Otherwise readers might not realise that beneath Miller's English-sounding name lurks a woman with no stake in 'our' history. Here we face the underlying toxicity of the myth of betrayal. Without the treachery of those who do not belong to 'us', Brexit would always have been wonderful. Since it is not, we know who to blame.

17 July 2019

*As Boris Johnson's progress towards 10 Downing Street
acquires the aura of inevitability, his books
give us some sense of who he is.*

In his only novel, *Seventy-Two Virgins*, published in 2004, Boris Johnson uses a strange word. The hero, like Johnson himself at the time, is a backbench Conservative member of the House of Commons. Roger Barlow is, indeed, a somewhat unflattering self-portrait – he bicycles to Westminster, he is unfaithful to his wife, he is flippantly racist and politically opportunistic, and he is famously dishevelled.

In the fond imagination of one Commons secretary who crossed his path he had the air of a man who had just burst through a hedge after running through a garden having climbed down a drainpipe on being surprised in the wrong marital bed.

Barlow, throughout the novel, is in constant fear that his political career is about to be ended by a tabloid scandal. In a moment of introspection, he reflects on this anxiety:

There was something prurient about the way he wanted to read about his own destruction, just as there was something weird about the way he had been impelled down the course he had followed. Maybe he wasn't a genuine *akratic*. Maybe it would be more accurate to say he had a *thanatos* urge [emphases added].

The novel is a mass-market comic thriller about a terrorist plot to capture the US president while he is addressing parliament in

331

London. The Greek terms stand out. In part, they function as signifiers of social class within a long-established code of linguistic manners: a sprinkling of classical phrases marks one out as a product of an elite private school (in Johnson's case, Eton) and therefore a proper toff. (Asked in June during the contest to replace Theresa May as Tory leader to name his political hero, Johnson chose Pericles of Athens.) The choice of *thanatos* is interesting, and the thought that he might have a death wish will ring bells for those who have followed the breathtaking recklessness of Johnson's career. But it is *akratic* that intrigues.

The Leave campaign that Johnson led to a stunning victory in the Brexit referendum of June 2016 owed much of its success to its carefully calibrated slogan 'Take Back Control'. *Akrasia*, which is discussed in depth by Socrates, Plato, and especially Aristotle in the *Nicomachean Ethics*, is the contrary of control. It means literally 'not being in command of oneself' and is translated variously as 'weakness of will', 'incontinence' and 'loss of self-control'. To Aristotle, an akratic is a person who knows the right thing to do but can't help doing the opposite. This is not just, as he himself seems to have intuited, Boris Johnson to a tee. It is also the reason why he embodies more than anyone else a Brexit project in which the very people who promised to take back control are utterly incapable of exercising it, even over themselves. 'Oh God, oh Gawd,' asks Barlow in a question that now echoes through much of the British establishment, 'why had he done it? Why had he put himself in this ludicrous position?'

To grasp how Johnson's akratic character has brought his country to a state approaching anarchy, it is necessary to return to the days immediately before 21 February 2016, when he announced to an expectant throng of journalists that he would support the Leave campaign. This was a crucial moment – polls have since shown that, in what turned out to be a very close-run referendum, Boris, as the mayor of London had branded himself, had a greater influence on voters than anyone else. 'Character is destiny, said the Greeks, and I agree,' writes Johnson in *The Churchill Factor*, his 2014 book about Winston Churchill, which carries the telling subtitle 'How One Man Made History'. While the book shows Johnson to be a true believer in the Great Man theory of history, his own moment of destiny plays it out as farce, the fate of a nation turning not on Churchillian resolution but on Johnsonian indecision. For Johnson was, in his own words, 'veering all over the place like a shopping trolley'. On Saturday 20 February, he texted Prime Minister David Cameron to say he was going to advocate for Brexit. A few hours later, he texted again to say that he might change his mind and back Remain.

Sometime between then and the following day, he wrote at least two different columns for the *Daily Telegraph* – his deadline was looming, so he wrote one passionately arguing for Leave and one arguing that the cost of Brexit would be too high. (Asked once if he had any convictions, Johnson replied, 'Only one – for speeding...') Then, early on Sunday evening, he texted Cameron to say that he was about to announce irrevocably that he was backing Leave. But, as Cameron told his communications director, Craig Oliver, at the time, Johnson added two remarkable things. One was that 'he doesn't expect to win, believing Brexit will be "crushed."' The other was staggering: '"He actually said he thought we could leave and still have a seat on the European Council – still making decisions."'

The expectation – perhaps the hope – of defeat is telling. Johnson's anti-EU rhetoric was always a Punch and Judy show, and without the EU to play Judy, the show would be over. But the belief that Britain would keep its seat on the European Council (which consists of the leaders of each member state and makes most of the EU's big political decisions), even if it left the EU, is mind-melting. Not only was Johnson unconvinced that he was taking the right side on one of the most important questions his country has faced since the Second World War, but he was unaware of the most basic consequence of Brexit. Britain had joined the Common Market, as it was then called, in 1973 precisely because it was being profoundly affected by decisions made in Brussels and was therefore better off having an equal say in those decisions. Johnson's belief that Britain would continue to have a seat at the European table after Brexit suggested a profound ignorance not just of his country's future but of its entire post-war past.

This ignorance is not stupidity – Johnson is genuinely clever and, as his fictional alter ego Barlow shows, quite self-aware. It is the studied carelessness affected by a large part of the English upper class whose manners and attitudes Johnson – in reality the product of a rather bohemian bourgeois background – thoroughly absorbed. Consequences are for the little people, seriousness for those who are paid to clean up the mess. In *Seventy-Two Virgins*, Barlow is anatomised by his sober-minded intern. (It is typical of Johnson's incestuously chummy rivalry with his fellow Old Etonian and rising Tory star that this lowly assistant is named Cameron.) She watches him in action at a constituency meeting: 'Barlow had given an intelligent answer... and then thrown it all away with some flip aside... Didn't he understand that these guys cared about this question?' Caring about the question is not Barlow's, or Johnson's, thing. Everything Johnson says is really a flip aside. As Cameron (the intern, but presumably also the prime minister) concludes, 'he is characterised by his political evasiveness, his moral evasiveness, and indeed, dammit, his sheer physical evasiveness'.

'Evasiveness' can be a polite term for lying, and it is impossible to understand Johnson without recalling that he has quite literally made a career of mendacity. At the end of that fateful weekend in February 2016, the *Telegraph*, which pays him £275,000 a year for a weekly column, dutifully spiked his sincere plea to Remain and published his anti-EU column. It cited as the main reason for Brexit that 'the more the EU does, the less room there is for national decision-making. Sometimes these EU rules sound simply ludicrous, like the rule that you can't recycle a teabag, or that children under eight cannot blow up balloons.' The truth is that some local councils in Britain itself had introduced rules against recycling teabags, which have nothing to do with the EU. As for children under eight not being allowed to blow up balloons, EU safety rules simply say that packets of balloons should carry the words 'Warning: children under eight can choke or suffocate.'

But Johnson has always understood that a vivid lie is much more memorable than a dull truth. He is a product of the tight little world of English class privilege in which the same people move from elite schools to elite universities to (often interchangeable) careers in politics and the media. (Johnson's contemporaries at Oxford included David Cameron, a fellow member of the aggressively elitist Bullingdon Club; his own main rivals for the Tory leadership, Jeremy Hunt and Michael Gove; and the political editors of the BBC and Channel 4 who now report on him.) From Oxford he soon sailed into a position as a graduate trainee at *The Times*. It was there that he learned a valuable lesson: it pays to fabricate stories. *The Times* had to fire him because he sexed up a dull story by inventing lurid quotes and attributing them to a real Oxford historian (who happened to be his own godfather). Instead of ending his journalistic career, this was the seed from which it blossomed. Almost immediately he was hired by the *Daily Telegraph*, which then employed him as its Brussels correspondent between 1989 and 1994.

The job of a Brussels correspondent is an odd one. It almost entirely consists of covering the EU, and therefore it carries a degree of prestige. But most of the time the EU is immensely dull. Johnson thus had a plum job but one with little public profile. His genius was to turn page 20 stories into page 1 stories by seizing on relatively inconsequential EU market regulations and inflating them into attacks by demented foreigners on the British way of life. He claimed the EU had considered 'plans for a maximum condom width of fifty-four millimetres', which would, of course, restrict the better-endowed Englishman. He spotted a regulation limiting harmful additives in packets of potato chips (called 'crisps' in Britain) and made it a question of national sovereignty. As he confessed in 2002, 'Some of my most joyous hours have been spent in a state of semi-incoherence, composing foam-flecked hymns of hate to the latest Euro-infamy: the ban on the prawn cocktail flavour crisp.'

The stories were fabulous bubbles of outrage (prawn-cocktail flavoured crisps were never banned), but the foam-flecked hymns of hate were real. Sonia Purnell, who was his deputy in the *Telegraph*'s Brussels office in the early 1990s, describes in her excellent biography, *Just Boris: A Tale of Blond Ambition*, how far he went to transform himself:

> from Bumbling Boris to Bilious Boris before penning yet another explosive tract. Most days, just before copy deadline, he would do this by a tried-and-tested method known as the 'four o'clock rant.'... After locking his door, he would then work himself up into a frenzy by hurling repeated four-letter abuse at a ragged yucca plant near his desk.

Johnson's anti-EU journalistic performances were a kind of method acting – and they required from his editors and his readers a willing suspension of disbelief.

This raises the two central questions about Johnson – does he believe any of his own claims, and do his followers in turn believe him? In both cases, the answer is yes, but only in the highly qualified way that an actor inhabits his role and an audience knowingly accepts the pretence. Johnson's appeal lies precisely in the creation of a comic persona that evades the distinction between reality and performance.

The Greek philosophers found *akrasia* mysterious – why would people knowingly do the wrong thing? But Johnson knows the answer: they do so, in England at least, because knowingness is essential to being included. You have to be 'in on the joke' – and Johnson has shown just how far some English people will go in order not to look like they are not getting it. The anthropologist Kate Fox, in her classic study *Watching the English*, suggested that a crucial rule of the national discourse is what she called The Importance of Not Being Earnest: 'At the most basic level, an underlying rule in all English conversation is the proscription of "earnestness."' Johnson has played on this to perfection – he knows that millions of his compatriots would rather go along with his outrageous fabrications than be accused of the ultimate sin of taking things too seriously.

'Boris being Boris' (the phrase that has long been used to excuse him) is an act, a turn, a travelling show. Johnson's father, Stanley, was fired from his job at the World Bank in 1968 when he submitted a satiric proposal for a $100 million loan to Egypt to build three new pyramids and a sphinx. But the son cultivated in England an audience more receptive to the half-comic, half-convincing notion that the EU might be just such an absurdist enterprise.

What he honed in his Brussels years is the practice of political journalism (and then of politics itself) as *Monty Python* sketch. He invented a version of the EU as a gigantic Ministry of Silly Walks, in which crazed bureaucrats with huge budgets develop ever more pointlessly complicated gaits. (In the original sketch, the British bureaucrats are trying to keep up with 'Le Marché Commun', the Common Market.) Johnson's Brussels is a warren of bureaucratic redoubts in which lurk a Ministry of Dangerous Balloons, a Ministry of Tiny Condoms and a Ministry of Flavourless Crisps. In this theatre of the absurd, it never matters whether the stories are true; what matters is that they are ludicrous enough to fly under the radar of credibility and hit the sweet spot where pre-existing prejudices are confirmed.

This running joke made Johnson not just highly popular as a comic anti-politician but, for many of his compatriots, the embodiment of that patriotic treasure, the English eccentric. There is a long tradition of embracing the eccentric (though in reality only the upper-class male eccentric) as proof of the English love of liberty and individualism in contrast to the supposed slavishness of the European continentals. No less a figure than John Stuart Mill wrote in *On Liberty* (1859) that 'precisely because the tyranny of opinion is such as to make eccentricity a reproach, it is desirable, in order to break through that tyranny, that people should be eccentric.' Mill associated eccentricity with 'strength of character', but Johnson has been able to turn it upside down – his very weakness of character (the chaos, the fecklessness, the mendacity) provides for his admirers a patriotically heartening proof that the true English spirit has not yet been chewed up in the homogenising maw of a humourless and excessively organised EU.

Here we must bear in mind that Johnson really did learn a great deal from his boyhood hero Churchill. What he emulated was not any kind of steadfastness or ability to lead but a self-conscious political theatricality. 'He was,' writes Johnson in *The Churchill Factor*, 'eccentric, over the top, camp, with his own special trademark clothes'. Johnson's use of 'camp' is an astute insight – he understands very well the strain of louchely histrionic Toryism that runs from Benjamin Disraeli through Churchill to the intellectual father of Brexit, Enoch Powell. Johnson, too, has 'his own special trademark clothes', albeit that he is the anti-dandy whose slovenly dishevelment is carefully cultivated as a sartorial brand.

Johnson, moreover, uses Churchill to lend his own cynicism and mendacity a paradoxical kind of gravity. In his book he argues that the great wartime leader "wasn't what people thought of as a man of principle; he was a glory-chasing goal-mouth-hanging opportunist... As for his political career – my word, what a feast of bungling!... His enemies detected in him a titanic egotism, a desire to find whatever wave or wavelet he could, and surf it long after it had dissolved into spume on the beach... Throughout his early career he was not just held to be untrustworthy – he was thought to be congenitally untrustworthy."

This is not just Boris in drag as Winston. It is intended to suggest a crazed logic. Churchill was an unprincipled opportunist, a serial bungler and a congenitally untrustworthy egotist; therefore, only someone who has all of these qualities in abundance can become the new Churchill that conservative England craves. It is a mark of how far Britain has fallen that, in what may indeed be its biggest crisis since 1940, so many Tories are willing to suspend disbelief in Johnson's pantomime caricature of the man who gave it the courage to 'stand alone' in that dark hour. So what if he has the V for Victory sign the wrong way around?

What, though, might a Johnson premiership actually look like? Donald Trump is the obvious point of reference. Johnson told a closed meeting in June 2018 that he was 'increasingly admiring' of Trump and suggested that the US president would be the ideal negotiator for Britain with the EU: 'He'd go in bloody hard... there'd be all sorts of breakdowns, all sorts of chaos... Everyone would think he'd gone mad. But actually, you might get somewhere.' Trump, for his part, openly endorsed Johnson a week before his recent state visit to Britain: 'I think Boris would do a very good job. I think he would be excellent.'

Both men see themselves, with good reason, as creatures who thrive on chaos. Johnson also shares with Trump a puerile fascination with gigantic and illusory infrastructure projects. As mayor of London, he left the city with large bills for an unbuilt airport on a fantasy island (known to his fans in the press as 'Boris Island') and a 'garden bridge' across the Thames for which the abandoned plans cost £46 million. He proposed, shortly after leading the campaign to take Britain out of the EU, to deal with the threat of isolation from the Continent by somehow erasing the English Channel and thus undoing 'the physical separation that took place at the end of the Ice Age'. He has proposed to deal with Brexit's threat to Northern Ireland's place in the UK by building a vast (and impossible) bridge linking it to Scotland.

Both he and Trump are racists, though Johnson's variety is much more arch and knowing. When he wrote in 2002 of Queen Elizabeth, on her visits to Commonwealth countries, being greeted by 'flag-waving piccaninnies' with 'watermelon smiles', he was (surely consciously) echoing Powell's infamous 'Rivers of Blood' diatribe, delivered thirty-five years earlier, which used the same curiously coy Christy's Minstrels term of racist abuse. Powell had spoken of the plight of another elderly English lady: 'When she goes to the shops, she is followed by children, charming, wide-grinning piccaninnies.' The word itself configures racism as an archaic, old-world, baroque notion, as if the racist epithet is being uttered not by a contemporary English politician but by a Southern belle in an old plantation novel.

In *Seventy-Two Virgins*, the journalist who is digging into Barlow's scandals is ethnically Asian, and Johnson calls her the 'pestilential Debbie Gujaratne'. He also gives us a Nigerian traffic warden with a comic 'black' accent: 'De law is de law… I cannot make de rules.' But this is all, unlike Trump's racism, wrapped in a coquettish, camp jokiness. When the Nigerian man is attacked by Serbs, Barlow thinks, 'Ah yes… a classic scene of our modern vibrant multicultural society, a group of asylum seekers in dispute with a Nigerian traffic warden.' Here, as always, Johnson claims the privileges of the clown while exercising the power of a politician.

Trump and Johnson are both serial philanderers. According to Purnell, Johnson once explained to another man that, though married, he had to have a lot of affairs because he was 'literally bursting with spunk'. But – and this is why his sexual life is relevant to his political prospects – these affairs were all conquest and no consequence. Johnson refused to pay the medical bills when his lover Petronella Wyatt had an abortion. The boyfriend of another of his lovers was left to pay the medical bills when she gave birth to what was almost certainly Johnson's child. As it is with sex, so with political power – the conquest of 10 Downing Street is Johnson's desire; the consequences of what he might do there are very much a secondary consideration.

Here, though, two differences between Trump and Johnson are important. First, Trump has been able to mobilise a visceral American nationalism. Johnson cannot articulate the powerful but inchoate English nationalism that has driven Brexit. In part this is because he is not really a nationalist – born in New York and raised for some of his childhood in Brussels, his fantasy world is much more a reconstituted 'global Britain' than the Little England imagined by many of his followers. (This divide is one of the insoluble contradictions of Brexit: its leaders, Johnson included, are globalists, while its followers are English nationalists.) In part, too, it is because Johnson cannot disentangle himself from the United Kingdom. He insists that the 'union [of Britain and Northern Ireland] comes first', even though it is abundantly clear that most of those who voted for Brexit and most Tory party members are quite happy to see Scotland and Northern Ireland depart. There is little sense that Johnson has any idea of how he might channel this English nationalism into a reinvented British patriotism or unleash it without destroying the UK.

Secondly, Trump sustains his base through the relentless repetition of the same slogans. He is brutally consistent. Johnson, especially on the all-consuming question of Brexit, is still 'veering all over the place like a shopping trolley'. He was – as a disastrously incompetent foreign secretary – part of the government that negotiated the withdrawal agreement with the EU, including the controversial 'backstop' provisions that would prevent the creation of a hard border between the Irish Republic and Northern Ireland. He resigned in 2018 and denounced the withdrawal agreement claiming that it would make the EU 'our colonial masters'. In March this year he voted in the House of Commons for the withdrawal agreement, backstop, colonial masters, and all. And then he ran for the Tory leadership on a promise to tear up the backstop even if it means a catastrophic no-deal Brexit.

So while Trump's anarchism shades into authoritarianism, Johnson's shades into a kind of insouciant nihilism. The joker's evasiveness that has taken him to the brink of power will be no use to him if he crosses that threshold and has to make fateful decisions. Brexit is finally moving beyond a joke. But what lies ahead for Johnson in those uncharted waters? His best joke was not meant to be one. In November 2016 he claimed that 'Brexit means Brexit and we are going to make a titanic success of it'. In this weirdly akratic moment of British history, most of those who support Johnson actually know very well that Brexit is the *Titanic* and that his evasive actions will be of no avail. But if the ship is going down anyway, why not have some fun with Boris on the upper deck? There is a fatalistic end-of-days pleasure in the idea of Boris doing his Churchill impressions while the iceberg looms ever closer. When things are too serious to be contemplated in sobriety, send in the clown.

20 July 2019

England wins the cricket World Cup. The team's
Irish captain knocks xenophobia for six.

If there were to be a new referendum on Brexit in the UK, what
should the slogan be for the Remainers? Last time out, the Leave
campaign owed much of its appeal to a brilliantly constructed
catchphrase: Take Back Control. In a rerun, it would have another
obvious zinger: Tell Them Again. So how would you counter that in
a few words? My suggestion would be: We're Better Than This. And
the implicit 'we' would not be the British. It would be the English.

Of the 17.4 million votes cast for Brexit in 2016, 15.2 million were
in England – 87 per cent of the total. It is to England that any anti-
Brexit campaign must speak. And what it must say is that England
is surely about something more than wilful self-harm. If I were
running that campaign, I'd start by putting on a loop a clip from the
press conference given on Monday morning by an Irishman, Eoin
Morgan, who had captained the English cricket team to the World
Cup title the previous day.

In an unbearably tense climax to the match against New Zealand, England enjoyed a stroke of outrageous good fortune.
Morgan, who is from Rush in north Co. Dublin, and who previously played for Ireland, was asked: 'Do you think the luck of an
Irishman got England over the line?' He responded: 'We had Allah
with us as well. I spoke to [England bowler] Adil [Rashid]. He said
Allah was definitely with us. I said we had the rub of the green. It
actually epitomises our team. It has quite diverse backgrounds and
cultures… To actually find humour in the situation that we were
in at the time was pretty cool.'

Morgan is pretty damn cool himself. His reply was witty, warm and good-natured. But it was also a masterclass in political batsmanship. Morgan was bowled a harmless and well-intentioned cliché about Irishness and he knocked it out of the park. It sailed gracefully over the boundaries of a closed-in nationalism and out into the wide-open spaces of a whole other England.

Morgan may or may not have been aware of an idiotic tweet from Jacob Rees-Mogg at the end of the final: 'We clearly don't need Europe to win…' But he surely knew very well that the same people who still sing 'Two world wars and one World Cup' at football matches against Germany would try to catch and claim his own team's achievements. He left them grasping at the air as the ball flew way above their heads.

Morgan is an immigrant and the son of an immigrant. His mother Olivia is from Ipswich and lived her early life in England until the family moved to Waterford. He is comfortable with a dual identity, with being both Irish and English.

And this has made him a perfect leader for an English side that also stars bowler Jofra Archer, born in Barbados to a Liverpudlian father; all-rounder Ben Stokes, born in New Zealand; batsman Jason Roy, born in South Africa; and Moeen Ali and Adil Rashid, both born in England to Pakistani immigrant parents.

Morgan has, by all accounts, done a splendid job in creating an atmosphere of mutual respect. Ali wrote in the *Guardian* on Tuesday about how 'guys took time out very early on to talk to us about our religion and our culture. They have made adjustments for us and we have for them.' Some of this is very simple – like not spraying Ali and Rashid with champagne during the celebrations because alcohol is taboo in Islam.

We shouldn't read too much into any of this. When France won the football World Cup in 1998 with a thrilling team that starred players of African descent such as Lilian Thuram and the great Zinedine Zidane – the team was nicknamed Black Blanc Beur (Black White Arab) – the moment supposedly defined the dawn of a post-racial France. Just four years later, the neo-fascist

Jean-Marie Le Pen advanced to the second-round run-off in the French presidential election. No doubt many people with Zidane's name on their replica France shirts voted for Le Pen, just as many people who wept with pride at England's victory on Sunday are fed up with bloody immigrants and vote accordingly.

Sport is not real life. But it's not entirely divorced from it either. And Morgan's elegant and benign reminder of the possibilities of a more open and complex Englishness could not be more salient. For it doesn't speak only to the hard English nationalists, who in truth will not pay much attention to it anyway. Its more important message is actually to Remainers. If they want to win, they have to address the English question.

Since the beginning of the century there has been a huge shift in the way English people identify themselves, away from 'British' and towards 'English'. And there is a very close relationship between identifying as English and supporting Brexit. With some honourable exceptions, liberals have tended to respond to this shift by turning up their noses in disdain.

George Orwell once claimed that 'England is perhaps the only great country where intellectuals are ashamed of their own nationality'. Not without reason: displays of Englishness have been associated with racism, football hooliganism and yobbery. But there is and always has been another England. And that other England has always been multicultural – Celtic/Roman/Saxon/ Norman/Irish/Jewish/Pakistani/Caribbean and so on. 'Thus from a mixture of all kinds began, / That het'rogeneous thing, an Englishman', wrote Daniel Defoe in the eighteenth century. He added: 'scarce one family is left alive, / Which does not from some foreigner derive'.

That other England is no more perfect than anywhere else, but it does have traditions of openness and egalitarianism that run at least as deep as the traditions of xenophobia and paranoia. If Britain is to get out of the terrible mess it has created for itself, it won't be done by telling the English they should be ashamed of themselves. It will be done by encouraging them to be proud of the things they should be proud of – those immense achievements in social justice (the building of the National Health Service for example), in fighting fascism, in science, in the arts and culture and in the absorption of migrants that have so enriched humanity.

It is not a good sign that they have to look to an Irish sportsman for a lesson in leadership. But with political leadership apparently about to pass to a man with no pride in himself, let alone in the real country he wants to represent, the bar is not all that high. Who could not look at the likely next prime minister and say: England is better than this?

23 July 2019

Boris Johnson wins the Tory leadership race on a platform
that centres on the threat of a no-deal Brexit. But he
will have to find a way to sell a capitulation as a triumph.

Blessed are the poo-polishers, for they shall see the kingdom of Brexit.

A little over a year ago, when Theresa May browbeat her recalcitrant cabinet into endorsing her Brexit plan at Chequers, Boris Johnson, then foreign secretary, repeatedly complained that arguing for the plan would be like 'polishing a turd'.

He added sarcastically: 'Luckily we have some expert turd polishers', while, as the *Mail on Sunday* reported at the time, 'shooting a glance at one of Mrs May's spin doctors'.

Turdism, as we might call it, subsequently enjoyed a brief flowering at Westminster. In the debate on the withdrawal agreement in March, one Tory MP, Steve Double, agonised over the choices: 'One option – if you will excuse my language, Mr Speaker – is a turd of a deal, which has now been taken away and polished so that it is a polished turd, but it might be the best turd that we have before us. The alternative would be to stop Brexit altogether.'

It is worth pointing out that turds really can be polished. In the Discovery Channel's series *Mythbusters*, in 2008, the hosts Adam Savage and Jamie Hyneman brought in an expert in the Japanese pastime known as dorodango, in which children create spheres of mud, dust them with fine soil and then polish them to a high gloss with a cloth. They tried the technique on ostrich and lion faeces and proved that it also works splendidly on poo.

Last week, we learned that the department of international trade in London has launched a scheme to recruit school leavers with no other qualifications and train them as trade experts. My sources tell me that the word has also gone out to Japanese school-children to come over and teach Johnson dorodango.

The question on which the fate of Britain may now turn is whether Johnson can persuade the European Union to put a bit of gloss on the withdrawal agreement and then sell it to parliament not just as 'the best turd that we have before us' but as the finest poo known to humanity.

For Johnson has always been right about one thing: the withdrawal agreement is obviously worse for Britain than staying in the EU. As he put it in September, even the Chequers plan (which was not achieved) was 'substantially worse than the status quo'. This is the fundamental and inescapable truth of the entire Brexit process. Membership of the EU is the status quo; the withdrawal deal and close alignment with the customs union and single market is a Status Quo tribute band.

And it's not going to get any better. Reopening the withdrawal agreement would be disastrous for the EU. The EU is a delicate fabric held together by rules, procedures and commitments. Undoing the agreement by ditching the backstop would not just unravel what has been achieved on Brexit – it would unstitch the whole fabric. No one – and certainly no small member state – would ever again be able to believe what the EU says. So there will be no meaningful change. Whatever is added will be gloss.

What could be buffed up? Any amount of language could be ladled on to the (rather thin) political declaration, but none of it will have legal force. What could be added to the legally binding withdrawal agreement is, perhaps, a grand international task force to work on 'alternative arrangements' for control of the Irish border so that the backstop never has to be invoked.

Have it chaired by a big global figure, pack it with experts and feed it money. Make a big fuss of it and hope that the noise drowns out the awkward truth that while technology can work marvels with compliant traders, it can't do much with people who want to evade compliance.

Now, if you do want someone to sell something like this as a fabulous victory, Johnson is your man. He has all the right character traits – a complete absence of principle (asked if he has any convictions, he replied that he has just one: for speeding) and an endless capacity for mendacity. He does grandiose bluster like no one else. Who better to step down from a Spitfire that has flown him back from a dramatic summit in Brussels and announce: 'I hold in my hand a piece of paper…'?

We must never forget that the hard Brexiteers have put their trust in a man who resigned from government in 2017 and denounced the withdrawal agreement for making the EU 'our colonial masters'. In March he voted in the House of Commons for the withdrawal agreement, backstop, colonial masters and all. He switched back to diehard opposition for the leadership race. There is no reason to believe he will not reverse himself yet again. It is his nature.

And as for all the bluster about no deal, I would guess that Johnson is secretly delighted that parliament will put a stop to it. He can and will blame those weak-willed MPs for losing their nerve. It will be their fault that the EU didn't crumble. If it had not been for Johnson's magnificent last-minute dorodango, all would have been lost. Hold your nose and pass the polish.

TIMELINE

24 July 2019: Boris Johnson formally takes over as prime minister.

25 July 2019: Johnson makes a statement in the House of Commons and commits to the October date for Brexit and – while hoping for a renegotiation of the withdrawal agreement – refuses to rule out the possibility of a 'no-deal' Brexit.

4 September 2019: With the Commons passing Hilary Benn's European Union (Withdrawal) (No. 6) Bill, effectively ruling out a no-deal Brexit, Johnson moves a motion to hold an early general election. The motion is defeated.

9 September 2019: Johnson prorogues parliament.

24 September 2019: The Supreme Court passes a unanimous judgement that the decision to prorogue parliament was unlawful. The Speaker of the House of Commons announces that the House will sit again the next day.

3 October 2019: The prime minister delivers a statement to the Commons, outlining more unrealistic government's proposals for a new Brexit deal.

8 October 2019: The government publishes the No-Deal Readiness Report, detailing the UK's preparedness ahead of Brexit on 31 October.

10 October 2019: Boris Johnson and Leo Varadkar engage in three hours of Brexit talks in Liverpool.

They later release a statement saying 'they agreed that they could see a pathway to a possible deal'.

17 October 2019: Johnson capitulates and accepts the withdrawal agreement, with the Northern Ireland-only backstop originally agreed in December 2017. This is a betrayal of his repeated assurances to the DUP that no British prime minister could ever agree to a 'border in the Irish Sea'.

19 October 2019: Johnson, having sworn to die in a ditch before doing so, writes to Donald Tusk, in accordance with the Benn Act, to ask for a Brexit extension.

21 October 2019: The European Union (Withdrawal Agreement) Bill is introduced to parliament.

22 October 2019: The EU (Withdrawal Agreement) Bill passes its second reading, but the programme motion setting out the timetable is defeated. Johnson withdraws the legislation.

28 October 2019: EU ambassadors agree to a Brexit extension to 31 January 2020.

30 October 2019: Parliament passes the Early Parliamentary General Election Bill, which sets the date for a general election to take place on 12 December.

25 July 2019

*Johnson's strategy is based on the EU believing that
he is telling the truth when he threatens to walk away
without a deal. But the problem is that nobody
believes a word he says.*

As Boris Johnson walked up to the podium at 10 Downing Street to make his first address as prime minister, they should have played Leonard Cohen's 'Everybody Knows' as his fanfare: 'Everybody knows that the boat is leaking / Everybody knows that the captain lied.' For the one thing that can be said in Johnson's defence is that he is not a conman. Yes, of course, he speaks fluent falsehood as his native language. But he deceives no one. Everybody knows.

The Tory MPs who backed him, the party members who voted for him so overwhelmingly, the media cheerleaders who hail his accession – they all know exactly what he's like. They don't believe him – they just wilfully suspend their disbelief. They cannot say they were taken in by a plausible charlatan – they choose to applaud the obviously implausible, to crown the man they know to be the Great Pretender. They go along with the fiction that Johnson is a Prince Hal who will metamorphose into the hero to lead England to a new Agincourt, while knowing damn well that he will always be a Falstaff for whom honour is just 'a word'.

Here is the most extraordinary aspect of this weird succession. All governments may end in failure but they are supposed at least to begin with some kind of gravity and some element of faith. As long ago as 1997, Johnson wrote: 'Politics is a constant repetition, in cycles of varying length, of one of the oldest myths in human culture, of how we make kings for our societies, and how after a while we kill them to achieve a kind of rebirth.'

But King Boris starts out with no clothes. There are no vestiges of solemn dignity to drape the nakedness of his mendacity and fecklessness. The usual arc of a premiership runs from illusion to disillusion, from great expectations to more or less bitter disappointments. Even Theresa May, let us remember, seemed, at this same moment in the cycle in 2016, sincere and serious and deserving of some goodwill. The disillusion took a little while to set in. Johnson cannot disillusion anyone, for no one is under any illusion that he is truthful or trustworthy, honourable or earnest. His fitness for the highest office is not about to be tested – it is the most conspicuous absence in modern British political history.

The knowingness is all. Johnson's genius has always lain in his ability to create a self-conscious collusion: complicity with the fiction known as Boris. He doesn't have to have any character because he *is* a character. He is very good at making stuff up because he started with the biggest invention of all: himself. Sonia Purnell, in her excellent biography *Just Boris*, describes his careful disarrangement of his hair before TV appearances: 'His famous dishevelled look is actually, however, the product of a brisk, artful rearrangement with his fingers (just before the cameras roll) rather than any naturally occurring disorder.'

And Johnson's rise to No. 10 is not a naturally occurring disorder either. It is the product of three decades of performances of the show called Boris Being Boris, an artful rearrangement of the standards of truthfulness and competence to which those who aspired to a public life had to at least pretend. His master at Eton, Martin Hammond, reported of him in 1982 that he regarded himself as being 'free of the network of obligation which binds everyone else'. And his public career in journalism, showbusiness and politics has been all about preparing the notion that he should indeed be free, not just of the network of obligation, but of the ties to honesty and dignity that (however tenuous they become over time) politicians profess to be bound by.

Johnson's fictions have always had a kind of postmodern quality – everybody knows they are fictions. His recent brandishing of a kipper to embody another Euro-infamy was a kind of camp self-parody in which the performance is everything and the relationship to truth simply irrelevant. In this sense, there is no more deception than there is at a pantomime. The point is not to make a claim about reality. It is to draw the audience into a knowingly comic complicity with unreality, so that, when the EU says 'but we never banned prawn cocktail flavour crisps', everyone can shout out together, 'Oh yes you did!'

This has one enormous political advantage and Johnson has exploited it so superbly that he is now prime minister: he could never be found out because his mendacity was never hidden. Just three months before the Brexit referendum, Johnson was publicly and forensically exposed as a liar by his own party colleague Andrew Tyrie, who cross-examined him before the House of Commons Treasury Committee and showed his claims about various EU regulations to be grossly distorted. In a courtroom drama, Johnson would have been led away in tears and handcuffs. But the hearing was not even a minor media story. Why? Because 'Boris lies' is like Jonathan Swift's 'Celia shits'. Have I got news for you? No. Everybody knows already.

It works because, with Brexit, a lot of people want to be lied to (it's all going to be fabulous; the EU will shred the withdrawal agreement; the Irish will panic and do as they're told). And if that is your desire, Johnson has another Leonard Cohen number for you: 'I'm Your Man'. But – and this is the fundamental problem of his accession to power – a lot of people don't want to be lied to.

Insofar as he has a strategy, Johnson's plan is all based on the power of a lie, or to use the polite term, a bluff. The bluff is a no-deal Brexit. The basic belief of Johnson and those around him is that the way to get a great deal out of the EU is to pretend that you are quite happy to crash out without one. But bluffing only works if you do not already have a reputation as one of the world's biggest bluffers. In this poker game, Johnson doesn't have a tell. He *is* the tell. To put him into No. 10 is to erect a neon sign over Downing Street that says: 'Don't believe a word of it.' The knowingness that Johnson has exploited to such great effect works within a circle of collusion. Outside the circle, knowingness is just plain old knowledge. Everybody knows that Johnson is the lying captain of a very leaky boat. Nobody in Europe is about to climb aboard.

27 July 2019

When it comes to Brexit, it is not the devil that is in the details. It is real life. The details are workers, jobs, families and communities. They are the hours and the days and how people get to spend them, for richer, for poorer, in sickness and in health. And one of the things even his fans will concede about the new British prime minister is that he doesn't do detail. Boris Johnson is a big picture man – which is a nice way of saying that he can't be bothered with the specifics of real-world consequences. His appeal to the Tory party faithful who voted for him so overwhelmingly is precisely that he allows them to fantasise about easy simplicity in a world of ferocious complexity.

To be fit for public office is to accept the network of obligation that connects every decision you make with the man feeding his kids, the woman paying her rent, the child beginning school, the old person in the hospital ward. And for Johnson this network of obligation does not exist – or, rather, it exists, but only for other people. He is the exception to his own demands. The carefully contrived eccentricity that constitutes (for some) his charm is also a way of saying: I'm not bound by common standards or principles. I make my own rules because, like Great Britain, I am exceptional.

In this, Johnson's accession to the highest office is a fitting expression of the deluded British exceptionalism that has driven Brexit. Insofar as it can be called a project at all, it is a rejection of the idea that Britain can ever be an ordinary country, a mere equal in the network of mutual obligation that is the EU. Ordinariness is defeat, humiliation, intolerable incarceration in an unnatural condition.

Johnson has long embodied this sense of exceptionalism at a personal level – he believes he can get away with anything because, for the most part, he has. Lies, serial infidelity, the waste of vast amounts of public money on self-indulgent 'big picture' schemes – he is exceptionally good at escaping their consequences. The Brexiteers have chosen him in the belief that somehow this magic can transfer itself from the personal to the political, that under Johnson Britain can be as free of the bonds of duty and the tedium of details as he is.

But the paradox of this wishful thinking is that there really is a great machine for obliterating detail. It is called the European Union. Its customs union and single market have successfully removed almost all the mind-numbing detail from trade within the EU. International trade – which is to say in reality the livelihoods of families and communities – is a horrible mess of dreary minutiae. What tariffs apply? Does this comply with our standards and safety rules? How much VAT is owed and to whom? How much of this complex object was made in what country?

The irony is that by making all of this go away, the EU has allowed it to be forgotten. Businesses don't have vast departments to process this stuff. Neither do national governments. But when you decide to leave the EU, you demolish the dykes, the wave of complexity floods back in and you are drowned in detail.

Details such as, for example, the 1,100 juggernauts that arrive in Britain from the EU every single morning, carrying components to the car and engine assembly plants that directly employ 186,000 real live people. Or the five minutes that is the average allotted time for one of those components to leave the truck and be actually placed into whatever part of the car it is meant for. Or the £50,000 per minute that border delays alone would cost that industry in the UK in the event of a no-deal Brexit. Or the 46.5 per cent fall in inward investment in those plants between 2017 and 2018 because of fears of no deal. Or the fact that virtually none of the mass-market cars assembled in the UK is made from components more than 50 per cent sourced in the UK, which means that none of these cars would qualify as British in any glorious trade deal that Johnson might hope to do with, say, Donald Trump.

Details, details. A health certificate for a consignment of food costs £200 (€223) from the UK's department of agriculture. In the case of a no-deal Brexit, exporters in just one sector (seafood) in just one local council area in Northern Ireland (Newry and Mourne) would need 60,000 of these certs every year. That's £12 million (€13.3 million) extra costs in this one tiny area alone – money these businesses simply don't have. To prepare one certificate of origin will cost a business about £400 (€446) – even small exporters will need huge numbers of these as well. And so on. But who cares? For Johnson, there are no details that do not come with a four-letter attachment. They are all 'mere' details.

Johnson told the Brexiteers and the Tory members what they want to hear – that all of this complexity can be wished away. He gave them the fantasy of a 'clean break' Brexit that is just Tinkerbell in reverse – if you believe strongly enough in it, it will happen. This make-believe is childish but it is not innocent. For at its heart lies a vicious assumption of superiority: the people whose jobs will be lost or whose lives will be made poorer are unwanted little distractions. They are mud in the clear waters of Brexit, pesky flies in its healing balm of British salvation. They don't matter enough to be told the truth, which is that they are not making a sacrifice for Brexit – they are being sacrificed to it.

But the details will have their revenge. In the real world, they do not take well to those who ignore them. They insist on having their say. For Johnson, crossing the threshold into 10 Downing Street is entering a universe he has never inhabited before, one in which specifics and particulars will tie him down like Gulliver among the Lilliputians. He has always been able to deal with facts he does not like by inventing his own ones and waving his fabrications about as props in his own solipsistic drama, like the kippers he lied about with such gusto at the final hustings of the leadership campaign.

Very soon, this pantomime of national liberation will find there is one rule that even Boris Johnson cannot evade: the tyranny of fact.

10 August 2019

The reasons why Ireland cannot give in to Johnson's pressure
to ditch the backstop are also to do with details: the cumulative
small changes that have transformed life on the island.

To get a sense of what has happened on the island of Ireland over the last twenty years, we could think about just two people. Both are involved in public life, though neither is a politician. But in both cases, what they are doing was unimaginable in 1998 when the Belfast Agreement was signed. They are the unthinkable Susan Fitzgerald and the unthinkable Drew Harris. Just to stop for a moment and contemplate who they are and the positions they now hold is to realise how the texture of life on the island has changed. It is to touch the delicate fabric that current events threaten to rip up.

The most visible icon of Protestant identity in Belfast is the looming yellow mass of the great gantry cranes that stand over the vast dry dock of the Harland & Wolff (H&W) shipyard. They are not that old (dating to the late 1960s and early 1970s) but they came to symbolise the great power and skill of the North's heritage of engineering and heavy manufacturing.

And that heritage in turn symbolised the division between the industrial North and the agricultural South, a distinction that mapped roughly on to the sectarian divide between Protestant and Catholic. The identification of H&W with Protestantism was not, of course, accidental – it was created and maintained by violence and exclusion.

H&W went into administration on Tuesday. The remaining workers at H&W are now fighting for survival.

The great citadel that once employed 35,000 men has shrunk to a workforce of 130, but those jobs matter more than the mere numbers. They have a psychological importance that outweighs their economic significance. They embody an identity. The H&W workers have occupied the yard and they staged a protest last week when Boris Johnson visited Stormont.

But who is leading them and speaking for them? The regional organiser of their union, Unite, Susan Fitzgerald. You don't have to listen to Fitzgerald for more than a few seconds to realise from her accent that she is a working-class Dubliner.

She's a powerfully articulate and passionate voice for the H&W workers and her background shouldn't be of any great interest. But it is – because it is not all that long ago that someone (even a man) with her accent would have been run out of the shipyard.

A Dublin woman speaking for the H&W workers would have seemed about as likely as Ian Paisley commentating on the All-Ireland hurling final – in Irish. Yet here she is fighting for a resonant part of Ulster Protestant culture, and by all accounts the H&W workers are very glad to have her on their side.

Think, then, of another highly symbolic institution, An Garda Síochána. It is a product of Irish revolutionary nationalism, and of the IRA's war on its predecessor, the Royal Irish Constabulary (RIC). And it is now headed by a product of the RIC's own successor, the Royal Ulster Constabulary (RUC).

Drew Harris's father, Alwyn, was the RUC district superintendent in Lisburn. On 8 October 1989, he and his wife were driving to the Harvest Thanksgiving service at their local Presbyterian church when a Semtex bomb planted on the car by the IRA exploded and killed him. He was mourned by many in the Catholic community.

He was, for the IRA and its supporters North and South, a 'legitimate target'. But the civil rights activist Fr Denis Faul, who had worked with him to stop harassment of local families by British troops, said he was 'exactly the kind of officer on whom a trustworthy police force could be built'.

People who have watched the new Garda commissioner go about the job of trying to do exactly that south of border would agree that Drew Harris is in that respect very much his father's son. He seems set to make a huge contribution to public and civic life in the Republic by fixing a police force broken by years of poor management.

But even a few years ago he would never have got the chance to do so. It would have been unthinkable for a Presbyterian policeman from an RUC family, twice decorated by Queen Elizabeth, to be given arguably the single most sensitive job in the South with access to all of the state's secrets. It would probably have been unthinkable for someone like Harris even to want the job.

Yet, as with Fitzgerald and the H&W workers, there is a widespread recognition that we are lucky to have him. This is what transformational change looks like: things that were unimaginable become real. Impossibilities are now facts. Fitzgerald and Harris exemplify a much larger dismantling of the small borders, the intimate hindrances of fear and prejudice.

Sectarianism is not dead – very far from it. We have not, in that great tautological cliché, simply put the past behind us. But the ground has shifted. The absence of violence has made movement possible. Some of this movement is literal: the occupants of the forty-five million vehicles crossing the border every year. But more of it is psychological. Mental barriers have not quite come down but they have become much more passable.

The idea of sharing the island has acquired a daily, ordinary substance. It is not a political manifesto or a constitutional claim. It is Irish life.

People have always been much more open and fluid than politics. Left to themselves, they fall in love with each other and make friendships and escape from tribal prisons. This is the natural state of affairs, the default setting of social life. If you want to stop it, you have to use extreme weapons of bigotry and violence. As the floodwaters of enforced hostility have ebbed, we begin to see this basic human landscape once more. It looks wonderfully ordinary.

But like everything marvellous, this change is delicate and precarious. We all know that it is not complete, that it has not been going on long enough to be robust.

The very fact that the positions of Susan Fitzgerald and Drew Harris are worth remarking on highlights this fragility. The change will be secure when it is taken for granted – and that cannot yet be done. It needs to be protected and insisted on.

And, really, we do have to insist. The already relentless campaign in the Tory press and its political wing to define the political developments that have made this change possible as nothing more than a plot against Brexit will become, in the next three months, ever nastier.

There are people who don't know what has happened and who, even if they did know, would not care. We know, we care and we have a right to say that we should be left alone to get on with the long process of accepting each other.

13 August 2019

Knowing how to make a grand entrance is all very well but, as the Brexit saga reminds us, the ability to make a dignified exit is even more important. There is a lovely French phrase, *l'esprit de l'escalier*, that signifies the moment at the bottom of the staircase when you think of what you should have said as you were leaving. The Brexiteers have not yet decided what it is they should have said before the decision to depart was made in June 2016. The words of Captain Lawrence Oates as he left the tent to walk into the blizzard near the bitter end of Robert Falcon Scott's doomed expedition to the South Pole, seem to be as much as they can manage: we are going out now, and we may be some time.

But there is more than one exit taking place now, more than one union that is about to be left behind. One certainty in these days of confusion is that whatever Boris Johnson is camping up most ludicrously is the thing that is in deepest trouble. When Johnson, like some tinpot dictator awarding himself decorations and accolades, granted himself the hitherto unheard-of title of minister for the union, there could be no more convincing proof that the union is in deep doo-doo. If you have to have a minister for potatoes, it can only be because there is potato blight. If the state you're in needs a minister to affirm its very existence, you are in a pretty bad state.

This creates, however, a historic challenge for Ireland, North and South. It may seem, on the face of it, to promise the fulfilment of the old Irish nationalist dream – a unitary insular state. The end of a century-long story is in sight: partition is about to be undone. Perhaps it is, but not in the way that Irish nationalism always imagined. What we may be about to experience is not so much Northern Ireland leaving the UK as Northern Ireland (and Scotland) being abandoned by England. The grand narrative of Irish nationalism has always been that perfidious Albion was desperate to hold on to the great prize of the Six Counties and had to be forced or cajoled into giving it up. This was never true, but it is now starkly and demonstrably false.

Every single survey of both Leave voters and Tory party members over the last three years has shown that they are not unionists. They want Brexit, and if the price of Brexit is the end of the union, so be it. So the story here is not Irish nationalists overcoming at last the doughty resistance of Ulster unionists to a united Ireland. It is English nationalists saying, 'here's your bowler hat, what's your hurry?' The act of departure is coming from the 'wrong' direction – it is England's exodus from its long, voluntary self-exile in the imperial state that the brilliant Scottish thinker Tom Nairn calls Ukania. And it is not the severing of a union – it is the implosion of a union.

Ukania was created in the eighteenth century to serve a particular purpose – the creation and governance of a global empire. One of the world's first and most aggressive nationalisms – Englishness – was folded into it. There is a long-term logic to the idea that, with empire gone, Englishness will unfold itself again. The problem for the rest of our archipelago is that it is doing so in a form (Brexit) that is both chaotic and self-contradictory. The Leave voters are saying 'we don't give a monkey's about the union'; their champion Johnson is telling them 'the union comes first'.

Karl Marx wrote that people 'make their own history, but they do not do so in circumstances of their own choosing'. History, including Irish history, is indeed being made – but not in circumstances of Ireland's choosing. If unity is indeed a live possibility, it is being driven by forces outside of our control. We are in a movie we did not write and are not directing. But what we do know is that we are all too capable of botched exits ourselves.

In one of those little jokes that history likes, we will be facing all of this while marking the centenary of a very bad Irexit from the

UK, one that gave us partition, a civil war, a sectarian Protestant state in the North and an economically miserable and socially oppressive Catholic state in the South. If the next Irish exit from Ukania is to be better than the last one, we cannot wait to talk about it until we are at the bottom of the stairs.

3 September 2019

Johnson's attempt to prorogue parliament suggests
that Britain's democracy is built on feudalism
and its unwritten constitution is feeble.

There are two things we know about revolutions. One is that they get more radical as they go along. The revolutionaries start out demanding specific reforms and end up imagining that they are inaugurating a whole new world. The other is that revolutions expose the great cracks in the *ancien régime* that should have been obvious all along. In retrospect, after the upheaval, it is clear that the old system was doomed by its own failure to manage necessary change.

Brexit is a very strange kind of revolution – the heroic over-throw of imaginary oppression, in which tragedy and farce are not sequential but simultaneous and deeply interwoven. But it is a revolution nonetheless, and it is conforming to these patterns. A goal that was unutterable in 2016 – the Year Zero of No Deal – is now mainstream policy. And the *ancien régime* of the Westminster system is having all its delusions mercilessly exposed by, of all places, Italy.

One thing that still unites the warring factions in England is the belief that Westminster is 'the mother of all parliaments' and the envy of the democratic world. Well, it sure looks like the mother of all something right now, but it's not parliamentary democracy. Consider what has happened. Boris Johnson was elected leader of the Tory party by 92,153 people. He was then appointed prime minister by a hereditary monarch with no parliamentary involve-ment whatsoever. Since 24 July, when he became prime minister, he has appeared just once in the House of Commons to answer questions. And he has now used those monarchical powers to prorogue parliament and make himself even more unaccountable to it. The one virtue of Johnson's brazenness is that he has surely made obvious to his compatriots what outsiders can see – that the system in which all of this is possible is a democracy built around a solid core of feudalism.

To grasp the absurdity of this spectacle, we might turn to one of England's great minds, Jonathan Sumption. He is simultaneously one of his country's most distinguished lawyers, recently retired from the UK's Supreme Court, and one of its leading historians, whose superb ongoing multi-volume history of the Hundred Years War is much better than *Game of Thrones*. Last week, the London *Times* asked him to pronounce on the legality of Johnson's prorogation of parliament. 'I don't think what the prime minister has said he is going to do is unlawful,' he said. But he added: 'It might be considered unconstitutional in as much as it might be argued to be contrary to a longstanding convention of the constitution.'

So what Johnson is doing is probably unconstitutional but probably not unlawful. I don't think most people in England have any idea how utterly nonsensical this seems to all the rest of us. It's like saying that a man is almost certainly dead but nonetheless in quite good health. In any other democracy, if it's unconstitutional, it's unlawful. Only in the United Kingdom of Absurdistan can it possibly be otherwise. And the heart of the absurdity is that great tautology, the 'unwritten constitution'.

The British constitution is so fine a thing that it would be positively insulting, even dangerous, to actually write it down. The people who need to know what it is are able to divine its mysteries – ordinary subjects are not among them. Johnson, for all his habitual mendacity, is exposing the truth that this arcane system of accretions and conventions is of little use when a shameless chancer is given the keys of the kingdom. His manoeuvre is not even a coup – when you can do all this lawfully, who needs coups?

Until very recently, most people in England would have pointed to Italy, with its infamous political instability, as the great counter-example that proved the wisdom of the British system. Last week, both countries were faced at the same time with a remarkably similar challenge: a radical right-wing opportunist seeking to bring down his own government and force a general election in which he would run not so much for parliament as against parliament. Matteo Salvini, leader of the pre-fascist League, has been governing in coalition with the populist Five Star movement. He tried to pull off pretty much the same trick as Johnson and for the same reason: to position himself as the voice of 'the people' against the political 'elites'.

But Salvini was stopped – for two reasons. First, enough people within the political system were willing to stop fighting each other and start fighting the radical right. Second, Italy has a written democratic constitution with an elected president who could manage the process of creating an alternative government. The UK does not have the second of these things, and it is not at all clear that its parliamentarians can manage the first.

How weak does your constitution need to be when it can't even stand up to a bluffer like Boris Johnson? How puny is it when it comes so badly out of a comparison with a country that is a byword for democratic fragility? It has come to something when an Italian might well look at the goings-on at the 'mother of parliaments' and exclaim 'Mamma mia!'

7 September 2019

Michael Gove launches a £100 million advertising campaign urging Britons to 'Get Ready' for a no-deal Brexit.

The American humourist James Thurber recalled in his memoir a local character from his childhood in Columbus, Ohio: the Get-Ready Man. 'The Get-Ready Man was a lank unkempt elderly gentleman with wild eyes and a deep voice who used to go about shouting at people through a megaphone to prepare for the end of the world, "GET READY! GET READ-Y!" he would bellow, "THE WORLLLD IS COMING TO AN END!" His startling exhortations would come up, like summer thunder, at the most unexpected times and in the most surprising places.'

Thurber's favourite memory of him was his invasion of a production of Shakespeare's suitably apocalyptic play, *King Lear*. 'The Get-Ready Man added his bawlings to the squealing of Edgar and the ranting of the King and the mouthing of the Fool, rising from somewhere in the balcony to join in. The theatre was in absolute darkness and there were rumblings of thunder and flashes of lightning offstage. Neither father nor I, who were there, ever completely got over the scene, which went something like this:

Get-Ready Man: The Worllld is com-ing to an End!

Fool: This cold night will turn us all to fools and madmen!

Edgar: Take heed o' the foul fiend: obey thy paren—

Get-Ready Man: Get Rea-dy!

Edgar: Tom's a-cold!

Get-Ready Man: The Worr-uld is coming to an end!…

They found him finally, and ejected him, still shouting. The theatre, in our time, has known few such moments.'

This last week in British politics has been like the mad scenes in *King Lear*, with the Get-Ready Man as the chorus. The political theatre, in our time, has known few such moments. It began – if anyone can remember back that far – with the launch of the £100 million Get Ready publicity campaign by Michael Gove, with a rolling programme of giant display ads and TV, radio and online commercials. According to the London *Times* there was also 'a substantial order placed for branded mugs and T-shirts'. And all of it is meant to shout: 'GET READY! GET READ-Y!' 'NO DEAL IS COMING!' Or, as the Westminster parliament put it instead: no it's not.

So while the Get-Ready Men – Gove, Boris Johnson and the prime minister Dominic Cummings – were bawling out their warnings through an incredibly expensive megaphone, a little bit of *King Lear* was playing out in the House of Commons. The play, after all, is about the collapse of political authority in Britain, caused by nothing more than a caprice. It shows the potentially terrible consequences of political self-indulgence. But in this Westminster production, there was a twist.

As everything falls apart, Lear conjures the image of state power as a farmer's dog barking at a beggar: 'There thou mightst behold the great image of authority: a dog's obeyed in office.' The twist in this week's surreal version of the play is that while a dog may be obeyed in office, Boris Johnson is not. The 'great image of authority' is an impotent prime minister running through a bad student debating routine of hammy harangues, bad jokes and schoolboy insults ('big girl's blouse!', 'chicken!') while losing vote after vote and being powerless even to resign and run to the country.

At the heart of this collapse of authority is a game of *Call My Bluff* that Johnson has lost. Bluffing is not Johnson's only weapon – he does bluster and bullying as well – but it has been at the core of what passes for a strategy. He is good at it: after all, he has bluffed his way into 10 Downing Street. But, having got there, he has in fact been trying to pull off an outrageous double bluff. On the one hand, Johnson has been trying to make the EU believe that he really is perfectly happy to leave with no deal on 31 October, in the belief that they will get scared and rush to mollify him with last-minute concessions. But he has also been trying to do the opposite: to convince sceptics in his own parliament, and especially in his own party, that he doesn't really want no-deal after all and is only threatening it as a negotiating ploy.

It would take a political genius to pull this off, and Johnson, as we saw this week, is not quite one of those. The ploy has always been innately absurd. It assumes that there are two entirely different audiences, one in Brussels and one in London, and that neither has any idea of the show that is being performed for the other. It ends up scaring the wrong people. The 'GET READY! GET READ-Y!' 'NO DEAL IS COMING!' manic street preacher act is meant for the Europeans and the Irish. But it can only be played out in Britain itself. Johnson has managed to preach the approaching apocalypse in the wrong churches. In the corridors of Brussels, it has left everybody entirely unmoved. But it sure put the wind up at Westminster.

It is also innately self-contradictory. It relies on no-deal Brexit being imagined as simultaneously terrible and harmless. To work as a threat, it has to be a portent of doom, a vision of hell that can be avoided only if the EU repents before it is too late. To be acceptable domestically, it has to be just (in the official, endlessly repeated phrase) 'a bump in the road'.

Johnson tried to close this gaping hole in the only way he knows: by lying. He and his toadies insisted that the megaphone diplomacy was working. Serious negotiations were under way in Brussels and the Europeans, scared to death, were on the brink of making great concessions. The only thing that could deprive Britain of this great triumph was weakness on the home front. Using the language of the Second World War that is so bizarrely encoded in the whole Brexit project, Johnson talks of 'collaboration' and 'surrender' and draws implicitly and explicitly on the belief that this is all a test of nerve and that the Brits always win those through sheer pluck.

But there are still – just about – enough people in parliament who cannot swallow such a big lie. Johnson's last resort, of course, is to try to create, through a general election, a parliament in his own image: careless about truth, reckless about consequences, bent only on keeping office at any price. When it comes, as it must soon, it will be an election that pits the true English spirit against the collaborators and the surrender monkeys, the treacherous Scot and the perfidious foreigner, that sets 'the people' against the 'elites'. It will offer the true believers a vision of redemption through pain – pain made acceptable by the assurance that the 'citizens of nowhere' will suffer even more. It will be very nasty. Get ready.

1 October 2019

Last month, Boris Johnson, anticipating an imminent general election, sprayed a golden shower of money all over the various departments of the British state. I have an unhealthy interest in one novel arm of that state: the new ministry for the union. In July, Johnson, not content with rising to the office of prime minister, gave himself a title none of his predecessors had ever held, or indeed heard of: minister for the union. I got to wondering what kind of budget this grand new institution might have. Since Johnson insists that 'the union comes first' in all his thoughts, I imagined it must be very large. Here is the exciting news from the spending package: '£10 million of additional funding to strengthen the links between the four nations of the union as the UK leaves the EU, supporting the work of the prime minister as minister for the union. Of this, £5 million will be allocated to the Territorial Offices.'

I have to confess that I had no idea what the Territorial Offices might be – something to do with Gibraltar or the British Virgin Islands? But no, Territorial Offices is the actual official term for the Office of the Secretary of State for Scotland, the Office of the Secretary of State for Wales and the Northern Ireland Office. The term seems wonderfully resonant: Edinburgh, Cardiff and Belfast being 'out in the territories'. But what really interests me is that Johnson's own budget as minister for the union, to be spent on strengthening the ties that bind together England, Wales, Scotland and Northern Ireland, is £5 million. By contrast, £8.3 billion has been committed to planning for a no-deal Brexit. So £10 million to save the union, £8.3 billion to tear it apart. The order of priorities is rather evident.

An obvious question arises here: is the union in danger or is it not? Clearly, Johnson thinks it is: you don't need a minister for the union if the union is just going about its prescribed business of existing. And just as clearly, he thinks it is not: if the very existence of your state is being threatened, £10 million is an entirely meaningless response. The truth, of course, is that Johnson, like Theresa May before him, is trying to paper over a very wide crack. Everyone who can read the polls knows that Leave voters, Tory voters and even the members of the Conservative and Unionist Party don't give a curse if the breakup of the union is the price to be paid for Brexit. But no one in government can acknowledge that truth – instead there must be a pretence that the 'precious, precious union', as the Gollum-like May called it, is to be saved at all costs. Hence the nonsense.

For £5 million, I could tell Johnson how to shore up the union: stay in the EU single market and customs union. But I don't think that is what the minister for the union has in mind. I also wonder how his budget squares with Theresa May's big idea for strengthening the union after Brexit. She unveiled it at last year's Tory party conference: a grand Festival of Great Britain and Northern Ireland in 2020. It will be 'a moment of national celebration and help attract new inward business and investment'.

May promised to spend £120 million on it. Though some of it will apparently be spent on French champagne. The idea, so far as I can trace it, sprang from the genius of Jacob Rees-Mogg, who told the *Express* in January 2018: 'A Festival of Brexit would be excellent. There should be a huge celebration and in the spirit of friendship of our European neighbours, upon leaving we should drink lots of champagne to say that though we may be leaving the European Union, we don't dislike Europe.' This seems a pretty good plan, and the same thinking could surely be applied to strengthening the ties between the four UK nations. If guzzling champagne (will there be a bottle for everyone who attends the festival?) will show the French that there are no hard feelings after Brexit, how could 'we' show that 'we don't dislike the Scots, Welsh and Northern Irish'? Serve haggis, leeks and soda farls?

But the serious point in all of this is that the Brexit endgame may well be played out precisely on this soggy terrain of contradictions and hypocrisy. The idea of the union undoubtedly still has a strong place in the psychology of Conservatism, and the DUP has been able to play on that sentimental attachment in its opposition to a Northern Ireland-only backstop. But its reality is that Conservatism is being replaced by a militant assault on the institutions of the UK state. Unionism is wrapped up in that strange fabric, the British constitution. Where does it stand when the fabric is being ripped up by Johnson and his cabal? If they show such contempt for parliament and the law, how likely is it that they will really 'die in the last ditch' to preserve a union that their own political base no longer cares about? I see your £10 million and I raise you a sceptical eyebrow.

3 October 2019

Johnson unveils his proposals for a new Brexit deal that will 'honour the result of the referendum and deliver Brexit on 31 October'. They are based on the long discredited idea that the UK, including Northern Ireland, can leave the customs union and single market and yet not create a hard border in Ireland.

When Boris Johnson described his long-awaited proposals for changes to the Brexit withdrawal treaty as a compromise, he was not wrong. Two questions arise, however. What is being compromised? And who is Johnson compromising with?

The answer to the second is obvious: the proposals are a compromise, not with the EU, but with the DUP. And what is being compromised is the credibility of the UK as a partner in any international negotiations. Though the EU and the Irish government are too polite to say so directly, Johnson's plan destroys any remaining sense that the current regime in London is capable of sticking even to its own self-declared principles.

Ever since its victory in the referendum of June 2016, the Brexit project has been dogged by its inability to transcend its own origins. The referendum was always driven by the internal politics of the Conservative Party. Its purpose, from the point of view of the man who called it, David Cameron, was to silence the increasingly turbulent anti-EU faction in his own party and see off the threat of Nigel Farage. And it has never been able to move on from being an internal negotiation to being an external one. The only thing that has really changed is that 'internal' Tory politics came, after the 2017 election, to include the DUP.

And so here we are again. Political compromise is about two sides with different agendas meeting each other halfway. It is easy to see why Johnson might be sincere in thinking he has achieved this – but only if the two sides are Johnson himself with his need to look like he is coming up with some vaguely credible alternative to the backstop and the DUP with its 'blood red line' of Northern Ireland leaving the EU on exactly the same terms as the rest of the UK.

This week's proposals do indeed represent a significant shift in this internal dynamic: both Johnson and the DUP now agree that Northern Ireland may in fact leave on different terms. It may (or may not) stay effectively within the EU single market for an indefinite number of four-year periods.

To that extent, we do not have to assume that Johnson is lying and that his proposals exist only to provoke the EU to reject them. We just have to assume that he is, like Cameron and Theresa May before him, so consumed with the internal politics of Brexit that he finds it impossible to think realistically about the real negotiations.

The problem, of course, is that the DUP – and its hardline supporters in the European Research Group faction of the Tories – are not Johnson's real interlocuters on the actual process of Brexit. He is supposed to be convincing Brussels (and Dublin) that he has a better way of achieving what the backstop does, which is to guarantee that there will be no new border-related infrastructure or checks on the island of Ireland. Instead, he has effectively resiled from the most basic commitments his government has made.

These commitments are not just rhetorical. They are legal. They are rooted in international law, which is what the Belfast Agreement is. But it is easy to forget that they are also in British law – ironically in the very act under which Brexit is supposed to be conducted. Section 10(2)(b) of the European Union (Withdrawal) Act 2018 explicitly commits the UK not to 'create or facilitate border arrangements between Northern Ireland and the Republic of Ireland after exit day which feature physical infrastructure, including border posts, or checks and controls, that did not exist before exit day and are not in accordance with an agreement between the United Kingdom and the EU'.

This could not be clearer: what is ruled out is not just posts on the border but any infrastructure, any checks, and any controls that do not currently exist.

This, remember, is not just an Irish or EU demand. It has been the official British line all throughout this process. The whole backstop problem arises, not as some kind of dastardly Irish or European plot, but because Britain just can't live up to this commitment if Northern Ireland leaves either the single market or the customs union.

This is the tyranny of fact: there is nowhere in the world where two different customs and/or market regimes have a frontier across which trade flows without checks, controls and infrastructure. But all the energy among the Brexiteers has gone into trying to escape this inescapable reality.

They have been in search of a magical technology that make the facts on the ground disappear. And ever since it became clear that this technology does not exist, the internal project has been what Whitehall officials privately call 'keeping the corpse warm'.

The corpse is now cold. Johnson's proposals acknowledge that even if all the magical technology works, there will still be checks, controls and (implicitly) infrastructure. The British government has broken its own solemn legal and political commitments. Faced with a choice between compromising with reality and fatally compromising trust, Johnson has chosen the second option.

5 October 2019

Will Brexit end like Emmerdale *or* Crossroads?

If Brexit is a soap opera, which soap opera is it? It has to be an English one, of course, and not one of your trendy, niche, late-night cleveralities either – whatever else we can say about Brexit, it is a saga for a mass audience. It is daytime TV with wobbly sets, incredible characters and wildly erratic plot lines.

So the shortlist really comes down to two: *Crossroads* and *Emmerdale*. These are two long-running soaps that found themselves in deep trouble because the writers had lost the plot and audiences were in equal measure perplexed and bored.

The usual twists to the characters or injections of super-melodramatic storylines wouldn't do. The show-runners had to resort to drastic measures. Specifically, they had to write their way out of a dead end. Their respective exit strategies give us two very different ways of thinking about the Brexit endgame. It is tempting to imagine a new Brexit referendum in which the question is: do you want to be in *Crossroads* or do you want to be in *Emmerdale*?

Boris Johnson is currently an *Emmerdale* man. When *Emmerdale* was in need of an extreme reboot in 1993, the scriptwriters went all apocalyptic. A passing plane exploded in mid-air, conveniently scattering burning wreckage around precise locations in and around the village to incinerate the most boring members of the cast. Johnson will surely be aware that the disaster didn't just rejuvenate *Emmerdale* by freeing it from the shackles of plausibility, it pushed its way up the hierarchy of English soaps. It proved that a willingness to embrace catastrophe could unleash great potential. And the cataclysm became a benchmark of English resilience.

In March 2000, after a bus crash, a cheery *Emmerdale* character said, 'Well, we have survived a plane crash. I am sure we can survive this' – just as we now hear in the vox pops (and presumably in Dominic Cummings's focus groups) 'We survived the Blitz, I am sure we can survive a no-deal Brexit.'

The *Emmerdale* option is the choice of the hard Leavers: a purifying crash-and-burn as a prelude to a much more thrilling series of 'our island story'.

Crossroads, on the other hand, is the option for the diehard Remainers. With *Crossroads*, the question was how to put a dying show out of its misery. How could it be brought to a sudden close? In the final episode in 2003, the owner of the Crossroads hotel, Angel (played by Jane Asher), realises the entire show had all been a reverie – 'I've just woken up from an amazing dream and dreamt that I owned a hotel called Crossroads.' She returned to her real-life job as a supermarket checkout assistant in Birmingham called Angela. This is the option favoured by some Remainers: Brexit was all just a bad dream. As James Joyce (surely an unacknowledged inspiration for *Crossroads*) put it: 'History is a nightmare from which I am trying to awake.' The dark Angel of English nationalism can just rub her eyes and go back to being nice, quiet, smiley Angela on the checkouts. It is 22 June 2016, again, and all is right with the world.

So which is it to be, *Emmerdale* or *Crossroads*? Wipe out half the village, or pretend it was all just a bad dream? Neither, of course. Brexit is not a soap opera. It is admittedly quite a show and, up to a point, entertaining: a camp performance with its own peculiar blend of farce and tragedy. But it is also a profound political, social and economic crisis with multigenerational consequences. It may have gone on for far too long already and viewers may be inclined to switch off, but the scriptwriters can't just resort to extreme narrative leaps. However tempting the alternative endgames, the thing cannot be escaped. It has to be worked through.

The problem with the *Emmerdale* scenario is not the obvious one. Apocalypse Now may not sound like a great idea to most people, but to those who fancy it – the hard core of no-deal zealots – Brexit has acquired a quasi-religious quality.

Its true believers are an end-of-the-world cult, waiting for the Rapture. Pain is good: it will wash away the sins of a half-century of shameful submission to Europe. Death is good: it will be followed by the resurrection of England.

In this seam of the reactionary imagination, England has only ever really been itself when it has been at war. A return to some version of wartime conditions is not a threat – it is a promise. So the real problem with the *Emmerdale* option is not the crash. It is that even the embrace of destruction doesn't really move the story on. To deepen the agony is merely to prolong it: after the apocalyptic Brextinction comes a Brexternity of new negotiations with the EU. The narrative, after the shock, will become even more tedious.

If you think the withdrawal agreement is dreary, you haven't even begun to imagine the profound existential ennui of trying to hammer out a trade deal with twenty-seven countries, each of which has a veto.

But the *Crossroads* solution doesn't work either. The referendum result of June 2016 is not a bad dream. It is history – and history has no reverse gear. It happened, and while what happened can be revisited, re-argued and redressed, it cannot be merely wished away. A stew of grievances that had long been simmering had a powerful heat put under it. It boiled over and it cannot simply be put back in the pan. Brexit can't be defeated by decreeing that it was all a moment of madness that occurred during a temporary sleep of reason.

This incoherent revolution demands, not a mere restoration of the *ancien régime*, but a better revolution, one that radically overhauls the political system, restores public and egalitarian values and convinces people that they really do have a democratic voice.

Brexit has never really been about the EU – indeed, it has exposed a great ignorance about the EU and how it works, not just in the general population but in a large section of the political class. Brexit is about England and its deep unhappiness with itself.

It is certainly a great exercise in displacement and distraction, and Johnson is a master of those tactics. But Johnson can't be countered without a serious engagement with what is being displaced and what is being distracted from.

There is a deep crisis of belonging and it has many dimensions: economic, social, cultural, national, democratic.

Brexit won't address any of these problems – indeed, it is much more likely to exacerbate them. But those who want to stop Brexit can't content themselves with merely pointing this out. They must themselves address that crisis. That can't be done by simply reviving the tired old show of a dying imperial state. It needs an entirely new series.

15 October 2019

I try not to be a pedant, but I do get annoyed when people use 'disinterested' when they mean 'uninterested'. To be disinterested is to be impartial, to deal honestly with other people without seeking to advance one's own interests. To be uninterested is not to care about what happens to those people. One of the reasons Brexit has been such a mess is that the British government has seriously confused these two attitudes to Northern Ireland. It has managed, under both Theresa May and Boris Johnson, simultaneously to abandon its duty to be disinterested and to be fundamentally uninterested. If a Brexit deal is finally to emerge, it will be because the British have been forced to grasp the profound stupidity of this combination.

The Belfast Agreement is very clear on the idea of disinterested government. It requires that 'whatever choice is freely exercised by a majority of the people of Northern Ireland, the power of the sovereign government with jurisdiction there shall be exercised with rigorous impartiality on behalf of all the people in the diversity of their identities and traditions'. This requirement has been openly flouted since May's ill-starred election of 2017 in which the Tories lost their majority in parliament. Impartiality has been abandoned in favour of a formal alliance with one party, the DUP, whose support lies almost entirely within one politico-religious tradition.

But this abandonment of the duty to be disinterested has gone hand in hand with a lack of interest. The Tories have been fundamentally indifferent to the desires of most people in Northern Ireland, to the realities of life for the border communities, to the fragility of the peace process and to the consequences of the re-creation of a hard border. In this, they have been faithful to the instincts of their own voters and members: 75 per cent of Tory voters say the collapse of the peace process in Northern Ireland is a price worth paying for Brexit and 60 per cent of party members say Northern Ireland leaving the UK is an acceptable consequence of Brexit.

It is quite a feat to be both nakedly partial and essentially unconcerned and its consequence is, of course, utter incoherence. The abandonment of impartiality led to a rhetoric of the 'precious, precious union'. But the lack of real interest in that peculiar part of the union known as Northern Ireland has made British governments incapable of addressing the real problems of the peace process and the border with any credibility or indeed honesty: we passionately love Northern Ireland but not enough to take its specific history and geography seriously. This, in essence, is why the Brexit tractor has been stuck in the muddy fields of Fermanagh and Tyrone, spinning its wheels ever more frantically but going nowhere.

The most ludicrous effect of this contradiction has been the wilful erasure of an obvious truth that both the British government and the DUP themselves accepted and articulated in the immediate period after the Brexit referendum: that Northern Ireland is different from Britain and that therefore Brexit would have to be different for Northern Ireland. It is hard to remember, after so much nonsense, that this was once a truth universally acknowledged in post-referendum discourse.

The British government's first substantial Brexit plan, the white paper of February 2017, says: 'The government recognises that Northern Ireland's particular circumstances present a range of particular challenges to be taken into account when preparing for our exit from the EU.' Even before that, Arlene Foster (yes, that Arlene Foster) had put her name beside that of Martin McGuinness in a joint letter of August 2016 to May stressing that 'this region [i.e. Northern Ireland] is unique' and actually demanding that the prime minister be aware of the 'unique aspects of negotiations that arise from the Border'.

But the result of the 2017 election created a toxic collusion in which the DUP, drunk on the illusion of power, spun the fantasy that Brexit could be exactly the same for Northern Ireland as for Somerset or Warwickshire and May (against her better judgement) indulged it. Out went 'particular' and 'unique'; in came 'exactly the same'. More than two years have been wasted on the pursuit of a proposition that both the British government and the DUP knew to be unreal. But in the manual of Brexit for slow learners, the last chapter of this volume was always going to be the same as the first: go back to the plain truth that Northern Ireland is unique and that, if it really has to endure Brexit, it must have a bespoke version. Its Brexit suit cannot be off the peg – it must be made to measure.

If a deal is now to be possible, Boris Johnson must restore some semblance of disinterestedness by acknowledging that Northern Ireland is not the DUP. And he must, however belatedly, try to seem interested in the realities of the place and its communities. It would be too much to expect either of these conversions to be sincere. But they are the key to the one thing that really interests Johnson: his own survival.

18 October 2019

The revised withdrawal agreement returns to the very thing the Tories had rejected before: a carving out of Northern Ireland from the rest of the UK. Brexit trumps the union. Johnson betrays the DUP.

So the backstop has become the frontstop. British prime minister Boris Johnson and his allies will claim victory: the hated backstop has been ditched. It is in Ireland's interests not to contradict that claim too vehemently – allowing the Brexiteers to save face is a necessary part of the process.

Given that Johnson came to office in July declaring that he would not even begin to negotiate with the European Union unless it agreed in advance to scrap the backstop, there is a lot of face to save. If a good outcome for Ireland is to be achieved, a certain amount of strategic amnesia will be required. We must forget, for example, Johnson's speech to the DUP conference less than a year ago, warning that if Northern Ireland had to continue to follow EU rules, it would 'leave Northern Ireland behind as an economic semi-colony of the EU and we would be damaging the fabric of the union with regulatory checks and even customs controls between GB and NI'. We must not say too loudly that this is exactly what Johnson has now agreed to do.

But let's be clear nonetheless. The backstop has not been 'ditched' or 'scrapped'. It has been triggered. It was an 'unless and until' conditional concept – if the British do not get a frictionless free trade deal with the EU and if the 'alternative arrangements' of hitherto uninvented technologies do not make all the problems of the border go away, this is what will happen. Most of that conditionality has now been removed. The backstop is now up-front – those 'regulatory checks and even customs controls between GB and NI' will be, if the deal is passed at Westminster, an open and direct fact.

This should not be a surprise to anyone, even the DUP. As early as August 2016, Arlene Foster put her name beside that of Martin McGuinness on a joint letter to Theresa May stressing that 'this region [Northern Ireland] is unique' and actually demanding that the then prime minister be aware of the 'unique aspects of negotiations that arise from the Border'. The new text of the Irish protocol to the withdrawal agreement repeats that same key word, 'unique'. It appears four times in all, twice in one of the opening sentences: 'It is necessary to address the unique circumstances on the island of Ireland through a unique solution.'

That solution may be Byzantine in detail but it is, in essence, obvious. There have always been just four options for any British government: no deal, a new referendum, a deal like May's that keeps all of the UK very closely aligned to the single market and the customs union or a bespoke, very soft Brexit for Northern Ireland. Parliament has blocked the first, Johnson is against the next two, so the unique solution for Northern Ireland's unique circumstances is all that remains. If the DUP did not want it, it should have supported May. By refusing to do so, it made its choice by default. It used its power in the only way it seems comfortable: negatively, to block May's deal. It has ended up with the one that is, from a unionist perspective, much worse.

Having failed miserably in his efforts to bluff the EU into capitulating on the backstop, all Johnson could really do was, in his own phrase, 'polish a turd' – or in more polite terms turn 'semi-colony of the EU' into 'great new deal'. There are two coats of polish. One is the complex mechanism for securing consent from the Northern Ireland assembly. This is, on paper at least, the one serious concession the Irish government and EU have made to Johnson – it sustains in ghostly form the idea of a time limit to the backstop. But, in reality, the crucial changes that make alignment with the EU the default option and that deprive the DUP of a veto make the concession much more minor than it seems.

The other coat of polish is one that Éamon de Valera, of all people, would have recognised. The irony of the plan for Northern Ireland to remain legally in the UK customs regime, while in practice following the EU's, is that its most obvious precedent is in Irish nationalism. De Valera's solution to the conundrum of getting on with governing twenty-six counties while claiming jurisdiction over thirty-two was the handy dualism of de jure/de facto: the North would be claimed de jure as part of the state while recognising that de facto it was not. There is something almost amusing in this Jesuitical device now defining Northern Ireland itself – UK by law, EU by fact.

The precedent would be enough to give the DUP nightmares – if it were not already having them. In one sense, the party is right to claim that the new deal will, over time, loosen Northern Ireland's place within the union. But this is merely the working out of Brexit itself, which of course it supports enthusiastically. There has been ample warning to the DUP that, given a choice between the 'precious, precious union' and Brexit, Johnson and his allies (and their voters) would always go for the latter. Now, the prime minister they so foolishly trusted has made that brutally clear. Those of them who are biblically inclined might ruefully recall Psalm 146: put not thy trust in princes.

30 October 2019

David Reynolds's Island Stories *considers the relationship
between Brexit and notions of British history.*

For diehard Brexiteers, the most potent image of their project
is the 'clean break'. It is in itself a rather attractive notion,
especially in our culture of personal makeovers and radical
transformations. Brexit is the New You. It proposes a Year Zero
and an Independence Day – points of origin at which a whole other
story of British greatness begins. Like most revolutions, it imagines
a sloughing off of history, especially, of course, the history of half a
century of deep entanglement with the European Union. It offers
a free programme of collective rehab, a political version of the
Scientologists' goal of 'going clear'.

Yet one of the many incoherences of the Brexit project is that
it cannot sustain even this rhetoric of a magical escape from the
past. It proposes a giant leap into a glorious future but what is to
follow from the great rupture has always been fuzzy. There is,
instead, an awful lot of past.

There is Jacob Rees-Mogg's ecstatic effusion at the Tory conference in 2017: 'We need to be reiterating the benefits of Brexit!...
Oh, this is so important in the history of our country... It's
Waterloo! It's Crécy! It's Agincourt! We win all these things!'
There is the same genius's laugh-a-minute literary pageant *The
Victorians*, whose dead white males are paraded as the exemplars
and progenitors of the post-Brexit future. There are Boris Johnson's
literary and rhetorical Churchill impersonations. There are the
zombie refrains of empire in the dream of Global Britain.

Above all, there is the constant harking back to the Second

World War, to the Dunkirk spirit and the Blitz spirit and, more darkly, to a rhetoric (aimed at the infidels) of appeasement, collaboration and, in Johnson's endlessly repeated term for the Benn act that sought to prevent a no-deal exit, of surrender. In a plaintive appeal to party members last April, the Tories' great lost leader Matt Hancock (remember him?) agonised that 'we have got to sound like we actually like this country. We have got to be patriots of the Britain of now and not the Britain of 1940.' But neither the Britain of now nor the putative future Britain can hold a candle to the imagined flame of past glory.

In this mixed-up discourse, the Brexit project can't decide whether it is a revolution or a restoration. If, like the characters in Philip Pullman's *His Dark Materials* it has an animal daemon to represent its true self, is it a beautiful butterfly emerging from the cocoon of European slavery or a homing pigeon returning to the comfortable roost of old England?

It wants, perhaps, to be both, to suggest simultaneously that all things will be made new in the buccaneering, disruptive, hyper-globalised capitalism that will be unleashed once freedom is gained; and that everything is just going back to the way it was meant to be before the terrible mistake of 1973. In this sense, the contradictory notions of history also expose the much deeper contradiction of Brexit – for most of those who are driving it, it is a radical breach in the British post-war social order; for most of those in the back of the bus, it is supposed to be a refurbishment and strengthening of that same social order.

Complicating all of this is the way the very potency of the idea of a restoration of the past is itself a restoration of the past. As David Reynolds points out in his concise, elegant and lucid revisiting of key themes in British history in the light of Brexit, Margaret Thatcher, in her very first election campaign, when she was just twenty-four, said: 'Britain's prestige in the eyes of the world has gone down and down... it is our earnest desire to make Great Britain great again.' That was in 1950, just after the triumph of the Second World War and before the shock of the Suez Crisis.

Yet here, in this proto-Trump rhetoric, there is already the notion of intolerable national decline: if British greatness has to be regained, it has by definition been lost.

Decline – or rather declinist rhetoric – is one of Reynolds's four themes. As an overriding notion in British political psychology, it has the odd quality of being at once inevitable and irrelevant. Inevitable because 'greatness' as defined by the empire was an extraordinary episode of political gigantism. Great Britain became Greater Britain as a result of a historically freakish conjunction of circumstances. It could not possibly sustain a situation in which it accounted for 33 per cent of the world's exports of manufactured goods or one in which it controlled nearly a quarter of the world's population.

But this inevitable retreat is irrelevant because Britain's descent from these impossible heights went hand in hand with great improvements in the lives of its own inhabitants. Given a choice between continuing to hold India captive and building a National Health Service, there is little doubt that ordinary people in Britain would have chosen the dignity of good healthcare over imperial 'greatness'.

Reynolds gives a nicely crisp account of all of this, but he might have risked a further thought. If it is true that a story of relative decline does not really matter to most people so long as their own circumstances are improving, then perhaps when people's lives stop improving, as they did as a result of static wages and austerity, they become susceptible to declinism. Their lives, they may come to accept, are not great because Britain is no longer great. This sleight-of-mind is surely one of the central and most effective tactics of Brexit. It suggests that membership of the EU, in which Britain is 'reduced' to the normality of being one country among twenty-eight, is the real reason why people's own life chances have been reduced.

It is possible to make this false connection because of Reynolds's second theme, the persistent ambivalence in English politics about whether or not it is possible to stand aloof from continental

Europe. It goes back a long way, certainly more than 1,000 years, and even in the post-war era it has weighed heavily on both main parties. It is good to be reminded by Reynolds that even in the infamous Bruges speech of 1988 that gave its name to the Eurosceptic wing of the Tory party, Thatcher insisted starkly: 'Our links to the rest of Europe, the continent of Europe, have been the dominant factor in our history.' (Not, note, empire, industrialism or Protestantism, which she might have chosen.) And equally that it was a Labour leader, Hugh Gaitskell, who insisted in 1962 that 'we are not just a part of Europe – at least not yet. We have a different history.' Here we see that the very notion of British history has long been deeply uncertain: is it fundamentally shaped by Europe or is it 'different'?

One great appeal to difference is the profound exceptionalism that was seemingly endorsed by imperial success, the notion, as the historian and Whig politician Thomas Babington Macaulay put it in 1833 of the British as a 'people blessed with far more than an ordinary measure of political liberty and intellectual light'. But the other is the history that the Brexiteers have been most anxious to ignore: the complex, fraught and often violent nature of the interrelationships of England, Scotland, Wales and, of course, Ireland.

There is here not history but histories. The 'island story' is neither; it pertains not to an island but to an archipelago and it contains multiple, shifting and sometimes competing narratives. Reynolds provides a very useful primer on the delusions of an English mentality in which, as John Pocock put it in a ground-breaking essay in 1974, the Welsh, Scots and Irish 'appear as peripheral peoples when, and only when, their doings assume the power to disturb the tenor of English politics'.

This myopia has been inextricable from the delusion of a 'clean break'. The 'peripheral peoples' of the Irish borderlands have been the ghosts at the Brexit feast and their insistence on being heard has radically changed the tenor of English politics. Johnson's deal with Brussels, which essentially jettisons Northern Ireland, can be seen as a last desperate attempt to go clear from history. But even if it succeeds, the Scots, the Welsh and even the English may prove to have historical imperatives of their own that cannot be wished away.

2 November 2019

Brexit will never be laid to rest. It may
even be destined to meander on forever.

There are some fine and historic ditches in and around these islands: Offa's Dyke that marks the old boundaries of England and Wales, the Black Pig's Dyke that did a similar service for northern and southern Ireland, Grim's Ditch that runs through several southern English counties. But surely none will have so storied a place in history as The Ditch That Boris Johnson Didn't Die In.

The British prime minister promised in early September that he would be 'dead in a ditch' before he would agree to extend his country's membership of the European Union beyond 31 October. That means, surely, that as of 11 p.m. Brussels time on Thursday, Johnson is the first self-acknowledged member of the undead to occupy 10 Downing Street.

This was not, admittedly, Johnson's first encounter with mortality in a roadside trench. In his 2002 book, *Friends, Voters, Countrymen: Jottings on the Stump*, he boasted of his great journalistic campaign to save Britain's 'heritage' of exotic-flavoured crisps from interfering food Nazis in Brussels.

Imagining a British crisp company executive, he wrote that such a man knows of the Tories 'that we are a capitalist party that will help him sell as much deep-fried potato as he likes... we will die in the last ditch to preserve the prawn cocktail flavour crisp'. In Johnson's world, leaving the EU and preserving the prawn cocktail flavour crisp are matters of equal gravity, equally worthy of the blood of martyrs.

There is, nonetheless, something apt about Johnson's joining of the undead, for the project he, more than anyone else, embodies has a strange kind of zombie or vampire existence, forever killing itself off only to return again to stalk the earth. Brexit posits an Independence Day, a great moment of national rebirth. That's standard practice for revolutions. But consider how many dates have been officially inscribed as British independence days by London or Brussels or both.

The first was 29 March 2019. It could not be met. The UK and the EU then agreed to extend Article 50 – the legal mechanism for exiting the EU – until 22 May, subject to MPs approving the withdrawal agreement, or failing that, until 12 April. After MPs rejected the deal for the third time, Theresa May wrote to Donald Tusk requesting an extension until 30 June 2019. The EU then agreed two options – an extension until 1 June if the UK didn't hold elections for the European Parliament – or an extension to 31 October if it did. And now we have three more possible dates for Brexit agreed by Johnson and the EU: 30 November or 31 December 2019, or 31 January 2020.

Queen Elizabeth only has two birthdays; post-Brexit Britain has nine – so far. The date with destiny has turned out to be a whole box of dates. With Brexit, a deadline is a line that is drawn forever and then dies away.

What we glimpse in these moments is that, with the Brexit referendum, time went out of joint. Britain began simultaneously to occupy two completely different temporal worlds. In one, Brexit was hurtling ever faster forward, towards a known and supposedly unbreakable appointment with fate. Not just known but chosen. It was entirely a matter for the British to start the timer, to say to their imagined destiny, as in an old-fashioned romantic movie: let's make a date to meet under the clock at 11 p.m. on 29 March 2019. The very hour was specified in law. And it was supposed to be irrevocable. When Theresa May triggered Article 50, she told parliament that 'there can be no turning back'.

And yet, there has been nothing but turning back. In any rational process, the two years allowed by the Lisbon Treaty for Britain to negotiate a withdrawal agreement with Brussels would have been a time of urgency and immediacy. The country had twenty-four months in which to undo nearly half a century of profound legal, economic and political entanglement with the EU. This was also the biggest constitutional change in the nature of the UK since Irish independence in 1922. Even if Brexit were a good idea, it was obviously an immense task. Each of the 730 available days mattered, and one might have expected British hearts to beat faster as each one of them was marked off on the calendar.

But there was instead a strange meandering, every movement towards a feasible agreement followed by a looping back into previously discarded impossibilities. Take the most notorious example, the 'backstop' agreement to ensure that whatever final trading arrangements might be agreed between the UK and the EU, the Irish border would remain open and invisible. It was agreed formally by Theresa May in December 2017, contradicted by some of her ministers in the following weeks, agreed again by May in March 2018 in a draft withdrawal agreement, included in the final withdrawal agreement in November 2018, and effectively repudiated by May in January 2019. And then, eventually, the whole thing looped all the way back to December 2017 and the original version of the backstop that May (under pressure from Arlene Foster) had rejected.

All of this gave Johnson's 'do or die' rhetoric about leaving the EU on 31 October a certain potency. In his shameless way, he has exploited public exasperation at the very mess he did so much to make. Having created the monster, he could pose as the Van Helsing of Brexit, the one man who could track it down to its lair and put a stake through its heart so it could never again suck the lifeblood out of British politics and society.

It is striking that the appeal of the whole project has ceased to lie in the wondrous future it once promised. It is now just what the torturer says to his victim: I can make it stop. 'Get Brexit Done', the slogan endlessly repeated by Johnson (presumably it tested well in the focus groups), pretty much boils down to: let's get this horrible thing over with. It is a long way from the sunny uplands.

But, of course, it won't be done. Even if the withdrawal agreement is passed, the much more complicated trade negotiations begin. More profoundly, all the reasons why Britain joined the EU in the first place (the reality that it is profoundly affected by what happens in continental Europe and thus needs to have a say in shaping what happens there) will simply return. The brave new world will look very like the old world of 1972. Back to the future; forward to the past – Brexit has a way of defying linear time. There is no last ditch, just an endless series of looping paths that will meander across the landscape unless and until the whole thing is ditched.

5 November 2019

It is, of course, impossible to identify the weirdest aspect of Brexit. But up there somewhere has to be the desire of some of the hard Brexiteers to think of England as Ireland – specifically the Irish Free State of the 1920s and 1930s. That state was formed out of a political and military uprising against Britain, led by Sinn Féin and the Irish Republican Army. Members of the Conservative and Unionist Party are not supposed to be in favour of that sort of thing. But some like to imagine themselves as leaders of a national revolt by a plucky underdog against the imperial might of the European Union. In this bizarre exercise, Michael Collins and Éamon de Valera become role models for the country they fought against.

Owen Paterson, a former secretary of state for Northern Ireland and an ardent Brexiteer, recently cited Collins when explaining to the House of Commons why he would support Boris Johnson's revised withdrawal agreement, even though he was not happy with it. Collins, the effective leader of the IRA at the time, negotiated the compromise treaty with the British in 1921 that settled for an Irish Free State rather than a full republic. Paterson quoted his speech to the Dáil in support of the treaty: 'Now as one of the signatories of the document I naturally recommend its acceptance. I do not recommend it for more than it is. Equally I do not recommend it for less than it is. In my opinion it gives us freedom, not the ultimate freedom that all nations desire and develop to, but the freedom to achieve it.'

Paterson added that Johnson's compromise 'begins the process of establishing our full freedom, and I hope that I do not suffer the same fate as Michael Collins in wanting to see that delivered'.

Collins was killed in an ambush during the civil war that followed the split in the IRA over the treaty. The logic of Paterson's analogy is that he risks the same fate at the hands of his colleagues in Brexit's army of liberation – perhaps with Mark Francois as Collins's eventual nemesis, de Valera.

This posturing may be ludicrous, but it has a serious purpose. The allure of the Irish settlement is that the Irish Free State didn't last very long. Much of what Collins agreed to in the treaty was gradually expanded into a more radical form of separation from Britain. In July 2018, the Conservative MEP Daniel Hannan directly compared Theresa May's Chequers proposals to the approach of the pro-treaty side in the early years of Irish independence: 'When the Irish Free State left the UK, in 1921, there were all sorts of conditions about treaty ports and oaths of supremacy and residual fiscal payments. And what very quickly became apparent was not just that those things were unenforceable once the split had been realised; it was that everyone in Britain kind of lost interest in enforcing them. And although there were some difficulties along the way in the 1920s, it turned out to have been better to have grabbed what looked like an imperfect independence and then build on it rather than risking the entire process.'

The message is: grab Brexit now and over time we can make the split from Europe even more radical. The Brexiteers wrap the green flag round them to cover a more barefaced project: when we have our 'freedom', we can tear up any commitments we make now. In all the pantomime dressing up of English Tories as Irish revolutionaries, it is easy to miss the point that what they really mean is that, once 'the split' has been finalised, the withdrawal treaty will in time become unenforceable. Britain can walk away from it.

There are, however, two obvious problems. One is that the analogy itself is ludicrous: the EU is not an empire and it has not sent the Black and Tans to suppress demands for freedom. The other is with what Hannan, with such charming insouciance, calls 'some difficulties along the way in the 1920s' in Ireland. These little local difficulties were partition, deadly pogroms in the North, a bitter civil war in the South and the ghost of unfinished business that returned in the Troubles from 1968 to 1998. In the Brexiteers' blithe analogies, it seems that equivalent events in the decade that is to follow eventual approval of Johnson's deal – the breakup of the union, civil disorder and violence and long-term tribal divisions – would be mere bumps on the road to English freedom.

For if the events of a century ago in Ireland really have to be used as an analogy for Brexit, there is only one valid parallel – the botched exit. Irish nationalists had, arguably, many better reasons for wanting to leave a multinational union (in their case two unions, the UK and the empire) than the Brexiteers have for their departure from the EU. They were also creatures of their own time – the freedom of small nations was, after all, the British rallying cry in the Great War that had so recently ended. Perhaps it is not just patriotic bias that makes me imagine Michael Collins and W. B. Yeats to be slightly more serious figures than Boris Johnson or even Owen Paterson; but, be that as it may, they blew it.

They wanted a unified new Ireland that would be able to leave its sectarian divisions behind. They got two narrowly sectarian states, one Catholic, one Protestant. They got civil war. The new Irish state, poor and enclosed, was not much of a homeland: half its population emigrated. They botched the exit and it took Ireland seventy-five years to begin to overcome the consequences. James Connolly, the most far-sighted of the nationalist revolutionaries of 1916, feared that a bad departure from the empire would lead to a 'carnival of reaction' in both parts of a divided Ireland. He was sadly right.

The divisions of the 1920s were cemented in place. The left was sidelined as tribal politics took hold. In the Free State (and later in the Republic), party allegiances were defined not by questions of social justice but according to who took what side in the civil war. Brexit has the capacity to have the same long-term distorting effect on English politics. The question for future generations could be not what you think the future should be but what did your side do in the Brexit wars?

So be careful what you wish for. Leaving a union is hard – don't do it unless you have to. And if you really must do it, do it with all the grace and generosity you can muster. Don't play at civil war – it's a game that everyone loses. Don't, on the one hand, work yourself up into such paroxysms of self-pity that you imagine England as early twentieth-century Ireland while, on the other, assuming that what happened to Ireland then could not possibly happen to you now.

And remember that if you botch the exit, the carnival of reaction may be coming to a town near you.

7 December 2019

It is a mark of the strangeness of current British politics that an epoch-making election is being contested by two would-be losers. Boris Johnson is prime minister because he led a Leave campaign in the 2016 referendum that, as he assured David Cameron at the time, he expected to be 'crushed'. And Jeremy Corbyn had no real intention of becoming leader of the Labour Party for any great length of time. Historians of the future may struggle to understand how things of such consequence have been determined more by accident than by design.

Labour ought to be headed for a great victory on 12 December, one that could change Britain as radically as Clement Attlee's triumph over Winston Churchill did in 1945. The ambient noise in most parts of the UK is about the state of the health service and social care, cuts to police numbers and the melting away of local facilities, from buses to libraries to playing fields. The Conservatives have been in power for almost a decade and their fingerprints are all over the austerity policies that have brought the country to this pass. They have also shredded their own brand, abandoning any claims to pragmatism, competence or indeed conservatism. They are led by a man who has very low levels of public trust and who has to dodge TV debates and interviews because he is so liable to self-destruct in a welter of lies and bluster.

Labour should be walking it. But the party has no chance at all of winning a majority and it could well suffer catastrophic losses in its own traditional heartlands. A large part of this failure can be named in advance: Jeremy Corbyn. Corbyn is relentlessly vilified by the Tory press and there is no doubt that this is a huge factor in the election. But talk to anyone on the ground in those crucial areas of the Midlands and the North, including those who want Labour to win, and they will tell you that traditional Labour voters are, as perhaps the best journalistic diviner of the popular mood in Britain, John Harris, puts it, 'bitterly dismissive of Jeremy Corbyn'.

Polling bears this out. Corbyn is regarded favourably in YouGov's large-scale surveys by 21 per cent of voters and unfavourably by 61 per cent. The authoritative British Election Study last March showed that the relatively benign view of him in the 2017 election campaign had by then evaporated. Asked to rate him out of 10, voters gave him 2.6 for competence, 2.8 for likeability and (crushingly for a man who can claim to have been true to his principles for a very long time), just 3 for integrity.

These dire figures are not all down to anti-Corbyn propaganda: even voters who say they were impressed by him in the 2017 campaign now rate him at dreadfully low levels. More than half (54 per cent) of those who voted Labour in 2017 wanted Corbyn to be replaced as party leader before this election.

Corbyn is so widely disliked that he has created an electoral paradox that probably deserves to be named after him. The Corbyn Effect is that bad opinion polls for his party are good news because people are more likely to vote for their local Labour MP if they are convinced that there is no chance of Corbyn becoming prime minister. It is not a distinction any party leader can be proud of.

But it does require explanation. Corbyn is, by all accounts, a nice man with a largely avuncular presence. He can become peevish under pressure but he is quite fluent in debates and generally retains his dignity and his innate politeness. He is not corrupt or venal. He clearly cares about social justice and equality. He does not come across as cynical or crazed by ambition. He is not a sociopath. He is up against an opponent in Johnson from whom just 13 per cent of voters say they would buy a used car. So why are so many traditional Labour voters so 'bitterly dismissive' of Corbyn?

One reason has to do with ambition. It is the misfortune of the British to be faced with a choice between a man who has far too much of it and a man who has far too little. Johnson developed as a child the demented desire to be 'world king' – he hungers for power above all else and is willing to do and say anything to get it. But Corbyn is at the opposite end of the spectrum. Nothing in his political career before he became party leader suggested the slightest appetite for power. This may be personally admirable, but it is politically disabling.

Politics is about power. Voters may not trust those who are too obviously power-hungry, but a politician who is not drawn to power is like a plumber who doesn't like pipes or a carpenter allergic to wood. Corbyn has been a politician since 1974 and a member of Parliament since 1983. In his thirty-two years at Westminster before he became leader of the Opposition, he made no effort to be on the Labour front bench or, when the party was in government, to hold office.

He was happy to be a campaigner, taking up causes, many of them admirable (he was an early champion of LGBT rights, for example, and of the Guilford Four and Birmingham Six), many not (he voted against the Anglo-Irish Agreement of 1985, a key step in the peace process, because Sinn Féin opposed it). He was comfortable with those who already shared his view of the world – his role was to galvanise and reinforce, not to persuade.

But he had no legislative achievements and avoided the difficult choices that come with power. And avoided, too, the kind of broad alliance-building that those who want power have to engage in. If Corbyn had more ambition, he would have forced himself outside his comfort zones of like-minded left-wingers. The way he has been as leader, surrounded by a bubble of hardliners who tell him what he wants to hear, is the way he was as a comfortably marginal backbencher. Their disastrous inability even to tolerate his own (elected) deputy leader Tom Watson is a result of Corbyn's profound uneasiness with challenges from within.

In 2015, when he agreed to stand as a token left-wing candidate for the Labour leadership, his pristine lack of ambition was part of the appeal: as he put it, 'I am much too old for personal ambition.' It is indeed crucial to understand that even the comrades in the hard-left Campaign Group who put him forward as a candidate to succeed Ed Miliband had absolutely no notion of Corbyn as a potential prime minister. Subsequent Corbyn boosters like the *Guardian* columnist Owen Jones did not want him to stand at the time and argued that a 'soft left' candidate should be supported instead. (Keir Starmer or Angela Eagle were seen as the best options.)

Most of those on the hard left who did want to run a candidate favoured John McDonnell, a far more obviously adept politician than Corbyn. But McDonnell himself was utterly demoralised. 'This,' he wrote in *Labour Briefing*, 'is the darkest hour that socialists in Britain have faced since the fall of the Attlee government in 1951.' When Corbyn's name began to be discussed, it was as a short-term, interim figure who could hold the arena open for debate while a more credible leader emerged. As Jon Lansman, who went on to found the pro-Corbyn Momentum movement, put it: 'Could we find someone who would be a caretaker leader, who could do it in order to have a debate about the future direction of the party and then have another leadership election two years later? It was in that context that we began to think about people like Jeremy.'

There is no evidence that Corbyn, in putting himself forward, thought of himself as doing anything other than fulfilling a duty to provoke debate. As Alex Nunns puts it in his definitive account of the 2015 Labour leadership campaign, *Candidate*, 'In all probability Corbyn was volunteering for a couple of weeks of lobbying and media appearances, a chance to raise the issue of austerity and, when he failed to make the ballot, to demonstrate that the leadership election rules were rigged against the left.'

This is where accident took over. Right up to the deadline for nominations, Corbyn did not have the thirty-five nominations from Labour MPs necessary to be a candidate for the leadership. Oddly, the Corbyn Effect started here – he got the crucial extra nominations from Labour veterans such as Frank Field and Margaret Beckett, purely on the basis that he had no chance of winning and that a broad debate would be healthy. What no one – including Corbyn himself – had thought through was that Labour's voting system had been thrown wide open to new members of the party and that there was an incoming tide of anger at the centrist politics that had produced austerity, insecurity and inequality and a new appetite for socialist and environmental radicalism.

Corbyn, instead of being at best a two-year caretaker figure, became the lightning rod for a genuinely transformational energy. His accession to the party leadership has allowed Labour to put forward serious alternatives to the feral capitalism that has unleashed brutal environmental destruction and levels of social inequality that are incompatible with democracy. But there is something tragic in this – the great current of insurgency has been channelled to a politician who has no great interest in power, no experience of using it and no ability to convince voters that he knows what to do with it.

The brutal truth is that no one (including those closest to him ideologically) would have chosen the unambitious Corbyn as the person to implement the most ambitious governmental programme in the UK since 1945. There is a vast gap between the scale of the political task Labour has set itself – a profound rebalancing of the economy and society – and the evidence of Corbyn's capacities. His inability even to deal credibly with an issue as egregious as anti-Semitism in his own party generates a deep public cynicism about his ability to implement such sweeping change. The mismatch is viciously corrosive. Corbyn is a victim of his own radicalism – he is cruelly dwarfed by the sheer size of the task Labour has set for itself. Corbyn is the Wizard of Oz inside the great edifice of Corbynism.

Nowhere is this inadequacy exposed more brutally than with Brexit. The issue is not so much whether he has been right or wrong on the defining question of his years as leader. It is that he has been a study in powerlessness. He was conspicuous only by his absence in the 2016 referendum. And his promise to remain 'neutral' if there is a second referendum, as if he were the Queen staying above the fray, does not come across as regal. It comes across as an extraordinary inability to use power to shape his country's destiny. It means, too, that he is unable to take the fight to Johnson, to expose for what it is the most pernicious reactionary project in contemporary British history. Being neutral on Brexit means being neutral on the ways it will set back every progressive environmental, social and economic cause that Corbyn believes in. At the heart of his public persona, there is a contradiction that diminishes him. If he cannot say what he believes on the question that is dividing voters, voters cannot believe Corbyn on all the other questions he cares about.

Envoi

*A moment of history in Brussels brings back memories
of a very different one seven years ago.*

On Friday, a very ordinary thing happened. A man packed up his stuff, closed the door and left his office for good. There was no ceremony to mark the big moment. It was like Bruegel's great painting of the fall of Icarus where, in the foreground, people are going about their mundane business and you have to look very hard to see the boy just about to disappear beneath the waves. As the poet William Carlos Williams has it, 'unsignificantly / off the coast / there was / a splash quite unnoticed / this was / Icarus drowning'. The man is called Julian King. Unless something dramatic happens in the UK election, he will be the last British member of the EU Commission. And from an Irish perspective, his departure has a peculiar poignancy.

The *Guardian* got a photograph of King preparing to leave. Behind him are the last objects ready to be carried away from the Berlaymont building in Brussels: two bankers' boxes sealed with duct tape; a Union Jack cushion and two wrapped-up pictures. One of them, you can just about see through the bubble wrap, is a portrait of the Queen.

The whole thing seems like a desultory version of the end-of-empire moments that ran through the second half of the twentieth century, the great winding-up replayed as a mere wind-up, the jokey little cushion serving as a mock-heroic version of the imperial flag being hauled down at sunset as the troops and the memsahibs wait in the bay to sail back to Blighty. The banality of this particular instant in history seems quite apt, for this is not an epic retreat from empire, just a wilfully foolish retreat from influence.

Britain is still a member of the EU and there is no legal basis for its government's refusal to nominate a successor to King. It is, on that level, another gesture, another piece of Brexit showbusiness. Yet it carries a charge of its own – after nearly half a century of engagement, there is this week a resonant absence: no British member of the commission. As a way of saying that something big is ending, it works: this feels like a point of no return.

But the particular poignancy for Ireland is the identity of the man who has been forced to be the lead actor in this piece of political theatre. Eight years ago, King was the British ambassador in Dublin. He was a key figure in what also felt – but in a completely different way – like a point of no return. King did a great deal to create the exquisite choreography of Queen Elizabeth's state visit to Ireland in 2011, the first time in 100 years that a reigning British monarch could come to what is now the Irish Republic.

That visit, I think, caught most of us by surprise. These things are generally not that interesting. But from the moment the Queen bowed her head so respectfully at the Garden of Remembrance, honouring those who had died as rebels against the British empire, it was clear that something extraordinary was going on. Ghosts were being exorcised: not just the ghosts of Irish resentment but those of British condescension. This drama was beautifully scripted. It touched the sites of pain: the raw nerve of Bloody Sunday in 1920 when the Queen visited Croke Park, the memories of the futile sacrifice of Irish troops at Gallipoli and the Somme when she went to Dublin's long-neglected war memorial.

And King had a large part in the crafting of that speech in Dublin Castle, when the British monarch began with those words, so often tokenistic clichés, now made electric: 'A Úachtaráin agus a chairde...' The speech was not just historic, it was about 'the weight of history', 'the complexity of our history, its many layers and traditions', the need to be 'able to bow to the past, but not be bound by it'. It acknowledged, gently but unmistakably, the legacy